ABOUT THIS PUBLICATION

FOR SERVICE ASSISTANCE

Customer Service Department
1.704.898.0770

North Carolina General Statues is published by The Muliti-Media Group of Greater Charlotte in Charlotte, North Carolina. Copyright 2015 by the Multi-Media Group of Greater Charlotte. This book or parts thereof may not be reproduced in any form, stored in a retrieval system, or transmitted in any form by any means—electronic, mechanical, photocopy, recording or otherwise—without prior written permission of the publisher, except as provided by United States of America copyright law.

The records required by U.S. Code 2257(a) through (c) and the pertinent regulations 28 C.F.R. Cli. 1, Part 75 with respect to this publication and all materials associated with such records are maintained by The Multi-Media Group of Greater Charlotte, Publisher and available for review by Attorney General.

www.visionbooks.org

Copyright © 2015 by MMGGC
All rights reserved!

TID: 4989448
ISBN (10) digit: 1502305798
ISBN (13) digit: 978-1502305794

123-4-56789-01239-Paperback
123-4-56789-01239-Hardback

First Edition

090520140547

Printed in the United States of America

2015 EDITION

North Carolina Criminal Law And Procedure-Pamphlet # 32

Printed In conjunction with the Administration of the Courts

North Carolina Criminal Law and Procedure
Pamphlet Reference Guide

Chapters	Pamphlet
Chapter 1 Civil Procedure	1
Chapter 1 Civil Procedure (Continue)	2
Chapter 1A Rules of Civil Procedure	2
Chapter 1B Contribution.	2
Chapter 1C Enforcement of Judgments.	2
Chapter 1D Punitive Damages.	2
Chapter 1E Eastern Band of Cherokee Indians.	2
Chapter 1F North Carolina Uniform Interstate Depositions and Discovery Act.	2
Chapter 2 - Clerk of Superior Court [Repealed and Transferred.]	3
Chapter 3 - Commissioners of Affidavits and Deeds [Repealed.]	3
Chapter 4 - Common Law	3
Chapter 5 - Contempt [Repealed.]	3
Chapter 5A - Contempt	3
Chapter 6 - Liability for Court Costs	3
Chapter 7 - Courts [Repealed and Transferred.]	3
Chapter 7A – Judicial Department	3
Chapter 7A – Continuation (Judicial Department)	4
Chapter 7A – Continuation (Judicial Department)	5
Chapter 7B - Juvenile Code	5
Chapter 8 - Evidence	6
Chapter 8A - Interpreters for Deaf Persons [Recodified.]	6
Chapter 8B - Interpreters for Deaf Persons	6
Chapter 8C - Evidence Code	6
Chapter 9 - Jurors	6
Chapter 10 - Notaries [Repealed.]	6
Chapter 10A - Notaries [Recodified.]	6
Chapter 10B - Notaries	6
Chapter 11 - Oaths	6
Chapter 12 - Statutory Construction	6
Chapter 13 - Citizenship Restored	6
Chapter 14 - Criminal Law	7
Chapter 14 –Criminal Law (Continuation)	8
Chapter 15 - Criminal Procedure	9
Chapter 15A - Criminal Procedure Act (Continuation)	10
Chapter 15A - Criminal Procedure Act (Continuation)	11
Chapter 15B - Victims Compensation	11
Chapter 15C - Address Confidentiality Program	11
Chapter 16 - Gaming Contracts and Futures	11
Chapter 17 - Habeas Corpus	11

Chapter 17A - Law-Enforcement Officers [Recodified.]	11
Chapter 17B - North Carolina Criminal Justice Education and Training System [Recodified.] Chapter 17C - North Carolina Criminal Justice Education and Training Standards Commission	11
	11
Chapter 17D - North Carolina Justice Academy	11
Chapter 17E - North Carolina Sheriffs' Education and Training Standards Commission	11
Chapter 18 - Regulation of Intoxicating Liquors [Repealed.]	12
Chapter 18A - Regulation of Intoxicating Liquors [Repealed.]	12
Chapter 18B - Regulation of Alcoholic Beverages	12
Chapter 18C - North Carolina State Lottery	12
Chapter 19 - Offenses against Public Morals	12
Chapter 19A - Protection of Animals	12
Chapter 20 - Motor Vehicles	13
Chapter 20 - Motor Vehicles (Continuation)	14
Chapter 20 - Motor Vehicles (Continuation)	15
Chapter 20 - Motor Vehicles (Continuation)	16
Chapter 21 - Bills of Lading	17
Chapter 22 - Contracts Requiring Writing	17
Chapter 22A - Signatures	17
Chapter 22B - Contracts Against Public Policy	17
Chapter 22C - Payments to Subcontractors	17
Chapter 23 - Debtor and Creditor. r 24 - Interest	17
Chapter 24 – Interest	17
Chapter 25 – Uniform Commercial Code	18
Chapter 25 – Uniform Commercial Code (Continuation)	19
Chapter 25A – Retail Installment Sales Act	20
Chapter 25B - Credit	20
Chapter 25C - Sales of Artwork	20
Chapter 26 - Suretyship	20
Chapter 27 - Warehouse Receipts [Repealed.]	20
Chapter 28 - Administration [Repealed.]	20
Chapter 28A - Administration of Decedents' Estates	20
Chapter 28B - Estates of Absontees in Military Service	20
Chapter 28C - Estates of Missing Persons	20
Chapter 29 - Intestate Succession	21
Chapter 30 - Surviving Spouses	21
Chapter 31 - Wills	21
Chapter 31A - Acts Barring Property Rights	21
Chapter 31B - Renunciation of Property and Renunciation of Fiduciary Powers Act	21
Chapter 31C - Uniform Disposition of Community Property Rights at Death Act	21
Chapter 32 - Fiduciaries	21
Chapter 32A - Powers of Attorney	21
Chapter 33 - Guardian and Ward [Repealed and Recodified.]	21

Chapter 33A - North Carolina Uniform Transfers to Minors Act	21
Chapter 33B - North Carolina Uniform Custodial Trust Act	21
Chapter 34 - Veterans' Guardianship Act	22
Chapter 35 - Sterilization Procedures	22
Chapter 35A - Incompetency and Guardianship	22
Chapter 36 - Trusts and Trustees [Repealed.]	22
Chapter 36A - Trusts and Trustees	22
Chapter 36B - Uniform Management of Institutional Funds Act [Repealed.]	22
Chapter 36C - North Carolina Uniform Trust Code	22
Chapter 36D - North Carolina Community Third Party Trusts, Pooled Trusts	23
Chapter 36E - Uniform Prudent Management of Institutional Funds Act	23
Chapter 37 - Allocation of Principal and Income [Repealed.]	23
Chapter 37A - Uniform Principal and Income Act	23
Chapter 38 - Boundaries	23
Chapter 38A - Landowner Liability	23
Chapter 39 - Conveyances	23
Chapter 39A - Transfer Fee Covenants Prohibited	23
Chapter 40 - Eminent Domain [Repealed.]	23
Chapter 40A - Eminent Domain	23
Chapter 41 - Estates	23
Chapter 41A - State Fair Housing Act	23
Chapter 42 - Landlord and Tenant	23
Chapter 42A - Vacation Rental Act	23
Chapter 43 - Land Registration	23
Chapter 44 - Liens	24
Chapter 44A - Statutory Liens and Charges	24
Chapter 45 - Mortgages and Deeds of Trust	24
Chapter 45A - Good Funds Settlement Act	24
Chapter 46 - Partition	24
Chapter 47 - Probate and Registration	25
Chapter 47A - Unit Ownership	25
Chapter 47B - Real Property Marketable Title Act	25
Chapter 47C - North Carolina Condominium Act	25
Chapter 47D - Notice of Settlement Act [Expired.]	25
Chapter 47E - Residential Property Disclosure Act	25
Chapter 47F - North Carolina Planned Community Act	25
Chapter 47G - Option to Purchase Contracts	25
Chapter 47H - Contracts for Deed	25
Chapter 48 - Adoptions +	26
Chapter 48A - Minors	26
Chapter 49 - Bastardy	26
Chapter 49A - Rights of Children	26
Chapter 50 - Divorce and Alimony	26
Chapter 50A - Uniform Child-Custody Jurisdiction and	

Enforcement Act	26
Chapter 50B - Domestic Violence	26
Chapter 50C - Civil No-Contact Orders	26
Chapter 51 - Marriage	26
Chapter 52 - Powers and Liabilities of Married Persons	27
Chapter 52A - Uniform Reciprocal Enforcement of Support Act [Repealed.]	27
Chapter 52B - Uniform Premarital Agreement Act	27
Chapter 52C - Uniform Interstate Family Support Act	27
Chapter 53 - Banks	27
Chapter 53A - Business Development Corporations and North Carolina Capital Resource Corporations	28
Chapter 53B - Financial Privacy Act	28
Chapter 54 - Cooperative Organizations	28
Chapter 54A - Capital Stock Savings and Loan Associations [Repealed.]	28
Chapter 54B - Savings and Loan Associations	29
Chapter 54C - Savings Banks	29
Chapter 55 - North Carolina Business Corporation Act	30
Chapter 55A - North Carolina Nonprofit Corporation Act	31
Chapter 55B - Professional Corporation Act	31
Chapter 55C - Foreign Trade Zones	31
Chapter 55D - Filings, Names, and Registered Agents for Corporations, Nonprofit Corporations, and Partnerships	31
Chapter 56 - Electric, Telegraph and Power Companies [Repealed.]	31
Chapter 57 - Hospital, Medical and Dental Service Corporations [Recodified.]	31
Chapter 57A - Health Maintenance Organization Act [Recodified.]	31
Chapter 57B - Health Maintenance Organization Act [Recodified.]	31
Chapter 57C - North Carolina Limited Liability Company Act.	31
Chapter 58 - Insurance.	32
Chapter 58 - Insurance (Continuation)	33
Chapter 58 - Insurance (Continuation)	34
Chapter 58 - Insurance (Continuation)	35
Chapter 58 - Insurance (Continuation)	36
Chapter 58 - Insurance (Continuation)	37
Chapter 58 - Insurance (Continuation)	38
Chapter 58A - North Carolina Health Insurance Trust Commission [Recodified.]	38
Chapter 59 - Partnership.	39
Chapter 59B - Uniform Unincorporated Nonprofit Association Act.	39
Chapter 60 - Railroads and Other Carriers [Repealed and Transferred.]	39
Chapter 61 - Religious Societies	39
Chapter 62 - Public Utilities	39

Chapter 62 - Public Utilities (Continuation)	40
Chapter 62A - Public Safety Telephone Service And Wireless Telephone Service	40
Chapter 63 - Aeronautics	40
Chapter 63A - North Carolina Global TransPark Authority	40
Chapter 64 - Aliens	40
Chapter 65 – Cemeteries	40
Chapter 66 - Commerce and Business	41
Chapter 67 - Dogs	41
Chapter 68 - Fences and Stock Law	41
Chapter 69 - Fire Protection	41
Chapter 70 - Indian Antiquities, Archaeological Resources and Unmarked Human Skeletal Remains Protection	42
Chapter 71 - Indians [Repealed.]	42
Chapter 71A - Indians	42
Chapter 72 - Inns, Hotels and Restaurants	42
Chapter 73 - Mills	42
Chapter 74 - Mines and Quarries	42
Chapter 74A - Company Police [Repealed.]	42
Chapter 74B - Private Protective Services Act [Repealed.]	42
Chapter 74C - Private Protective Services	42
Chapter 74D - Alarm Systems	42
Chapter 74E - Company Police Act	42
Chapter 74F - Locksmith Licensing Act	42
Chapter 74G - Campus Police Act	42
Chapter 75 - Monopolies, Trusts and Consumer Protection	42
Chapter 75A - Boating and Water Safety	43
Chapter 75B - Discrimination in Business	43
Chapter 75C - Motion Picture Fair Competition Act	43
Chapter 75D - Racketeer Influenced and Corrupt Organizations	43
Chapter 75E - Unlawful Activities in Connection With Certain Corporate Transactions	43
Chapter 76 - Navigation	43
Chapter 76A - Navigation and Pilotage Commissions	43
Chapter 77 - Rivers, Creeks, and Coastal Waters	43
Chapter 78 - Securities Law [Repealed.]	43
Chapter 78A - North Carolina Securities Act	43
Chapter 78B - Tender Offer Disclosure Act [Repealed.]	43
Chapter 78C - Investment Advisers	43
Chapter 78D - Commodities Act	43
Chapter 79 - Strays [Repealed.]	43
Chapter 80 - Trademarks, Brands, etc.	44
Chapter 81 - Weights and Measures [Recodified.]	44
Chapter 81A - Weights and Measures Act of 1975.	44
Chapter 82 - Wrecks [Repealed.]	44
Chapter 83 - Architects [Recodified.]	44

Chapter 83A - Architects	44
Chapter 84 - Attorneys-at-Law	44
Chapter 84A - Foreign Legal Consultants	44
Chapter 85 - Auctions and Auctioneers [Repealed.]	44
Chapter 85A - Bail Bondsmen and Runners [Recodified.]	44
Chapter 85B - Auctions and Auctioneers	44
Chapter 85C - Bail Bondsmen and Runners [Recodified.]	44
Chapter 86 - Barbers [Recodified.]	44
Chapter 86A - Barbers	44
Chapter 87 - Contractors	44
Chapter 88 - Cosmetic Art [Repealed.]	44
Chapter 88A - Electrolysis Practice Act	44
Chapter 88B - Cosmetic Art	45
Chapter 89 - Engineering and Land Surveying [Recodified.]	45
Chapter 89A - Landscape Architects	45
Chapter 89B - Foresters	45
Chapter 89C - Engineering and Land Surveying	45
Chapter 89D - Landscape Contractors	45
Chapter 89E - Geologists Licensing Act	45
Chapter 89F - North Carolina Soil Scientist Licensing Act	45
Chapter 89G - Irrigation Contractors	45
Chapter 90 - Medicine and Allied Occupations	45
Chapter 90 - Medicine and Allied Occupations (Continuation)	46
Chapter 90 - Medicine and Allied Occupations (Continuation)	47
Chapter 90 - Medicine and Allied Occupations (Continuation)	48
Chapter 90A - Sanitarians and Water and Wastewater Treatment Facility Operators	48
Chapter 90B - Social Worker Certification and Licensure Act	48
Chapter 90C - North Carolina Recreational Therapy Licensure Act	48
Chapter 90D - Interpreters and Transliterators	48
Chapter 91 - Pawnbrokers [Repealed.]	48
Chapter 91A - Pawnbrokers Modernization Act of 1989	48
Chapter 92 - Photographers [Deleted.]	48
Chapter 93 - Certified Public Accountants	48
Chapter 93A - Real Estate License Law	49
Chapter 93B - Occupational Licensing Boards	49
Chapter 93C - Watchmakers [Repealed.]	49
Chapter 93D - North Carolina State Hearing Aid Dealers and Fitters Board.	49
Chapter 93E - North Carolina Appraisers Act	49
Chapter 94 - Apprenticeship	49
Chapter 95 - Department of Labor and Labor Regulations	49
Chapter 95 - Department of Labor and Labor Regulations (Continuation)	50
Chapter 96 - Employment Security	50
Chapter 97 - Workers' Compensation Act	50
Chapter 97 - Workers' Compensation Act (Continuation)	51

Chapter 98 - Burnt and Lost Records	51
Chapter 99 - Libel and Slander	51
Chapter 99A - Civil Remedies for Criminal Actions	51
Chapter 99B - Products Liability	51
Chapter 99C - Actions Relating to Winter Sports Safety and Accidents	51
Chapter 99D - Civil Rights	51
Chapter 99E - Special Liability Provisions	51
Chapter 100 - Monuments, Memorials and Parks	51
Chapter 101 - Names of Persons	51
Chapter 102 - Official Survey Base	51
Chapter 103 - Sundays, Holidays and Special Days	51
Chapter 104 - United States Lands	51
Chapter 104A - Degrees of Kinship	51
Chapter 104B - Hurricanes or Other Acts of Nature	51
Chapter 104C - Atomic Energy, Radioactivity and Ionizing Radiation [Repealed and Recodified.]	51
Chapter 104D - Southern States Energy Compact	51
Chapter 104E - North Carolina Radiation Protection Act	51
Chapter 104F - Southeast Interstate Low-Level Radioactive Waste Management Compact [Repealed]	51
Chapter 104G - North Carolina Low-Level Radioactive Waste Management Authority Act of 1987 [Repealed]	51
Chapter 105 - Taxation	51
Chapter 105 - Taxation (Continuation)	52
Chapter 105 - Taxation (Continuation)	53
Chapter 105 - Taxation (Continuation)	54
Chapter 105A - Setoff Debt Collection Act	55
Chapter 105B - Defaulted Student Loan Recovery Act	55
Chapter 106 - Agriculture	55
Chapter 106 - Agriculture (Continue)	56
Chapter 106 - Agriculture (Continue)	57
Chapter 107 - Agricultural Development Districts [Repealed.]	57
Chapter 108 - Social Services [Repealed and Recodified.]	57
Chapter 108A - Social Services	57
Chapter 108B - Community Action Programs	58
Chapter 108C Medicaid and Health Choice Provider Requirements.	58
Chapter 108D Medicaid Managed Care for Behavioral Health Services.	58
Chapter 109 - Bonds [Recodified.]	58
Chapter 110 - Child Welfare	58
Chapter 111 - Aid to the Blind	58
Chapter 112 - Confederate Homes and Pensions [Repealed.]	58
Chapter 113 - Conservation and Development	58
Chapter 113 - Conservation and Development (Continuation)	59

Chapter 113A - Pollution Control and Environment	59
Chapter 113A - Pollution Control and Environment (Continuation)	60
Chapter 113B - North Carolina Energy Policy Act of 1975	60
Chapter 114 - Department of Justice	60
Chapter 115 - Elementary and Secondary Education [Repealed.]	60
Chapter 115A - Community Colleges, Technical Institutes, and Industrial Education Centers [Repealed.]	60
Chapter 115B - Tuition and Fee Waivers	60
Chapter 115C - Elementary and Secondary Education	60
Chapter 115C - Elementary and Secondary Education (Continuation)	61
Chapter 115C - Elementary and Secondary Education (Continuation)	62
Chapter 115C - Elementary and Secondary Education (Continuation)	63
Chapter 115D - Community Colleges	63
Chapter 115E - Private Educational Facilities Finance Act [Recodified]	63
Chapter 116 - Higher Education	63
Chapter 116 - Higher Education (Continuation)	63
Chapter 116A - Escheats and Abandoned Property [Repealed.]	64
Chapter 116B - Escheats and Abandoned Property	64
Chapter 116C - Continuum of Education Programs	64
Chapter 116D - Higher Education Bonds	64
Chapter 117 - Electrification	64
Chapter 118 - Firemen's and Rescue Squad Workers' Relief and Pension Funds [Recodified.]	64
Chapter 118A - Firemen's Death Benefit Act [Repealed.]	64
Chapter 118B - Members of a Rescue Squad Death Benefit Act [Repealed.]	64
Chapter 119 - Gasoline and Oil Inspection and Regulation	64
Chapter 120 - General Assembly	65
Chapter 120 - General Assembly (Continuation)	66
Chapter 120 - General Assembly (Continuation)	67
Chapter 120C - Lobbying	67
Chapter 121 - Archives and History	67
Chapter 122 - Hospitals for the Mentally Disordered [Repealed.]	67
Chapter 122A - North Carolina Housing Finance Agency	67
Chapter 122B - North Carolina Agricultural Facilities Finance Act [Repealed.]	67
Chapter 122C - Mental Health, Developmental Disabilities, and Substance Abuse Act of 1985	67
Chapter 122C - Mental Health, Developmental Disabilities, and Substance Abuse Act of 1985 (Continuation)	68
Chapter 122D - North Carolina Agricultural Finance Act	68

Chapter 122E - North Carolina Housing Trust and Oil Overcharge Act	68
Chapter 123 - Impeachment	69
Chapter 123A - Industrial Development [Repealed.]	69
Chapter 124 - Internal Improvements	69
Chapter 125 - Libraries	69
Chapter 126 - State Personnel System	69
Chapter 127 - Militia [Repealed.]	69
Chapter 127A - Militia	69
Chapter 127B - Military Affairs	69
Chapter 127C - Advisory Commission on Military Affairs	69
Chapter 128 - Offices and Public Officers	69
Chapter 128 - Offices and Public Officers (Continuation)	70
Chapter 129 - Public Buildings and Grounds	70
Chapter 130 - Public Health [Repealed.]	70
Chapter 130A - Public Health	70
Chapter 130A - Public Health (Continuation)	71
Chapter 130A - Public Health (Continuation)	72
Chapter 130B - Hazardous Waste Management Commission [Repealed.]	72
Chapter 131 - Public Hospitals [Repealed.]	72
Chapter 131A - Health Care Facilities Finance Act	72
Chapter 131B - Licensing of Ambulatory Surgical Facilities [Repealed.]	72
Chapter 131C - Charitable Solicitation Licensure Act [Repealed.]	72
Chapter 131D - Inspection and Licensing of Facilities	72
Chapter 131E - Health Care Facilities and Services	72
Chapter 131E - Health Care Facilities and Services (Continuation)	73
Chapter 131F - Solicitation of Contributions	73
Chapter 132 - Public Records	73
Chapter 133 - Public Works	74
Chapter 134 - Youth Development [Recodified.]	74
Chapter 134A - Youth Services [Repealed.]	74
Chapter 135 - Retirement System for Teachers and State Employees; Social Security; Health Insurance Program for Children	74
Chapter 135 - Retirement System for Teachers and State Employees; Social Security; Health Insurance Program for Children	75
Chapter 136 - Transportation	75
Chapter 136 - Transportation (Continuation)	76
Chapter 137 - Rural Rehabilitation [Repealed.]	76
Chapter 138 - Salaries, Fees and Allowances	76
Chapter 138A - State Government Ethics Act	76
Chapter 139 - Soil and Water Conservation Districts	76

Chapter 140 - State Art Museum; Symphony and Art Societies	76
Chapter 140A - State Awards System	76
Chapter 141 - State Boundaries	76
Chapter 142 - State Debt	76
Chapter 143 - State Departments, Institutions, and Commissions	77
Chapter 143 - State Departments, Institutions, and Commissions (Continuation)	78
Chapter 143 - State Departments, Institutions, and Commissions (Continuation)	79
Chapter 143 - State Departments, Institutions, and Commissions (Continuation)	80
Chapter 143A - State Government Reorganization	80
Chapter 143B - Executive Organization Act of 1973	80
Chapter 143B - Executive Organization Act of 1973 (Continuation)	81
Chapter 143B - Executive Organization Act of 1973 (Continuation)	82
Chapter 143C - State Budget Act	83
Chapter 143D - The State Governmental Accountability and Internal Control Act	83
Chapter 144 - State Flag, Official Governmental Flags, Motto, and Colors	83
Chapter 145 - State Symbols and Other Official Adoptions.	83
Chapter 146 - State Lands	83
Chapter 147 - State Officers	83
Chapter 148 - State Prison System	84
Chapter 149 - State Song and Toast	84
Chapter 150 - Uniform Revocation of Licenses [Repealed.]	84
Chapter 150A - Administrative Procedure Act [Recodified.]	84
Chapter 150B - Administrative Procedure Act	84
Chapter 151 - Constables [Repealed.]	84
Chapter 152 - Coroners	84
Chapter 152A - County Medical Examiner [Repealed.]	84
Chapter 152A - County Medical Examiner [Repealed.] (Continuation)	85
Chapter 153 - Counties and County Commissioners [Repealed.]	85
Chapter 153A - Counties	85
Chapter 153B - Mountain Resources Planning Act	85
Chapter 153C - Uwharrie Regional Resources Act	85
Chapter 154 - County Surveyor [Repealed.]	85
Chapter 155 - County Treasurer [Repealed.]	85
Chapter 156 - Drainage	85
Chapter 156 – Drainage (Continuation)	86

Chapter 157 - Housing Authorities and Projects	86
Chapter 157A - Historic Properties Commissions [Transferred.]	86
Chapter 158 - Local Development	86
Chapter 159 - Local Government Finance	86
Chapter 159 - Local Government Finance (Continuation)	87
Chapter 159A - Pollution Abatement and Industrial Facilities Financing Act [Unconstitutional.]	87
Chapter 159B - Joint Municipal Electric Power and Energy Act	87
Chapter 159C - Industrial and Pollution Control Facilities Financing Act	87
Chapter 159D - The North Carolina Capital Facilities Financing Act	87
Chapter 159E - Registered Public Obligations Act	87
Chapter 159F - North Carolina Energy Development Authority [Repealed.]	87
Chapter 159G - Water Infrastructure	87
Chapter 159H - [Reserved.]	87
Chapter 159I - Solid Waste Management Loan Program and Local Government Special Obligation Bonds	87
Chapter 160 - Municipal Corporations [Repealed And Transferred.]	87
Chapter 160A - Cities and Towns	88
Chapter 160A - Cities and Towns (Continuation)	89
Chapter 160B - Consolidated City-County Act	89
Chapter 160C - Baseball Park Districts [Repealed.]	90
Chapter 161 - Register of Deeds	90
Chapter 162 - Sheriff	90
Chapter 162A - Water and Sewer Systems	90
Chapter 162B Continuity of Local Government in Emergency.	90
Chapter 163 Elections and Election Laws.	90
Chapter 163 Elections and Election Laws. (Continuation)	91
Chapter 164 Concerning the General Statutes of North Carolina.	92
Chapter 165 Veterans.	92
Chapter 166 Civil Preparedness Agencies [Repealed.]	92
Chapter 166A North Carolina Emergency Management Act.	92
Chapter 167 State Civil Air Patrol [Repealed.]	92
Chapter 168 Persons with Disabilities.	92
Chapter 168A Persons With Disabilities Protection Act.	92

Chapter 58.

Insurance.

Article 1.

Title and Definitions.

§ 58-1-1. Title of the Chapter.

Articles 1 through 64 of this Chapter may be cited and shall be known as the Insurance Law. (1899, c. 54; Rev., s. 4677; C.S., s. 6260.)

§ 58-1-5. Definitions.

In this Chapter, unless the context clearly requires otherwise:

(1)   "Alien company" means a company incorporated or organized under the laws of any jurisdiction outside of the United States.

(1a)   "Commercial aircraft" means aircraft used in domestic, flag, supplemental, commuter, or on-demand operations, as defined in Federal Aviation Administration Regulations, 14 C.F.R. § 119.3, as amended.

(2)   "Commissioner" means the Commissioner of Insurance of North Carolina or an authorized designee of the Commissioner.

(3)   "Company" or "insurance company" or "insurer" includes any corporation, association, partnership, society, order, individual or aggregation of individuals engaging or proposing or attempting to engage as principals in any kind of insurance business, including the exchanging of reciprocal or interinsurance contracts between Individuals, partnerships and corporations. "Company" or "insurance company" or "insurer" does not mean the State of North Carolina or any county, city, or other political subdivision of the State of North Carolina.

(4)   "Department" means the Department of Insurance of North Carolina.

(5)   "Domestic company" means a company incorporated or organized under the laws of this State.

(6) "Foreign company" means a company incorporated or organized under the laws of the United States or of any jurisdiction within the United States other than this State.

(7) "NAIC" means the National Association of Insurance Commissioners.

(8) Repealed by Session Laws 1999-219, s. 5.5.

(9) "Person" means an individual, partnership, firm, association, corporation, joint-stock company, trust, any similar entity, or any combination of the foregoing acting in concert.

(10) The singular form includes the plural, and the masculine form includes the feminine wherever appropriate. (1899, c. 54, s. 1; Rev., s. 4678; C.S., s. 6261; 1945, c. 383; 1971, c. 510, s. 1; 1987, c. 864, s. 34; 1995, c. 193, s. 1; 1999-219, s. 5.5; 2001-334, s. 18.2.)

§ 58-1-10. Contract of insurance.

A contract of insurance is an agreement by which the insurer is bound to pay money or its equivalent or to do some act of value to the insured upon, and as an indemnity or reimbursement for the destruction, loss, or injury of something in which the other party has an interest. (1899, c. 54, s. 2; Rev., s. 4679; C.S., s. 6262; 1945, c. 383.)

§ 58-1-15. Warranties by manufacturers, distributors, or sellers of goods or services.

(a) As used in this section:

(1) "Goods" means all things that are moveable at the time of sale or at the time the buyer takes possession. "Goods" includes things not in existence at the time the transaction is entered into; and includes things that are furnished or used at the time of sale or subsequently in modernization, rehabilitation, repair, alteration, improvement, or construction on real property so as to become a part of real property whether or not they are severable from real property.

(2) "Services" means work, labor, and other personal services.

(b) Any warranty made solely by a manufacturer, distributor, or seller of goods or services without charge, or an extended warranty offered as an option and made solely by a manufacturer, distributor, or seller of goods or services for charge, that guarantees indemnity for defective parts, mechanical or electrical breakdown, labor, or any other remedial measure, including replacement of goods or repetition of services, shall not be a contract of insurance under Articles 1 through 64 of this Chapter; however, service agreements on motor vehicles are governed by G.S. 66-370, 66-372, and 66-373. Service agreements on home appliances are governed by G.S. 66-371, 66-372, and 66-373.

(c) Nothing in this section affects the provisions of Article 28 of this Chapter. Any warranty or extended warranty made by any person other than the manufacturer, distributor, or seller of the warranted goods or services is a contract of insurance.

(d) Repealed by Session Laws 1989 (Regular Session, 1990), c. 1021, s. 3. (1959, c. 866; 1975, cc. 643, 788; 1977, c. 185; 1987, c. 369; 1989, c. 789, s. 2; 1989 (Reg. Sess., 1990), c. 1021, s. 3; 1991 (Reg. Sess., 1992), c. 1014, s. 2; 1995, c. 193, s. 2; 2007-95, s. 7.)

§ 58-1-20. Real property warranties.

(a) Any warranty relating to fixtures to real property issued by a person is a contract of insurance, except the following:

(1) A warranty made by a builder or seller of the real property;

(2) A warranty providing for the repair or replacement of the items covered by the warranty for defective parts and mechanical failure or resulting from ordinary wear and tear, and excluding from its coverage damage from recognizable perils, such as fire, flood, and wind, that neither relate to any defect in the items covered nor result from ordinary wear and tear.

(b) It is unlawful for any person to issue a warranty specified in subdivision (a)(2) of this section unless that person has posted a surety bond with the Secretary of State in the principal sum of not less than one hundred thousand dollars ($100,000). The bond must be issued by a surety company licensed to do business in this State and is subject to the approval of the Secretary of State. Any person to whom the warranty is issued may institute an action to recover against the warrantor and the surety bond for any breach of warranty.

(c) Persons issuing real property warranties shall comply with the requirements of G.S. 66-373. (1979, c. 773, s. 1; 1987, c. 864, s. 9; 1991, c. 644, s. 43; 2003-290, s. 1(a); 2007-95, s. 8.)

§ 58-1-25: Recodified as G.S. 66-370 by Session Laws 2007-95, ss. 2-5, effective October 1, 2007.

§ 58-1-30: Recodified as G.S. 66-371 by Session Laws 2007-95, ss. 2-5, effective October 1, 2007.

§ 58-1-35: Recodified as G.S. 66-372 by Session Laws 2007-95, ss. 2-5, effective October 1, 2007.

§ 58-1-36: Recodified as G.S. 66-373 by Session Laws 2007-95, ss. 2-5, effective October 1, 2007.

§ 58-1-40: Repealed by Session Laws 1993 (Reg. Sess., 1994), c. 730, s. 3.

§ 58-1-42: Recodified as G.S. 66-374 by Session Laws 2007-95, s. 6, effective October 1, 2007.

§§ 58-1-43, 58-1-50: Repealed by Session Laws 1993 (Reg. Sess., 1994), c. 730, s. 3.

Article 2.

Commissioner of Insurance.

§ 58-2-1. Department established.

The Department is hereby established as a separate and distinct department, which is charged with the execution of laws relating to insurance and other subjects placed under the Department. (1899, c. 54, s. 3; 1901, c. 391, s. 1; Rev., s. 4680; C.S., s. 6263; 1991, c. 720, s. 5.)

§ 58-2-5. Commissioner's election and term of office.

The chief officer of the Insurance Department shall be called the Commissioner of Insurance; whenever in the statutes of this State the words "Insurance Commissioner" appear, they shall be deemed to refer to and to be synonymous with the term "Commissioner of Insurance." He shall be elected by the people in the manner prescribed for the election of members of the General Assembly and State officers, and the result of the election shall be declared in the same manner and at the same time as the election of State officers is now declared. His term of office begins on the first day of January next after his election, and is for four years or until his successor is elected and qualified. If a vacancy occurs during the term, it shall be filled by the Governor for the unexpired term. (Rev., ss. 4680, 4681; 1907, c. 868; C.S., s. 6264; 1943, c. 170.)

§ 58-2-10. Salary of Commissioner.

The salary of the Commissioner shall be set by the General Assembly in the Current Operations Appropriations Act. In addition to the salary set by the General Assembly in the Current Operations Appropriations Act, longevity pay shall be paid on the same basis as is provided to employees of the State who are subject to the North Carolina Human Resources Act. (1899, c. 54, ss. 3, 8;

1901, c. 710; 1903, c. 42; c. 771, s. 3; Rev., s. 2756; 1907, c. 830, s. 10; c. 994; 1909, c. 839; 1913, c. 194; 1915, cc. 158, 171; 1917, c. 70; 1919, c. 247, s. 4; C.S., s. 3874; 1921, c. 25, s. 1; 1933, c. 282, s. 5; 1935, c. 293; 1937, c. 342; 1945, c. 383; 1947, c. 1041; 1949, c. 1278; 1953, c. 1, s. 2; 1957, c. 1; 1963, c. 1178, s. 6; 1967, c. 1130; c. 1237, s. 6; 1969, c. 1214, s. 6; 1971, c. 912, s. 6; 1973, c. 778, s. 6; 1975, 2nd Sess., c. 983, s. 21; 1977, c. 802, s. 42.12; 1983, c. 761, s. 206; 1983 (Reg. Sess., 1984), c. 1034, s. 164; 1987, c. 738, s. 32(b); 1991, c. 720, s. 4; 2013-382, s. 9.1(c).)

§ 58-2-15. Chief deputy commissioner.

The Commissioner shall appoint and may remove at his discretion a chief deputy commissioner, who, in the event of the absence, death, resignation, disability or disqualification of the Commissioner, or in case the office of Commissioner shall for any reason become vacant, shall have and exercise all the powers and duties vested by law in the Commissioner. He shall receive such compensation as fixed and provided by the Department of Administration. (1945, c. 383; 1987, c. 864, s. 19(a).)

§ 58-2-20. Chief actuary.

The Commissioner shall appoint and may remove at his discretion a chief actuary, who shall receive such compensation as fixed and provided by the Department of Administration. (1945, c. 383; 1987, c. 864, s. 19(b).)

§ 58-2-25. Other deputies, actuaries, examiners and employees.

(a) The Commissioner shall appoint or employ such other deputies, actuaries, economists, financial analysts, financial examiners, licensed attorneys, rate and policy analysts, accountants, fire and rescue training instructors, market conduct analysts, insurance complaint analysts, investigators, engineers, building inspectors, risk managers, clerks and other employees that the Commissioner considers to be necessary for the proper execution of the work of the Department, at the compensation that is fixed and provided by the Department of Administration. If the Commissioner considers it to be necessary for the proper execution of the work of the Department to contract with persons, except to fill authorized employee positions, all of those contracts, except those provided for in Articles 36 and 37 and Part 2 of Article 44 of this Chapter, shall be made pursuant to the provisions of Article 3C of Chapter 143 of the General Statutes.

Whenever the Commissioner or any deputy or employee of the Department is requested or subpoenaed to testify as an expert witness in any civil or administrative action, the party making the request or filing the subpoena and on whose behalf the testimony is given shall, upon receiving a statement of the cost from the Commissioner, reimburse the Department for the actual time and expenses incurred by the Department in connection with the testimony.

(b) The minimum education requirements for financial analysts and examiners referred to in subsection (a) of this section are a bachelors degree, with the appropriate courses in accounting as defined in 21 NCAC 8A.0309, and other courses that are required to qualify the applicant as a candidate for the uniform certified public accountant examination, based on the examination requirements in effect at the time of graduation by the analyst or examiner from an accredited college or university. (1945, c. 383; 1981, c. 859, s. 94; 1987, c. 864, s. 20; 1989 (Reg. Sess., 1990), c. 1069, s. 20; 1991, c. 681, s. 1; 2000-122, s. 4; 2006-145, s. 4.)

§ 58-2-30. Appointments of committees or councils.

(a) As used in this section, the term "committee" means a collective body that consults with and advises the Commissioner or his designee in detailed technical areas; and the term "council" means a collective body that consults with and advises the Commissioner or his designee as representative of citizen advice in specific areas of interest.

(b) The Commissioner may create and appoint committees and councils, each of which shall consist of no more than 13 members unless otherwise provided by law. The members of any committee or council shall serve at the pleasure of the Commissioner and may be paid per diem and necessary travel and subsistence expenses within the limits of appropriations and in accordance with G.S. 138-5. Per diem, travel, and subsistence payments to members of committees or councils that are created in connection with federal programs shall be paid from federal funds unless otherwise provided by law. (1985, c. 666, s. 44.)

§ 58-2-31. Seniors' Health Insurance Information Program.

The Seniors' Health Insurance Information Program is established within the Department as a statewide health benefits counseling program to provide the State's Medicare beneficiaries with counseling in Medicare, Medicare supplement insurance, long-term care insurance, and related health care coverage plans. (2011-196, s. 2.)

§ 58-2-35. Seal of Department.

The Commissioner, with the approval of the Governor, shall devise a seal, with suitable inscription, for his office, a description of which, with the certificate of approval by the Governor, shall be filed in the office of the Secretary of State, with an impression thereof, which seal shall thereupon become the seal of office of the Commissioner of the Department. The seal may be renewed whenever necessary. (1899, c. 54, s. 11; Rev., s. 4682; C.S., s. 6266; 1991, c. 720, ss. 4, 5.)

§ 58-2-40. Powers and duties of Commissioner.

The Commissioner shall:

(1) See that all laws of this State that the Commissioner is responsible for administering and the provisions of this Chapter are faithfully executed; and to that end the Commissioner is authorized to adopt rules in accordance with Chapter 150B of the General Statutes, in order to enforce, carry out and make effective the provisions of those laws. The Commissioner is also authorized to adopt such further rules not contrary to those laws that will prevent persons subject to the Commissioner's regulatory authority from engaging in practices injurious to the public.

(2) Have the power and authority to adopt rules pertaining to and governing the solicitation of proxies, including financial reporting in connection therewith, with respect to the capital stock or other equity securities of any domestic stock insurance company.

(3) Prescribe to the companies, associations, orders, or bureaus required by Articles 1 through 64 of this Chapter to report to the Commissioner, the necessary forms for the statements required. The Commissioner may change those forms from time to time when necessary to secure full information as to the standing, condition, and such other information desired of companies, associations, orders, or bureaus under the jurisdiction of the Department.

(4) Receive and thoroughly examine each financial statement required by Articles 1 through 64 of this Chapter.

(5) Report in detail to the Attorney General any violations of the laws relative to insurance companies, associations, orders and bureaus or the business of insurance; and the Commissioner may institute civil actions or criminal prosecutions either by the Attorney General or another attorney whom the Attorney General may select, for any violation of the provisions of Articles 1 through 64 of this Chapter.

(6) Upon a proper application by any citizen of this State, give a statement or synopsis of the provisions of any insurance contract offered or issued to the citizen.

(7) Administer, or the Commissioner's deputy may administer, all oaths required in the discharge of the Commissioner's official duty.

(8) Compile and make available to the public such lists of rates charged, including deviations, and such explanations of coverages that are provided by insurers for and in connection with contracts or policies of (i) insurance against loss to residential real property with not more than four housing units located in this State and any contents thereof or valuable interest therein and other insurance coverages written in connection with the sale of such property insurance and (ii) private passenger (nonfleet) motor vehicle liability, physical damage, theft, medical payments, uninsured motorists, and other insurance coverages written in connection with the sale of such insurance, as may be advisable to inform the public of insurance premium differentials and of the nature and types of coverages provided. The explanations of coverages

provided for in this section must comply with the provisions of Article 38 of this Chapter.

(9)   Repealed by Session Laws 2000-19, s. 3, effective on or after April 1, 1998.

(10)   Repealed by Session Laws 2013-5, s. 1(b), effective March 6, 2013. (1899, c. 54, s. 8; 1905, c. 430, s. 3; Rev., s. 4689; C.S., s. 6269; 1945, c. 383; 1947, c. 721; 1965, c. 127, s. 1; 1971, c. 757, s. 1; 1977, c. 376, s. 1; 1979, c. 755, s. 19; c. 881, s. 1; 1981, c. 846, s. 2; 1989, c. 485, s. 29; 1991, c. 644, s. 26; 1997-392, s. 3; 2000-19, s. 3; 2010-31, s. 24.2(a); 2013-5, s. 1(b).)

§ 58-2-45. Orders of Commissioner; when writing required.

Whenever by any provision of Articles 1 through 64 of this Chapter, the Commissioner is authorized to grant any approval, authorization or permission or to make any other order affecting any insurer, insurance agent, insurance broker or other person or persons subject to the provisions of Articles 1 through 64 of this Chapter, such order shall not be effective unless made in writing and signed by the Commissioner or by his authority. (1945, c. 383.)

§ 58-2-46. State of disaster automatic stay of proof of loss requirements; premium and debt deferrals; loss adjustments for separate windstorm policies.

Whenever (i) a state of disaster is proclaimed for the State or for an area within the State under G.S. 166A-19.21 or whenever the President of the United States has issued a major disaster declaration for the State or for an area within the State under the Stafford Act, 42 U.S.C. § 5121, et seq., as amended and (ii) if the Commissioner has issued an order declaring subdivisions (1) through (4) of this section effective for the specific disaster:

(1)   The application of any provision in an insurance policy insuring real property and its contents that are located within the geographic area designated in the proclamation or declaration, which provision requires an insured to file a proof of loss within a certain period of time after the occurrence of the loss, shall be stayed for the time period not exceeding the earlier of (i) the expiration of the disaster proclamation or declaration and all renewals of the proclamation or (ii)

the expiration of the Commissioner's order declaring subdivisions (1) through (4) of this section effective for the specific disaster, as determined by the Commissioner.

(2)   As used in this subdivision, "insurance company" includes a service corporation, HMO, MEWA, surplus lines insurer, and the underwriting associations under Articles 45 and 46 of this Chapter. All insurance companies, premium finance companies, collection agencies, and other persons subject to this Chapter shall give their customers who reside within the geographic area designated in the proclamation or declaration the option of deferring premium or debt payments that are due during the earlier of (i) [the time period covered by the proclamation or declaration or (ii)] the time period prior to the expiration of the Commissioner's order declaring subdivisions (1) through (4) of this section effective for the specific disaster, as determined by the Commissioner. This deferral period shall be 30 days from the last day the premium or debt payment may be made under the terms of the policy or contract. This deferral period shall also apply to any statute, rule, or other policy or contract provision that imposes a time limit on an insurer, insured, claimant, or customer to perform any act during the time period covered by the proclamation or declaration, including the transmittal of information, with respect to insurance policies or contracts, premium finance agreements, or debt instruments when the insurer, insured, claimant, or customer resides or is located in the geographic area designated in the proclamation or declaration. Likewise, the deferral period shall apply to any time limitations imposed on insurers under the terms of a policy or contract or provisions of law related to individuals who reside within the geographic area designated in the proclamation or declaration. Likewise, the deferral period shall apply to any time limitations imposed on insurers under the terms of a policy or contract or provisions of law related to individuals who reside within the geographic area designated in the proclamation or declaration. The Commissioner may extend any deferral period in this subdivision, depending on the nature and severity of the proclaimed or declared disaster. No additional rate or contract filing shall be necessary to effect any deferral period.

(3)   With respect to health benefit plans, after a deferral period has expired, all premiums in arrears shall be payable to the insurer. If premiums in arrears are not paid, coverage shall lapse as of the date premiums were paid up, and preexisting conditions shall apply as permitted under this Chapter; and the insured shall be responsible for all medical expenses incurred since the effective date of the lapse in coverage.

(4) In addition to the requirements of G.S. 58-45-35(e), for separate windstorm policies that are written by an insurer other than the Underwriting Association, losses shall be adjusted by the insurer that issued the property insurance and not by the insurer that issued the windstorm policy. The insurer that issued the windstorm policy shall reimburse the insurer that issued the property insurance for reasonable expenses incurred by that insurer in adjusting the windstorm losses. (2006-145, s. 3; 2012-12, s. 2(i); 2013-199, s. 22(a).)

§ 58-2-47. Incident affecting operations of the Department; stay of deadlines and deemer provisions.

Regardless of whether a state of emergency or disaster has been proclaimed under G.S. 166A-19.20 or G.S. 166A-19.21 or declared under the Stafford Act, whenever an incident beyond the Department's reasonable control, including an act of God, insurrection, strike, fire, power outage, or systematic technological failure, substantially affects the daily business operations of the Department, the Commissioner may issue an order, effective immediately, to stay the application of any deadlines and deemer provisions imposed by law or rule upon the Commissioner or Department or upon persons subject to the Commissioner's jurisdiction, which deadlines and deemer provisions would otherwise operate during the time period for which the operations of the Department have been substantially affected. The order shall remain in effect for a period not exceeding 30 days. The order may be renewed by the Commissioner for successive periods not exceeding 30 days each for as long as the operations of the Department remain substantially affected, up to a period of one year from the effective date of the initial order. (2006-145, s. 3; 2012-12, s. 2(j); 2013-199, s. 22(b).)

§ 58-2-50. Examinations, hearings, and investigations.

All examinations, hearings, and investigations provided for by this Chapter may be conducted by the Commissioner personally or by one or more deputies, investigators, actuaries, examiners or employees designated for the purpose. If the Commissioner or any investigator appointed to conduct the investigations is of the opinion that there is evidence to charge any person or persons with a criminal violation of any provision of this Chapter, the Commissioner may arrest with warrant or cause the person or persons to be arrested. All hearings shall, unless otherwise specially provided, be held in accordance with this Article and Article 3A of Chapter 150B of the General Statutes and at a time and place designated in a written notice given by the Commissioner to the person cited to appear. The notice shall state the subject of inquiry and the specific charges, if any. (1945, c. 383; 1969, c. 1009; 1995, c. 193, s. 6; 1999-219, s. 1.1.)

§ 58-2-52. Appeals and rate-making hearings before the Commissioner.

(a)   The Commissioner may adopt rules for the hearing of appeals by the Commissioner or the Commissioner's designated hearing officer under G.S. 58-36-35, 58-37-65, 58-45-50, 58-46-30, 58-48-40(c)(7), 58-48-42, and 58-62-51(c). These rules may provide for prefiled evidence and testimony of the parties, prehearing statements and conferences, settlement conferences, discovery, subpoenas, sanctions, motions, intervention, consolidation of cases, continuances, rights and responsibilities of parties, witnesses, and evidence.

(b)   Notwithstanding G.S. 150B-38(h), hearing procedures for rate filings made by the North Carolina Rate Bureau shall be governed by the provisions of Article 36 of this Chapter and G.S. 150B-39 through G.S. 150B-41. The Commissioner may adopt rules for those hearings.

(c)   Appeals under the statutes cited in subsection (a) of this section are not contested cases within the meaning of G.S. 150B-2(2). (1993, c. 409, s. 23; 1995, c. 193, s. 7.)

§ 58-2-53. Filing approvals and disapprovals; clarification of law.

Whenever any provision of this Chapter requires a person to file rates, forms, classification plans, rating plans, plans of operation, the Safe Driver Incentive Plan, or any other item with the Commissioner or Department for approval, the approval or disapproval of the filing is an agency decision under Chapter 150B of the General Statutes only with respect to the person making the filing or any person that intervenes in the filing. (2001-423, s. 2.)

§ 58-2-55. Designated hearing officers.

In any contested case under this Chapter or Article 9A or Article 9B of Chapter 143 of the General Statutes, the Commissioner may designate a member of his staff to serve as a hearing officer. When the Commissioner is unable or elects not to hear a contested case and elects not to designate a hearing officer to hear a contested case, he shall apply to the director of the Office of Administrative Hearings for the designation of an administrative law judge to preside at the hearing of a contested case. Upon receipt of the application, the Director shall, without undue delay, assign an administrative law judge to hear the case. (1989, c. 485, s. 30; 1999-393, s. 4.)

§ 58-2-60. Restraining orders; criminal convictions.

(a)   Whenever it appears to the Commissioner that any person has violated, is violating, or threatens to violate any provision of Articles 1 through 64, 65 and 66, 67, 69, 70, or 71 of this Chapter, or Article 9A of Chapter 143 of the General Statutes, he may apply to the superior court of any county in which the violation has occurred, is occurring, or may occur for a restraining order and injunction to restrain such violation. If upon application the court finds that any provision of said statutes has been violated, is being violated, or a violation thereof is threatened, the court shall issue an order restraining and enjoining such violations; and such relief may be granted regardless of whether criminal prosecution is instituted under any provision of law.

(b)   The conviction in any court of competent jurisdiction of any licensee for any criminal violation of the statutes referred to in subsection (a) of this section automatically has the effect of suspending the license of that person until such time that the license is reinstated by the Commissioner. As used in this subsection, "conviction" includes an adjudication of guilt, a plea of guilty, and a plea of nolo contendere. (1989, c. 485, s. 30.)

§ 58-2-65. License surrenders.

This section applies to persons or entities licensed under Articles 1 through 64, 65 and 66, 67, 69, 70, or 71 of this Chapter, or Article 9A of Chapter 143 of the General Statutes. When a licensee is accused of any act, omission, or misconduct that would subject the license to suspension or revocation, the licensee, with the consent and approval of the Commissioner, may surrender the license for a period of time established by the Commissioner. A person or entity who surrenders a license shall not thereafter be eligible for or submit any application for licensure during the period of license surrender. (1989, c. 485, s. 30.)

§ 58-2-69. Notification of criminal convictions and changes of address; service of notice; contracts for online services, administrative services, or regulatory data systems.

(a) As used in this section:

(1) "License" includes any license, certificate, registration, or permit issued under this Chapter.

(2) "Licensee" means any person who holds a license.

(b) Every applicant for a license shall inform the Commissioner of the applicant's residential address and provide the applicant's e-mail address to which the Commissioner can send electronic notifications and other messages. Every licensee shall give written notification to the Commissioner of any change of the licensee's residential or e-mail address within 10 business days after the licensee moves into the licensee's new residence or obtains a different e-mail address. This requirement applies if the change of residential address is by governmental action and there has been no actual change of residence location; in which case the licensee shall notify the Commissioner within 10 business days after the effective date of the change. A violation of this subsection is not a ground for revocation, suspension, or nonrenewal of the license or for the imposition of any other penalty by the Commissioner, though a licensee who violates this subsection shall pay an administrative fee of fifty dollars ($50.00) to the Commissioner.

(c) If a licensee is convicted in any court of competent jurisdiction for any crime or offense other than a motor vehicle infraction, the licensee shall notify the Commissioner in writing of the conviction within 10 days after the date of the conviction. As used in this subsection, "conviction" includes an adjudication of guilt, a plea of guilty, or a plea of nolo contendere.

(d) Notwithstanding any other provision of law, whenever the Commissioner is authorized or required to give any notice under this Chapter to a licensee, the notice may be given personally or by sending the notice by first-class mail to the licensee at the address that the licensee has provided to the Commissioner under subsection (b) of this section.

(e) The giving of notice by mail under subsection (d) of this section is complete upon the expiration of four days after the deposit of the notice in the post office. Proof of the giving of notice by mail may be made by the certificate of any employee of the Department.

(f) Notification by licensees under subsection (b) of this section may be accomplished by submitting written notification directly to the Commissioner or by using any online services approved by the Commissioner for this purpose.

(g) The Commissioner may contract with the NAIC or other persons for the provision of online services to applicants and licensees, for the provision of administrative services, for the provision of license processing and support services, and for the provision of regulatory data systems to the Commissioner. The NAIC or other person with whom the Commissioner contracts may charge applicants and licensees a reasonable fee for the provision of online services, the provision of administrative services, the provision of license processing and support services, and the provision of regulatory data systems to the Commissioner. The fee shall be agreed to by the Commissioner and the other contracting party and shall be stated in the contract. The fee is in addition to any applicable license application and renewal fees. Contracts for the provision of online services, contracts for the provision of administrative services, and contracts for the provision of regulatory data systems shall not be subject to Article 3, 3C, or 8 of Chapter 143 of the General Statutes or to Article 3D of Chapter 147 of the General Statutes. However, the Commissioner shall: (i) submit all proposed contracts for supplies, materials, printing, equipment, and contractual services that exceed one million dollars ($1,000,000) authorized by this subsection to the Attorney General or the Attorney General's designee for review as provided in G.S. 114-8.3; and (ii) include in all contracts to be awarded by the Commissioner under this subsection a standard clause which provides that the State Auditor and internal auditors of the Commissioner may audit the records of the contractor during and after the term of the agreement or contract to verify accounts and data affecting fees and performance. The Commissioner shall not award a cost plus percentage of cost agreement or contract for any purpose. (1998-211, s. 16; 2007-507, s. 15; 2009-566, s. 20; 2010-194, s. 6; 2011-196, s. 1; 2011-326, s. 15(f).)

§ 58-2-70. Civil penalties or restitution for violations; administrative procedure.

(a)   This section applies to any person who is subject to licensure or certification under this Chapter.

(b)   Whenever the Commissioner has reason to believe that any person has violated any of the provisions of this Chapter, and the violation subjects the license or certification of that person to suspension or revocation, the Commissioner may, after notice and opportunity for a hearing, proceed under the appropriate subsections of this section.

(c)   If, under subsection (b) of this section, the Commissioner finds a violation of this Chapter, the Commissioner may, in addition to or instead of suspending or revoking the license or certification, order the payment of a monetary penalty as provided in subsection (d) of this section or petition the Superior Court of Wake County for an order directing payment of restitution as provided in subsection (e) of this section, or both. Each day during which a violation occurs constitutes a separate violation.

(d)   If the Commissioner orders the payment of a monetary penalty pursuant to subsection (c) of this section, the penalty shall not be less than one hundred dollars ($100.00) nor more than one thousand dollars ($1,000). In determining the amount of the penalty, the Commissioner shall consider the degree and extent of harm caused by the violation, the amount of money that inured to the benefit of the violator as a result of the violation, whether the violation was committed willfully, and the prior record of the violator in complying or failing to comply with laws, rules, or orders applicable to the violator. The clear proceeds of the penalty shall be remitted to the Civil Penalty and Forfeiture Fund in accordance with G.S. 115C-457.2. Payment of the civil penalty under this section shall be in addition to payment of any other penalty for a violation of the criminal laws of this State.

(e)   Upon petition of the Commissioner the court may order the person who committed a violation specified in subsection (c) of this section to make restitution in an amount that would make whole any person harmed by the violation. The petition may be made at any time and also in any appeal of the Commissioner's order.

(f) Restitution to any State agency for extraordinary administrative expenses incurred in the investigation and hearing of the violation may also be ordered by the court in such amount that would reimburse the agency for the expenses.

(g) Nothing in this section prevents the Commissioner from negotiating a mutually acceptable agreement with any person as to the status of the person's license or certificate or as to any civil penalty or restitution.

(h) Unless otherwise specifically provided for, all administrative proceedings under this Chapter are governed by Chapter 150B of the General Statutes. Appeals of the Commissioner's orders under this section shall be governed by G.S. 58-2-75. (1985, c. 666, s. 35; 1987, c. 752, ss. 3-5; c. 864, s. 1; 1989, c. 485, s. 46; 1998-211, s. 15; 1998-215, s. 83(a).)

§ 58-2-75. Court review of orders and decisions.

(a) Any order or decision made, issued or executed by the Commissioner, except an order to make good an impairment of capital or surplus or a deficiency in the amount of admitted assets and except an order or decision that the premium rates charged or filed on all or any class of risks are excessive, inadequate, unreasonable, unfairly discriminatory or are otherwise not in the public interest or that a classification assignment is unwarranted, unreasonable, improper, unfairly discriminatory, or not in the public interest, shall be subject to review in the Superior Court of Wake County on petition by any person aggrieved filed within 30 days from the date of the delivery of a copy of the order or decision made by the Commissioner upon such person. A copy of such petition for review as filed with and certified to by the clerk of said court shall be served upon the Commissioner or in his absence upon someone in active charge of the Department within five days after the filing thereof. If such petition for review is not filed within the said 30 days, the parties aggrieved shall be deemed to have waived the right to have the merits of the order or decision reviewed and there shall be no trial of the merits thereof by any court to which application may be made by petition or otherwise, to enforce or restrain the enforcement of the same.

(b) The Commissioner shall within 30 days, unless the time be extended by order of court, after the service of the copy of the petition for review as provided in subsection (a) of this section, prepare and file with the clerk of the Superior

Court of Wake County a complete transcript of the record of the hearing, if any, had before him, and a true copy of the order or decision duly certified. The order or decision of the Commissioner if supported by substantial evidence shall be presumed to be correct and proper. The court may change the place of hearing,

(1)   Upon consent of the parties; or

(2)   When the convenience of witnesses and the ends of justice would be promoted by the change; or

(3)   When the judge has at any time been interested as a party or counsel.

The cause shall be heard by the trial judge as a civil case upon transcript of the record for review of findings of fact and errors of law only. It shall be the duty of the trial judge to hear and determine such petition with all convenient speed and to this end the cause shall be placed on the calendar for the next succeeding term for hearing ahead of all other cases except those already given priority by law. If on the hearing before the trial judge it shall appear that the record filed by the Commissioner is incomplete, he may by appropriate order direct the Commissioner to certify any or all parts of the record so omitted.

(c)   The trial judge shall have jurisdiction to affirm or to set aside the order or decision of the Commissioner and to restrain the enforcement thereof.

(d)   Appeals from all final orders and judgments entered by the superior court in reviewing the orders and decisions of the Commissioner may be taken to the appellate division of the General Court of Justice by any party to the action as in other civil cases.

(e)   The commencement of proceedings under this section shall not operate as a stay of the Commissioner's order or decision, unless otherwise ordered by the court. (1945, c. 383; 1947, c. 721; 1969, c. 44, s. 55; 1971, c. 703, s. 1.)

§ 58-2-80. Court review of rates and classification.

Any order or decision of the Commissioner that the premium rates charged or filed on all or any class of risks are excessive, inadequate, unreasonable, unfairly discriminatory or are otherwise not in the public interest or that a classification or classification assignment is unwarranted, unreasonable, improper, unfairly discriminatory or not in the public interest may be appealed to the North Carolina Court of Appeals by any party aggrieved thereby. Any such order shall be based on findings of fact, and if applicable, findings as to trends related to the matter under investigation, and conclusions of law based thereon. Any order or decision of the Commissioner, if supported by substantial evidence, shall be presumed to be correct and proper. For the purposes of the appeal the Insurance Commissioner, who shall be represented by his general counsel, shall be deemed an aggrieved party. (1971, c. 703, s. 2.)

§ 58-2-85. Procedure on appeal under § 58-2-80.

Appeals to the North Carolina Court of Appeals pursuant to G.S. 58-2-80 shall be subject to the following provisions:

(1)   No party to a proceeding before the Commissioner may appeal from any final order or decision of the Commissioner unless within 30 days after the entry of such final order or decision, or within such time thereafter as may be fixed by the Commissioner, by order made within 30 days, the party aggrieved by such decision or order shall file with the Commissioner notice of appeal.

(2)   Any party may appeal from all or any portion of any final order or decision of the Commissioner in the manner herein provided. Copy of the notice of appeal shall be mailed by the appealing party at the time of filing with the Commissioner, to each party to the proceeding to the addresses as they appear in the files of the Commissioner in the proceeding. The failure of any party, other than the Commissioner, to be served with or to receive a copy of the notice of appeal shall not affect the validity or regularity of the appeal.

(3)   Repealed by Session Laws 2009-566, s. 26, effective October 1, 2009, and applicable to appeals filed on or after that date.

(4)   The appeal shall lie to the Court of Appeals as provided in G.S. 7A-29. The procedure for the appeal shall be as provided by the rules of appellate procedure.

(5),   (6) Repealed by Session Laws 1975, c. 391, s. 11.

(7) The Court of Appeals shall hear and determine all matters arising on such appeal, as in this Article provided, and may in the exercise of its discretion assign the hearing of said appeal to any panel of the Court of Appeals.

(8) Unless otherwise provided by the rules of appellate procedure, the cause on appeal from the Commissioner of Insurance shall be entitled "State of North Carolina ex rel. Commissioner of Insurance (here add any additional parties in support of the Commissioner's order and their capacity before the Commissioner). Appellee(s) v. (here insert name of appellant and his capacity before the Commissioner), Appellant." Appeals from the Insurance Commissioner pending in the superior courts on January 1, 1972, shall remain on the civil issue docket of such superior court and shall have priority over other civil actions. Appeals to the Court of Appeals under G.S. 7A-29 shall be docketed in accordance with the rules of appellate procedure.

(9) In any appeal to the Court of Appeals, the complainant in the original complaint before the Commissioner shall be a party to the record and each of the parties to the proceeding before the Commissioner shall have a right to appear and participate in said appeal.

(10) An appeal under this section shall operate as a stay of the Commissioner's order or decision until said appeal has been dismissed or the questions raised by the appeal determined according to law. (1971, c. 703, s. 3; 1975, c. 391, s. 11; 2009-566, s. 26.)

§ 58-2-90. Extent of review under § 58-2-80.

(a) On appeal the court shall review the record in accordance with the rules of the Court of Appeals, and any alleged irregularities in procedures before the Commissioner, not shown in the record, shall be considered under the rules of the Court of Appeals.

(b) So far as necessary to the decision and where presented, the court shall decide all relevant questions of law, interpret constitutional and statutory provisions, and determine the meaning and applicability of the terms of any action of the Commissioner. The court may affirm or reverse the decision of the Commissioner, declare the same null and void, or remand the case for further proceedings; or it may reverse or modify the decision if the substantial rights of the appellants have been prejudiced because the Commissioner's findings, inferences, conclusions or decisions are:

(1)   In violation of constitutional provisions, or

(2)   In excess of statutory authority or jurisdiction of the Commissioner, or

(3)   Made upon unlawful proceedings, or

(4)   Affected by other errors of law, or

(5)   Unsupported by material and substantial evidence in view of the entire record as submitted, or

(6)   Arbitrary or capricious.

(c)   In making the foregoing determinations, the court shall review the whole record or such portions thereof as may be cited by any party and due account shall be taken of the rule of prejudicial error.

(d)   The court shall also compel action of the Commissioner unlawfully withheld or unlawfully or unreasonably delayed.

(e)   Upon any appeal, the rates fixed or any rule, regulation, finding, determination, or order made by the Commissioner under the provisions of Articles 1 through 64 of this Chapter shall be prima facie correct. (1971, c. 703, s. 4; 2009-566, s. 27.)

§ 58-2-95. Commissioner to supervise local inspectors.

The Commissioner shall exercise general supervision over local investigators of fires and fire prevention inspectors. Whenever the Commissioner has reason to believe that the local inspectors are not doing their duty, he or his deputy shall make special trips of inspection and take proper steps to have all the provisions of the law relative to the investigation of fires and the prevention of fire waste enforced. (1905, c. 506, s. 6; Rev., s. 4690; C.S., s. 6270; 1925, c. 89; 1969, c. 1063, s. 2.)

§ 58-2-100. Office of Commissioner a public office; records, etc., subject to inspection.

The office of the Commissioner shall be a public office and the records, reports, books and papers thereof on file therein shall be accessible to the inspection of the public, except that the records compiled as a part of an investigation for the crime of arson, that of unlawful burning, or of fraud, shall not be considered as public records and may be made available to the public only upon an order of court of competent jurisdiction. Provided that such records shall upon request be made available to the district attorney of any district if the same concerns persons or investigations in his district. (1899, c. 54, ss. 9, 77; Rev., s. 4683; 1907, c. 1000, s. 1; C.S., s. 6271; 1945, c. 383; 1951, c. 781, s. 11; 1955, c. 456; 1973, c. 47, s. 2.)

§ 58-2-105. Confidentiality of medical and credentialing records.

(a)   All patient medical records in the possession of the Department are confidential and are not public records pursuant to G.S. 58-2-100 or G.S. 132-1. As used in this section, "patient medical records" includes personal information that relates to an individual's physical or mental condition, medical history, or medical treatment, and that has been obtained from the individual patient, a health care provider, or from the patient's spouse, parent, or legal guardian.

(b)   Under Part 4 of Article 50 of this Chapter, the Department may disclose patient medical records to an independent review organization, and the organization shall maintain the confidentiality of those records as required by this section, except as allowed by G.S. 58-39-75 and G.S. 58-39-76.

(c)   Under Part 4 of Article 50 of this Chapter, all information related to the credentialing of medical professionals that is in the possession of the Commissioner is confidential and is a public record neither under this section nor under Chapter 132 of the General Statutes. (1989 (Reg. Sess., 1990), c. 1021, s. 4; 1993 (Reg. Sess., 1994), c. 678, s. 3; 2001-446, s. 5(a); 2002-187, s. 3.4.)

§ 58-2-110. Original documents and certified copies as evidence.

Every certificate, assignment, or conveyance executed by the Commissioner, in pursuance of any authority conferred on him by law and sealed with his seal of office, may be used as evidence and may be recorded in the proper recording offices, in the same manner and with like effect as a deed regularly acknowledged or proved before an officer authorized by law to take the probate of deeds; and all copies of papers in the office of the Commissioner, certified by him and authenticated by his official seal, shall be evidence as the original. (1899, c. 54, s. 11; Rev., s. 4684; C.S., s. 6272.)

§ 58-2-115. Admissibility of certificate as evidence of agent's authority.

In any case or controversy arising in any court of original jurisdiction within this State wherein it is necessary to establish the question as to whether any insurance or other corporation or agent thereof is or has been licensed by the Department to do business in this State, the certificate of the Commissioner under the seal of his office shall be admissible in evidence as proof of such corporation or agent's authority as conferred by the Department. (1929, c. 289, s. 1; 1991, c. 720, ss. 4, 5.)

§ 58-2-120. Reports of Commissioner to the Governor and General Assembly.

The Commissioner shall, from time to time, report to the Governor and the General Assembly any change or changes that in the Commissioner's opinion should be made in the laws relating to insurance and other subjects pertaining to the Department. (1899, c. 54, ss. 6, 7, 10; 1901, c. 391, s. 2; Rev., ss. 4687, 4688; 1911, c. 211, s. 2; C.S., s. 6273; 1927, c. 217, s. 5; 1945, c. 383; 1999-219, s. 8.)

§ 58-2-125. Authority over all insurance companies; no exemptions from license.

Every insurance company must be licensed and supervised by the Commissioner, and must pay all licenses, taxes, and fees as prescribed in the insurance laws of the State for the class of company, association, or order to which it belongs. No provision in any statute, public or private, may relieve any company, association, or order from the supervision prescribed for the class of companies, associations, or orders of like character, or release it from the payment of the licenses, taxes, and fees prescribed for companies, associations, and orders of the same class; and all such special provisions or exemptions are hereby repealed. It is unlawful for the Commissioner to grant or issue a license to any company, association, or order, or agent for them, claiming such exemption from supervision by his Department and release for the payment of license, fees, and taxes. (1903, c. 594, ss. 1, 2, 3; Rev., s. 4691; C.S., s. 6274; 1945, c. 383; 1991, c. 720, s. 4.)

§ 58-2-128. Interagency consultation.

(a) Purpose. - It is the stated intention of the Congress in P.L. 106-102, the Gramm-Leach-Bliley Act, that the Board of Governors of the Federal Reserve System, as the umbrella supervisor for financial holding companies, and the Commissioner, as the functional regulator of persons engaged in insurance activities, coordinate efforts to supervise persons that control both a depository institution and a person engaged in insurance activities regulated under State law. In particular, Congress believes that the Board and the Commissioner should share, on a confidential basis, information relevant to the supervision of persons that control both a depository institution and a person engaged in insurance activities, including information regarding the financial health of the consolidated organization and information regarding transactions and relationships between persons engaged in insurance activities and affiliated depository institutions. The purpose of this section is to encourage this coordination and confidential sharing of information and to thereby improve both the efficiency and the quality of the supervision of financial holding companies and their affiliated depository institutions and persons engaged in insurance activities.

(b) Commissioner's Authority. - Upon the request of the Board or the appropriate federal banking agency, the North Carolina Secretary of State, or the North Carolina Commissioner of Banks, the Commissioner may provide any examination or other reports, records, or other information to which the Commissioner has access with respect to a person that:

(1) Is engaged in insurance activities and regulated by the Commissioner.

(2) Is an affiliate of a depository institution or financial holding company.

Upon the request of the Board or the appropriate federal banking agency, the North Carolina Secretary of State, or the North Carolina Commissioner of Banks, the Commissioner may provide any examination or other reports, records, or other information to which the Commissioner has access with respect to any insurance producer.

(c) Privilege. - The provision of information or material under this section by the Commissioner does not constitute a waiver of, or otherwise affect, any privilege to which the information or material is otherwise subject.

(d) Definitions. - As used in this section, the terms:

(1) "Appropriate federal banking agency" and "depository institution" have the same meanings as in section 3 of the Federal Deposit Insurance Act, 12 U.S.C. § 1813.

(2) "Board" and "financial holding company" have the same meanings as in section 2 of the Bank Holding Company Act of 1956, 12 U.S.C. § 1841, et seq.

(3) "Insurance producer" or "producer" means a person required to be licensed under this Article to sell, solicit, or negotiate insurance. "Insurance producer" or "producer" includes an agent, a broker, and a limited representative. (2001-215, s. 1.)

§ 58-2-130: Repealed by Session Laws 1991, c. 681, s. 3.

§ 58-2-131. Examinations to be made; authority, scope, scheduling, and conduct of examinations.

(a) This section and G.S. 58-2-132 through G.S. 58-2-134 shall be known and may be cited as the Examination Law. The purpose of the Examination Law is to provide an effective and efficient system for examining the activities, operations, financial condition, and affairs of all persons transacting the business of insurance in this State and all persons otherwise subject to the Commissioner's jurisdiction; and to enable the Commissioner to use a flexible system of examinations that directs resources that are appropriate and necessary for the administration of the insurance statutes and rules of this State.

(b)   As used in this section and G.S. 58-2-132 through G.S. 58-2-134, unless the context clearly indicates otherwise:

(1)   "Commissioner" includes an authorized representative or designee of the Commissioner.

(2)   "Examination" means an examination conducted under the Examination Law.

(3)   "Examiner" means any person authorized by the Commissioner to conduct an examination.

(4)   "Insurance regulator" means the official or agency of another jurisdiction that is responsible for the regulation of a foreign or alien insurer.

(5)   "Person" includes a trust or any affiliate of a person.

(c)   Before licensing any person to write insurance in this State, the Commissioner shall be satisfied, by such examination and evidence as the Commissioner decides to make and require, that the person is otherwise duly qualified under the laws of this State to transact business in this State.

(d)   The Commissioner may conduct an examination of any entity whenever the Commissioner deems it to be prudent for the protection of policyholders or the public, but shall at a minimum conduct a financial examination of every domestic insurer not less frequently than once every five years. In scheduling and determining the nature, scope, and frequency of examinations, the Commissioner shall consider such matters as the results of financial statement analyses and ratios, changes in management or ownership, actuarial opinions, reports of independent certified public accountants, and other criteria as set forth in the NAIC Examiners' Handbook.

(e)   To complete an examination of any entity, the Commissioner may authorize an examination or investigation of any person, or the business of any person, insofar as the examination or investigation is necessary or material to the entity under examination.

(f) Instead of examining any foreign or alien insurer licensed in this State, the Commissioner may accept an examination report on that insurer prepared by the insurer's domiciliary insurance regulator. In making a determination to accept the domiciliary insurance regulator's report, the Commissioner may consider whether (i) the insurance regulator was at the time of the examination accredited under NAIC Financial Regulation Standards and Accreditation Program, or (ii) the examination is performed under the supervision of an NAIC-accredited insurance regulator or with the participation of one or more examiners who are employed by the regulator and who, after a review of the examination work papers and report, state under oath that the examination was performed in a manner consistent with the standards and procedures required by the regulator.

(g) If it appears that the insurer is of good financial and business standing and is solvent, and it is certified in writing and attested by the seal, if any, of the insurer's insurance regulator that it has been examined by the regulator in the manner prescribed by its laws, and was by the examination found to be in sound condition, that there is no reason to doubt its solvency, and that it is still permitted under the laws of such jurisdiction to do business therein, then, in the Commissioner's discretion, further examination may be dispensed with, and the obtained information and the furnished certificate may be accepted as sufficient evidence of the solvency of the insurer.

(h) Upon determining that an examination should be conducted, the Commissioner shall issue a notice of examination appointing one or more examiners to perform the examination and instructing them about the scope of the examination. In conducting the examination, an examiner shall observe the guidelines and procedures in the NAIC Examiners' Handbook. The Commissioner may also use such other guidelines or procedures as the Commissioner deems to be appropriate.

(i) Every person from whom information is sought and its officers, directors, and agents must provide to the Commissioner timely, convenient, and free access, at all reasonable hours at its offices, to all data relating to the property, assets, business, and affairs of the entity being examined. The officers, directors, employees, and agents of the entity must facilitate and aid in the examination. The refusal of any entity, by its officers, directors, employees, or agents, to submit to examination or to comply with any reasonable written request of the Commissioner or to knowingly or willfully make any false statement in regard to the examination or written request, is grounds for revocation, suspension, refusal, or nonrenewal of any license or authority held by the entity to engage in an insurance or other business subject to the Commissioner's jurisdiction.

(j) The Commissioner may issue subpoenas, administer oaths, and examine under oath any person about any matter pertinent to the examination. Upon the failure or refusal of any person to obey a subpoena, the Commissioner may petition the Superior Court of Wake County, and upon proper showing the Court may enter any order compelling the witness to appear and testify or produce documentary evidence. Failure to obey the Court order is punishable as contempt of court.

(k) When making an examination, the Commissioner may retain attorneys, appraisers, independent actuaries, independent certified public accountants, or other professionals and specialists as examiners. In the case of an examination of an insurer, the insurer shall bear the cost of retaining those persons.

(l) Pending, during, and after the examination of any entity, the Commissioner shall not make public the financial statement, findings, or examination report, or any report affecting the status or standing of the entity examined, until the entity examined has either accepted and approved the final examination report or has been given a reasonable opportunity to be heard on the report and to answer or rebut any statements or findings in the report. The hearing, if requested, shall be informal and private.

(m) Nothing in the Examination Law limits the Commissioner's authority to terminate or suspend any examination in order to pursue other legal or regulatory action under the laws and rules of this State and to use any final or preliminary examination report, any examiner or insurer work papers or other documents, or any other information discovered or developed during any examination in the furtherance of any legal or regulatory action that the Commissioner may consider to be appropriate. Findings of fact and conclusions made pursuant to any examination are prima facie evidence in any legal or regulator action. (1991, c. 681, s. 2; 1995, c. 360, s. 2(c); c. 517, s. 1; 1998-212, s. 26B(b), (c), (f); 2001-180, ss. 1, 2, 3; 2002-144, s. 6; 2002-187, ss. 2.1, 2.2; 2003-284, s. 22.2; 2004-124, s. 21.1.)

§ 58-2-132. Examination reports.

(a) All examination reports shall comprise only facts appearing upon the books, records, or other documents of the entity, its agents or other persons examined, or as ascertained from the testimony of its officers or agents or other persons examined concerning its affairs, and conclusions and recommendations that the examiners find reasonably warranted from the facts.

(b) No later than 60 days following completion of an examination, the examiners shall file with the Department a verified written examination report under oath. Upon receipt of the verified report, the Department shall send the report to the entity examined, together with a notice that affords the entity examined a reasonable opportunity of not more than 30 days to make a written submission or rebuttal with respect to any matters contained in the examination report. Within 30 days after the date of the examination report, the entity examined shall file affidavits executed by each of its directors stating under oath that they have received and read a copy of the report.

(c) At the end of the 30 days provided for the receipt of written submissions or rebuttals, the Commissioner shall fully consider and review the report, together with any written submissions or rebuttals and any relevant parts of the examiners' work papers and enter an order:

(1) Adopting the examination report as filed or with modifications or corrections. If the examination report reveals that the entity examined is operating in violation of any law, rule, or prior order of the Commissioner, the Commissioner may order the entity examined to take any action the Commissioner considers necessary and appropriate to cure the violation; or

(2) Rejecting the examination report with directions to the examiners to reopen the examination to obtain additional data, documentation of the information, and refiling under subdivision (1) of this subsection; or

(3) Calling for an investigatory hearing with no less than 20 days' notice to the insurer for purposes of obtaining additional documentation, data, and testimony.

(d) All orders entered under subdivision (c)(1) of this section shall be accompanied by findings and conclusions resulting from the Commissioner's consideration and review of the examination report, relevant examiner work papers, and any written submissions or rebuttals. Any such order shall be considered a final administration decision and shall be served upon the entity examined by certified mail. Any hearing conducted under subdivision (c)(3) of this section shall be conducted as a nonadversarial confidential investigatory proceeding as necessary for the resolution of any inconsistencies, discrepancies, or disputed issues apparent on the face of the filed examination report or raised by or as a result of the Commissioner's review of relevant work papers or by the written submission or rebuttal of the entity examined. Within 20 days after the conclusion of any such hearing, the Commissioner shall enter an order under subdivision (c)(1) of this section. The Commissioner may not appoint a member of the Department's examination staff as an authorized representative to conduct the hearing. The hearing shall proceed expeditiously with discovery by the entity examined limited to the examiner's work papers that tend to substantiate any assertions set forth in any written submission or rebuttal. The Commissioner may issue subpoenas for the attendance of any witnesses or the production of any documents the Commissioner considers to be relevant to the investigation, whether they are under the control of the Department, the entity examined, or other persons. The documents produced shall be included in the record, and testimony taken by the Commissioner shall be under oath and preserved for the record. Nothing in this section requires the Department to disclose any information or records that would show the existence or content of any investigation or activity of any federal or state criminal justice agency. In the hearing, the Commissioner shall question the persons subpoenaed. Thereafter the entity examined and the Department may present testimony relevant to the investigation. Cross-examination shall be conducted only by the Commissioner. The entity examined and the Department may make closing statements and may be represented by counsel of their choice.

(e) Upon completion of the examination report under subdivision (c)(1) of this section, the Commissioner shall hold the content of the examination report as private and confidential information for the 30-day period provided for written submissions or rebuttals. If after 30 days after the examination report has been submitted to it, the entity examined has neither notified the Commissioner of its acceptance and approval of the report nor requested to be heard on the report, the report shall then be filed as a public document and shall be open to public inspection, as long as no court of competent jurisdiction has stayed its publication. Nothing in the Examination Law prohibits the Commissioner from disclosing the content of the examination report, preliminary examination report or results, or any related matter, to an insurance regulator or to law enforcement officials of this or any other state or country or of the United States government at any time, as long as the person or agency receiving the report or related matters agrees in writing and is authorized by law to hold it confidential and in a manner consistent with this section. If the Commissioner determines that further regulatory action is appropriate as a result of any examination, the Commissioner may initiate such proceedings or actions as provided by law.

(f) All working papers, information, documents, and copies thereof produced by, obtained by, or disclosed to the Commissioner or any other person in connection with an examination, market analysis, market conduct action, or financial analysis shall be given confidential treatment, are not subject to subpoena, and shall not be made public by the Commissioner or any other person. The Commissioner may use the documents, materials, or other information in the furtherance of any regulatory or legal action brought as part of the Commissioner's official duties.

(g) In order to assist in the performance of the Commissioner's duties, the Commissioner may:

(1) Share documents, materials, or other information, including the confidential and privileged documents, materials, or information subject to subsection (f) of this section, with other state, federal, and international regulatory agencies, with the NAIC, and with state, federal, and international law enforcement authorities, provided that the recipient agrees to maintain the confidentiality and privileged status of the document, material, communication, or other information.

(2) Receive documents, materials, communications, or information, including otherwise confidential and privileged documents, materials, or information, from the NAIC, and from regulatory and law enforcement officials of other foreign or domestic jurisdictions, and shall maintain as confidential or privileged any document, material, or information received with notice or the understanding that it is confidential or privileged under the laws of the jurisdiction that is the source of the document, material, or information.

(3) Enter into agreements governing sharing and use of information consistent with this section.

(h) No waiver of an existing privilege or claim of confidentiality in the documents, materials, or information shall occur as a result of disclosure to the Commissioner under this section or as a result of sharing as authorized in subsection (g) of this section.

(i) A privilege established under the law of any state or jurisdiction that is substantially similar to the privilege established under this section shall be available and enforced in any proceeding in, and in any court of, this State.

(j) In this section, "department," "insurance regulator," "law enforcement official or authority," "NAIC," and "regulatory official or agency" include employees, agents, consultants, and contractors of those entities. (1991, c. 681, s. 2; 2001-180, s. 4; 2005-206, s. 2.)

§ 58-2-133. Conflict of interest; cost of examinations; immunity from liability.

(a) No person may be appointed as an examiner by the Commissioner if that person, either directly or indirectly, has a conflict of interest or is affiliated with the management of or owns a pecuniary interest in any person subject to examination. This section does not preclude an examiner from being:

(1) A policyholder or claimant under an insurance policy;

(2) A grantor of a mortgage or similar instrument on the examiner's residence to an insurer if done under customary terms and in the ordinary course of business;

(3) An investment owner in shares of regulated diversified investment companies; or

(4) A settler or beneficiary of a blind trust into which any otherwise nonpermissible holdings have been placed.

(b) Notwithstanding the requirements of G.S. 58-2-131, the Commissioner may retain from time to time, on an individual basis, qualified actuaries, certified public accountants, or other similar individuals who are independently practicing their professions, even though they may from time to time be similarly employed or retained by persons subject to examination under the Examination Law. In the case of an examination of an insurer, the insurer shall bear the cost of retaining those persons.

(c) The refusal of any insurer to submit to examination is grounds for the revocation, suspension, or refusal of a license. The Commissioner may make public any such revocation, suspension, or refusal of license and may give reasons for that action.

(d)   The provisions of G.S. 58-2-160 apply to examinations conducted under the Examination Law. (1991, c. 681, s. 2; 1995, c. 360, s. 2(d); 2002-144, s. 7; 2003-284, s. 22.2; 2004-124, s. 21.1.)

§ 58-2-134. Cost of certain examinations.

(a)   An insurer shall reimburse the State Treasurer for the actual expenses incurred by the Department in any examination of those records or assets conducted under G.S. 58-2-131, 58-2-132, or 58-2-133 under any of the following circumstances:

(1)   The insurer maintains part of its records or assets outside this State under G.S. 58-7-50 or G.S. 58-7-55 and the examination is of the records or assets outside this State.

(2)   The insurer requests an examination of its records or assets.

(3)   The Commissioner examines an insurer that is impaired or insolvent or is unlikely to be able to meet obligations with respect to known or anticipated claims or to pay other obligations in the normal course of business.

(4)   The examination involves analysis of the company's investment portfolio, a material portion of which comprises a sophisticated derivatives program, material holdings of collateralized mortgage obligations with high flux scores, unusual real estate or limited partnership holdings, high or unusual portfolio turnover, material asset movement between related parties, or unusual securities lending activities.

(b)   The amount paid by an insurer for an examination of records or assets under this section shall not exceed one hundred thousand dollars ($100,000), unless the insurer and the Commissioner agree on a higher amount. The State Treasurer shall deposit all funds received under this section in the Insurance Regulatory Fund established under G.S. 58-6-25. Funds received under this section shall be used by the Department for offsetting the actual expenses incurred by the Department for examinations under this section. (1998-212, s. 26B(d); 1999-435, s. 7; 2002-187, s. 2.3.)

§ 58-2-135: Repealed by Session Laws 1991, c. 681, s. 3.

§ 58-2-136. Insurer records sent to Department for examination; expenses.

(a) As used in this section, "records" means all data relating to the property, assets, business, and affairs of the insurer being examined.

(b) In addition to the Commissioner's authority in G.S. 58-2-185 through G.S. 58-2-200 to compel the production of records, in lieu of sending examiners to the location of an insurer's records to conduct an examination under the Examination Law, the Commissioner may require the insurer to send copies of its records to the Department. The chief executive or financial officer of the insurer shall certify under oath that the copies are true and accurate copies of the insurer's records. The insurer being examined shall pay all expenses associated with the examination. The insurer is not liable for the salaries and benefits of Department employees. The refusal by an insurer to pay for expenses under this subsection is grounds for the suspension, revocation, or refusal of a license.

(c) If the Commissioner sends examiners to the location of an insurer's records to conduct an examination under the Examination Law, the insurer shall pay for the travel and subsistence expenses and other administrative expenses associated with the examination. The insurer is not liable for the salaries and benefits of Department employees. The refusal by an insurer to pay for expenses under this subsection is grounds for the suspension, revocation, or refusal of a license. (2002-144, s. 8; 2003-284, s. 22.2; 2004-124, s. 21.1.)

§ 58-2-140: Repealed by Session Laws 1991, c. 681, s. 3.

§ 58-2-145: Repealed by Session Laws 1997-362, s. 7.

§ 58-2-150. Oath required for compliance with law.

Before issuing a license to any insurance company to transact the business of insurance in this State, the Commissioner shall require, in every case, in addition to the other requirements provided for by law, that the company file with the Commissioner the affidavit of its president or other chief officer that it accepts the terms and obligations of this Chapter as a part of the consideration of the license. (1899, c. 54, s. 110; 1901, c. 391, s. 8; Rev., s. 4693; C.S., s. 6276; 1991, c. 720, s. 4; 2004-199, s. 20(a); 2005-215, s. 1; 2006-105, s. 1.1.)

§ 58-2-155. Investigation of charges.

Upon his own motion or upon complaint being filed by a citizen of this State that a company authorized to do business in the State has violated any of the provisions of Articles 1 through 64 of this Chapter, the Commissioner shall investigate the matter, and, if necessary, examine, under oath, by himself or his accredited representatives the president and such other officer or agents of such companies as may be deemed proper; also all books, records, and papers of the same. In case the Commissioner shall find upon substantial evidence that any complaint against a company is justified, said company, in addition to such penalties as are imposed for violation of any of the provisions of Articles 1 through 64 of this Chapter, shall be liable for the expenses of the investigation, and the Commissioner shall promptly present said company with a statement of such expenses. If the company refuses or neglects to pay, the Commissioner is authorized to bring a civil action for the collection of these expenses. (1899, c. 54, s. 111; 1903, c. 438, s. 11; Rev., s. 4694; C.S., s. 6277; 1921, c. 136, s. 4; 1925, c. 275, s. 6; 1945, c. 383.)

§ 58-2-160. Reporting and investigation of insurance and reinsurance fraud and the financial condition of licensees; immunity from liability.

(a)   As used in this section, "Commissioner" includes an employee, agent, or designee of the Commissioner. A person, or an employee or agent of that person, acting without actual malice, is not subject to civil liability for libel, slander, or any other cause of action by virtue of furnishing to the Commissioner under the requirements of law or at the direction of the Commissioner reports or other information relating to (i) any known or suspected fraudulent insurance or reinsurance claim, transaction, or act or (ii) the financial condition of any licensee. In the absence of actual malice, members of the NAIC, their duly authorized committees, subcommittees, task forces, delegates, and employees, and all other persons charged with the responsibility of collecting, reviewing, analyzing, or disseminating the information developed from filings of financial statements or examinations of licensees are not subject to civil liability for libel, slander, or any other cause of action by virtue of their collection, review, analysis, or dissemination of the data and information collected from such filings or examinations.

(b) The Commissioner, acting without actual malice, is not subject to civil liability for libel or slander by virtue of an investigation of (i) any known or suspected fraudulent insurance or reinsurance claim, transaction, or act or (ii) the financial condition of any licensee; or by virtue of the publication or dissemination of any official report related to any such investigation, which report is published or disseminated in the absence of fraud, bad faith, or actual malice on the part of the Commissioner. The Commissioner is not subject to civil liability in relation to the collecting, reviewing, analyzing, or dissemination of information that is developed by the NAIC from the filing of financial statements with the NAIC or from the examination of insurers by the NAIC and that is communicated to the Commissioner, including any investigation or publication or dissemination of any report or other information in relation thereto, which report is published or disseminated in the absence of fraud, bad faith, negligence, or actual malice on the part of the Commissioner.

(c) During the course of an investigation of (i) a known or suspected fraudulent insurance or reinsurance claim, transaction, or act or (ii) the financial condition of any licensee, the Commissioner may request any person to furnish copies of any information relative to the (i) known or suspected claim, transaction, or act or (ii) financial condition of the licensee. The person shall release the information requested and cooperate with the Commissioner pursuant to this section. (1985 (Reg. Sess., 1986), c. 1013, s. 3; 1987, c. 864, s. 43; 1987 (Reg. Sess., 1988), c. 975, s. 3; 1989 (Reg. Sess., 1990), c. 1054, s. 1.)

§ 58-2-161. False statement to procure or deny benefit of insurance policy or certificate.

(a) For the purposes of this section:

(1) "Insurer" has the same meaning as in G.S. 58-1-5(3) and also includes:

a. Any hull insurance and protection and indemnity club operating under Article 20 of this Chapter.

b. Any surplus lines insurer operating under Article 21 of this Chapter.

c. Any risk retention group or purchasing group operating under Article 22 of this Chapter.

d. Any local government risk pool operating under Article 23 of this Chapter.

e. Any risk-sharing plan operating under Article 42 of this Chapter.

f. The North Carolina Insurance Underwriting Association operating under Article 45 of this Chapter.

g. The North Carolina Joint Insurance Underwriting Association operating under Article 46 of this Chapter.

h. The North Carolina Insurance Guaranty Association operating under Article 48 of this Chapter.

i. Any multiple employer welfare arrangement operating under Article 49 of this Chapter.

j. The North Carolina Life and Health Insurance Guaranty Association operating under Article 62 of this Chapter.

k. Any service corporation operating under Article 65 of this Chapter.

l. Any health maintenance organization operating under Article 67 of this Chapter.

m. The State Health Plan for Teachers and State Employees and any optional plans or programs operating under Part 2 of Article 3 of Chapter 135 of the General Statutes.

n. A group of employers self-insuring their workers' compensation liabilities under Article 47 of this Chapter.

o. An employer self-insuring its workers' compensation liabilities under Article 5 of Chapter 97 of the General Statutes.

p. The North Carolina Self-Insurance Security Association under Article 4 of Chapter 97 of the General Statutes.

q. Any reinsurer licensed or accredited under this Chapter.

(2) "Statement" includes any application, notice, statement, proof of loss, bill of lading, receipt for payment, invoice, account, estimate of property damages, bill for services, diagnosis, prescription, hospital or doctor records, X rays, test result, or other evidence of loss, injury, or expense.

(b) Any person who, with the intent to injure, defraud, or deceive an insurer or insurance claimant:

(1) Presents or causes to be presented a written or oral statement, including computer-generated documents as part of, in support of, or in opposition to, a claim for payment or other benefit pursuant to an insurance policy, knowing that the statement contains false or misleading information concerning any fact or matter material to the claim, or

(2) Assists, abets, solicits, or conspires with another person to prepare or make any written or oral statement that is intended to be presented to an insurer or insurance claimant in connection with, in support of, or in opposition to, a claim for payment or other benefit pursuant to an insurance policy, knowing that the statement contains false or misleading information concerning a fact or matter material to the claim is guilty of a Class H felony. Each claim shall be considered a separate count. Upon conviction, if the court imposes probation, the court may order the defendant to pay restitution as a condition of probation. In determination of the amount of restitution pursuant to G.S. 15A-1343(d), the reasonable costs and attorneys' fees incurred by the victim in the investigation of, and efforts to recover damages arising from, the claim, may be considered part of the damage caused by the defendant arising out of the offense.

In a civil cause of action for recovery based upon a claim for which a defendant has been convicted under this section, the conviction may be entered into evidence against the defendant. The court may award the prevailing party compensatory damages, attorneys' fees, costs, and reasonable investigative costs. If the prevailing party can demonstrate that the defendant has engaged in a pattern of violations of this section, the court may award treble damages. (1899, c. 54, s. 60; Rev., s. 3487; 1913, c. 89, s. 28; C.S., s. 4369; 1937, c. 248; 1967, c. 1088, s. 1; 1979, c. 760, s. 5; 1989 (Reg. Sess., 1990), c. 1054, s. 2; 1995, c. 43, s. 1; 1999-294, s. 3; 2005-400, s. 17; 2007-298, s. 8.1; 2007-323, s. 28.22A(o); 2007-345, s. 12.)

§ 58-2-162. Embezzlement by insurance agents, brokers, or administrators.

If any insurance agent, broker, or administrator embezzles or fraudulently converts to his own use, or, with intent to use or embezzle, takes, secretes, or otherwise disposes of, or fraudulently withholds, appropriates, lends, invests, or otherwise uses or applies any money, negotiable instrument, or other consideration received by him in his performance as an agent, broker, or administrator, he shall be guilty of a felony. If the value of the money, negotiable instrument, or other consideration is one hundred thousand dollars ($100,000) or more, violation of this section is a Class C felony. If the value of the money, negotiable instrument, or other consideration is less than one hundred thousand dollars ($100,000), violation of this section is a Class H felony. (1889, c. 54, s. 103; Rev., s. 3489; 1911, c. 196, s. 8; C.S., s. 4274; 1989 (Reg. Sess., 1990), c. 1054, s. 2; 1997-443, s. 19.25(n).)

§ 58-2-163. Report to Commissioner.

Whenever any insurance company, or employee or representative of such company, or any other person licensed or registered under Articles 1 through 67 of this Chapter knows or has reasonable cause to believe that any other person has violated G.S. 58-2-161, 58-2-162, 58-2-164, 58-2-180, 58-8-1, 58-24-180(e), or whenever any insurance company, or employee or representative of such company, or any other person licensed or registered under Articles 1 through 67 of this Chapter knows or has reasonable cause to believe that any entity licensed by the Commissioner is financially impaired, it is the duty of such person, upon acquiring such knowledge, to notify the Commissioner and provide the Commissioner with a complete statement of all of the relevant facts and circumstances. Such report is a privileged communication, and when made without actual malice does not subject the person making the same to any liability whatsoever. The Commissioner may suspend, revoke, or refuse to renew the license of any licensee who willfully fails to comply with this section. (1945, c. 382; 1987, c. 752, s. 2; 1989 (Reg. Sess., 1990), c. 1054, s. 2; 2007-443, s. 4.)

§ 58-2-164. Rate evasion fraud; prevention programs.

(a) The following definitions apply in this section:

(1) "Applicant" means one or more persons applying for the issuance or renewal of an auto insurance policy.

(2) "Auto insurance" means nonfleet private passenger motor vehicle insurance.

(3) "Eligible applicant" means a person who is an eligible risk under G.S. 58-37-1(4a).

(4) "Insurer" means a member of the North Carolina Rate Bureau that is licensed to write and is writing auto insurance in this State.

(5) "Nonfleet" means a motor vehicle as defined in G.S. 58-40-10(2).

(6) "Private passenger motor vehicle" means a motor vehicle as defined in G.S. 58-40-10(1).

(b) It shall be a Class 3 misdemeanor for any person who, with the intent to deceive an insurer, does any of the following:

(1) Present or cause to be presented a written or oral statement in support of an application for auto insurance or for vehicle registration pursuant to G.S 20-52(a)(4) and (a)(5), knowing that the application contains false or misleading information that states the applicant is an eligible risk when the applicant is not an eligible risk.

(2) Assist, abet, solicit, or conspire with another person to prepare or make any written or oral statement that is intended to be presented to an insurer in connection with or in support of an application for auto insurance or for vehicle registration pursuant to G.S. 20-52(a)(4) and (a)(5), if the person knows that the

statement contains false or misleading information that states the applicant is an eligible risk when the applicant is not an eligible risk.

In addition to any other penalties authorized by law, a violation of this subsection may be punishable by a fine of not more than one thousand dollars ($1,000) for each violation.

(c)   The insurer and its agent shall also take reasonable steps to verify that the information provided by an applicant regarding the applicant's address and the place the motor vehicle is garaged is correct. The insurer may take its own reasonable steps to verify residency or eligible risk status or may rely upon the agent verification of residency or eligible risk status to meet the insurer's verification obligations under this section. The agent shall retain copies of any items obtained under this section as required under the record retention rules adopted by the Commissioner and in accordance with G.S. 58-2-185. The agent may satisfy the requirements of this section by obtaining reliable proof of North Carolina residency from the applicant or the applicant's status as an eligible risk. Reliable proof of residency or eligible risk includes but is not limited to:

(1)   A pay stub with the payee's address.

(2)   A utility bill showing the address of the applicant-payor.

(3)   A lease for an apartment, house, modular unit, or manufactured home with a North Carolina address signed by the applicant.

(4)   A receipt for personal property taxes paid.

(5)   A receipt for real property taxes paid to a North Carolina locality.

(6)   A monthly or quarterly financial statement from a North Carolina regulated financial institution.

(7)   A valid unexpired North Carolina driver's license.

(8)   A matricula consular or substantially similar document issued by the Mexican Consulate for North Carolina.

(9)   A document similar to that described in subdivision (8) of this section, issued by the consulate or embassy of another country that would be accepted by the North Carolina Division of Motor Vehicles as set forth in G.S. 20-7(b4)(9).

(10) A valid North Carolina vehicle registration.

(11) A valid military ID.

(12) A valid student ID for a North Carolina school or university.

(d) In the absence of actual malice, neither an insurer, the authorized representative of the insurer, a producer, the Commissioner, an organization of which the Commissioner is a member, the North Carolina Reinsurance Facility, nor the respective employees and agents of such persons acting on behalf of such persons shall be subject to civil liability as a result of any statement or information provided or action taken pursuant to this section.

(e) In any action brought against a person that may have immunity under subsection (d) of this section for making any statement required by this section or for providing any information relating to any statement that may be requested by the Commissioner, the party bringing the action shall plead specifically in any allegation that subsection (d) of this section does not apply because the person making the statement or providing the information did so with actual malice. Subsections (d) and (e) of this section do not abrogate or modify any existing statutory or common law privileges or immunities.

(f) Every insurer shall maintain safeguards within its auto insurance business at the point of sale, renewal, and claim to identify misrepresentations by applicants regarding their addresses and the places their motor vehicles are garaged. Identified misrepresentations are subject to the requirements of Article 2 of this Chapter.

(g) If an applicant provides false and misleading information as to the applicant's or any named insured's status as an eligible applicant and that fraudulent information makes the applicant or any named insured appear to be an eligible applicant when that person is in fact not an eligible applicant, the insurer may do any or all of the following:

(1) Refuse to issue a policy.

(2) Cancel or refuse to renew a policy that has been issued.

(3) Deny coverage for any claim arising out of bodily injury or property damage suffered by the applicant. This subdivision does not apply to innocent third parties.

(h) In a civil cause of action for recovery based upon a claim for which a defendant has been convicted under this section, the conviction may be entered into evidence against the defendant and shall establish the liability of the defendant as a matter of law for such damages, fees, or costs as may be proven. The court may award the prevailing party compensatory damages including but not limited to any costs, losses, expenses, and attorneys' fees incurred in connection with any false statement of eligible risk status made in an application for insurance or incurred in connection with any claim submitted under a policy obtained as a result of a false statement of status as an eligible risk, attorneys' fees, costs, and reasonable investigative costs. If the prevailing party can demonstrate that the defendant has engaged in a pattern of violations of this section, the court may award treble damages. (2007-443, s. 3.)

§ 58-2-165. Annual, semiannual, monthly, or quarterly statements to be filed with Commissioner.

(a) Except as provided in subsection (a1) of this section, every insurance company shall file in the Commissioner's office, on or before March 1 of each year, a statement showing the business standing and financial condition of the company, association, or order on the preceding December 31, signed and sworn to by the chief managing agent or officer thereof, before the Commissioner or some officer authorized by law to administer oaths. Provided, the Commissioner may, for good and sufficient cause shown by an applicant company, extend the filing date of the company's annual statement, for a reasonable period of time, not to exceed 30 days. In addition, except as provided in subsection (a1) of this section, the Commissioner may require any insurance company, association, or order to file its statement semiannually, quarterly, or monthly.

(a1) A town or county mutual, organized under G.S. 58-7-75(5)d., is required to file only an annual statement or an audited financial statement that was prepared by a certified public accountant if for the preceding year it had a direct written premium of less than one hundred fifty thousand dollars ($150,000) and fewer than 400 policyholders. The Commissioner shall not require those mutuals to file statements semiannually, quarterly, or monthly.

(b) The Commissioner may require statements under this section, G.S. 58-2-170, and G.S. 58-2-190 to be filed in a format that can be read by electronic data processing equipment, provided that this subsection does not apply to an audited financial statement prepared by a certified public accountant that is submitted by a town or county mutual pursuant to subsection (a1) of this section.

(c) Except as provided herein, all statements filed under this section must be prepared in accordance with the appropriate NAIC Annual Statement Instructions Handbook and pursuant to the NAIC Accounting Practices and Procedures Manual and on the NAIC Model Financial Statement Blank, unless further modified by the Commissioner as the Commissioner considers to be appropriate. This subsection does not apply to statements filed by a town or county mutual organized under G.S. 58-7-75(5)d. if for the preceding year it had a direct written premium of less than one hundred fifty thousand dollars ($150,000) and fewer than 400 policyholders. (1899, c. 54, ss. 72, 73, 83, 90, 97; 1901, c. 706, s. 2; 1903, c. 438, s. 9; Rev., s. 4698; C.S., s. 6280; 1945, c. 383; 1957, c. 407; 1985, c. 666, ss. 50, 51; 1985 (Reg. Sess., 1986), c. 1013, s. 11; 1991, c. 681, s. 7; 1993, c. 504, s. 1; 1998-211, s. 22; 1999-192, s. 1.)

§ 58-2-170. Annual statements by professional liability insurers; medical malpractice claim reports.

(a) In addition to the financial statements required by G.S. 58-2-165, every insurer, self-insurer, and risk retention group that provides professional liability insurance in the State shall file with the Commissioner, on or before the first day of February in each year, in form and detail as the Commissioner prescribes, a statement showing the items set forth in subsection (b) of this section, as of the preceding 31st day of December. The annual statement shall not be reported or disclosed to the public in a manner or format which identifies or could reasonably be used to identify any individual health care provider or medical center. The statement shall be signed and sworn to by the chief managing agent or officer of the insurer, self-insurer, or risk retention group, before the Commissioner or some officer authorized by law to administer oaths. The Commissioner shall, in December of each year, furnish to each such person that provides professional liability insurance in the State forms for the annual statements. The Commissioner may, for good cause, authorize an extension of the report due date upon written application of any person required to file. An extension is not valid unless the Commissioner's authorization is in writing and signed by the Commissioner or one of his deputies.

(b) The statement required by subsection (a) of this section shall contain:

(1) Number of claims pending at beginning of year;

(2) Number of claims pending at end of year;

(3) Number of claims paid;

(4) Number of claims closed no payment;

(5) Number and amounts of claims in court in which judgment paid:

a. Highest amount

b. Lowest amount

c. Average amount

d. Median amount;

(6) Number and amounts of claims out of court in which settlement paid:

a. Highest amount

b. Lowest amount

c. Average amount

d. Median amount;

(7) Average amount per claim set up in reserve;

(8) Total premium collection;

(9) Total expenses less reserve expenses; and

(10) Total reserve expenses.

(c) Every insurer, self-insurer, and risk retention group that provides professional liability insurance to health care providers in this State shall file, within 90 days following the request of the Commissioner, a report containing information for the purpose of allowing the Commissioner to analyze claims. The report shall be in the form prescribed by the Commissioner. The form prescribed by the Commissioner shall be a form that permits the public inspection, examination, or copying of any information contained in the report: Provided, however, that any data or other characteristics that identify or could be used to identify the names or addresses of the claimants or the names or addresses of the individual health care provider or medical center against whom the claims are or have been asserted or any data that could be used to identify the dollar amounts involved in such claims shall be treated as privileged information and shall not be made available to the public. The Commissioner shall analyze these reports and shall file statistical and other summaries based on these reports with the General Assembly as soon as practicable after receipt of the reports. The Commissioner shall assess a penalty against any person that willfully fails to file a report required by this subsection. Such penalty shall be one thousand dollars ($1,000) for each day after the due date of the report that the person willfully fails to file: Provided, however, the penalty for an individual who self insures shall be two hundred dollars ($200.00) for each day after the due date of the report that the person willfully fails to file: Provided, however, that upon the failure of a person to file the report as required by this subsection, the Commissioner shall send by certified mail, return receipt requested, a notice to that person informing him that he has 10 business days after receipt of the notice to either request an extension of time or file the report. The Commissioner may, for good cause, authorize an extension of the report due date upon written application of any person required to file. An extension is not valid unless the Commissioner's authorization is in writing and signed by the Commissioner or one of his deputies.

(d) Every person that self-insures against professional liability in this State shall provide the Commissioner with written notice of such self-insurance, which notice shall include the name and address of the person self-insuring. This notice shall be filed with the Commissioner each year for the purpose of apprising the Commissioner of the number and locations of persons that self-insure against professional liability. (1975, 2nd Sess., c. 977, s. 6; 1985, c. 666, s. 53; 1987, c. 343.)

§ 58-2-171. Qualifications of actuaries.

The Commissioner may adopt rules setting forth requisite qualifications of consulting actuaries for the sole purpose of qualifying them to certify financial statements filed and rate filings made by entities under this Chapter as to the actuarial validity of those filings. The qualifications shall be commensurate with the degree of complexity of the actuarial principles applicable to the various statements filed or rate filings made. Nothing in this section affects the scope of practice or the professional qualifications of actuaries. (1995, c. 517, s. 2.)

§ 58-2-175: Repealed by Session Laws 1993, c. 452, s. 65.

§ 58-2-180. Punishment for making false statement.

If any person in any financial or other statement required by this Chapter willfully misstates information, that person making oath to or subscribing the statement is guilty of a Class I felony; and the entity on whose behalf the person made the oath or subscribed the statement is subject to a fine imposed by the court of not less than two thousand dollars ($2,000) nor more than ten thousand dollars ($10,000). (1899, c. 54, s. 97; Rev., s. 3493; C.S., s. 6281; 1985, c. 666, s. 13; 1989 (Reg. Sess., 1990), c. 1054, s. 5; 1993 (Reg. Sess., 1994), c. 767, s. 23.)

§ 58-2-185. Record of business kept by companies and agents; Commissioner may inspect.

All companies, agents, or brokers doing any kind of insurance business in this State must make and keep a full and correct record of the business done by them, showing the number, date, term, amount insured, premiums, and the persons to whom issued, of every policy or certificate or renewal. Information from these records must be furnished to the Commissioner on demand, and the original books of records shall be open to the inspection of the Commissioner when demanded. (1899, c. 54, s. 108; 1903, c. 438, s. 11; Rev., s. 4696; C.S., s. 6284; 1945, c. 383; 1991, c. 720, s. 4.)

§ 58-2-190. Commissioner may require special reports.

The Commissioner may also address to any authorized insurer, statistical organization, joint underwriting or joint reinsurance organization, or the North Carolina Rate Bureau or Motor Vehicle Reinsurance Facility, or its officers any inquiry in relation to its transactions or condition or any matter connected therewith. Every corporation or person so addressed shall reply in writing to the inquiry promptly and truthfully, and the reply shall be verified, if required by the Commissioner, by such individual, or by such officer or officers of a corporation, as he shall designate. (1945, c. 383; 1985 (Reg. Sess., 1986), c. 1027, s. 8; 2005-210, s. 1.)

§ 58-2-195. Commissioner may require records, reports, etc., for agencies, agents and others.

(a) The Commissioner is empowered to make and promulgate reasonable rules and regulations governing the recording and reporting of insurance business transactions by insurance agencies, agents, brokers and producers of record, any of which agencies, agents, brokers or producers of record are licensed in this State or are transacting insurance business in this State to the end that such records and reports will accurately and separately reflect the insurance business transactions of such agency, agent, broker or producer of record in this State. Information from records required to be kept pursuant to the provisions of this section must be furnished the Commissioner on demand and the original records required to be kept pursuant to the provisions of this section shall be open to the inspection for the Commissioner or any other authorized employee described in G.S. 58-2-25 when demanded.

(b) Every insurance agency transacting insurance business in this State shall at all times have appointed some person employed or associated with such agency who shall have the responsibility of seeing that such records and reports as are required pursuant to the provisions of this section are kept and maintained.

(c) Any person subject to the provisions of subsection (a) of this section who violates the provisions of this section or the rules and regulations prescribed by the Commissioner pursuant to the provisions of this section may after notice and hearing: for the first offense have his license or licenses (in case license be issued for more than one company in such person's case) suspended or revoked for not less than one month nor more than six months and for the second offense shall have his license or licenses (in case license be issued from more than one company in his case) suspended or revoked for the period of one year and such person shall not thereafter be licensed for one year from the date said revocation or suspension first became effective.

(d)   For the purpose of enforcing the provisions of this section the Commissioner or any other authorized employee described in G.S. 58-2-25 is authorized and empowered to examine persons, administer oaths and require production of papers and records relative to this section.

(e)   Whenever the Commissioner deems it to be prudent for the protection of policyholders in this State, he or any other authorized employee described in G.S. 58-2-25 shall visit and examine any insurance agency, agent, broker, adjuster, motor vehicle damage appraiser, or producer of record. The refusal of any agency, agent, broker, adjuster, motor vehicle damage appraiser, or producer of record to submit to examination is grounds for the revocation or refusal of a license. (1971, c. 948, s. 1; 1987, c. 629, ss. 14, 15; c. 752, s. 1; 1995, c. 360, s. 2(e).)

§ 58-2-200. Books and papers required to be exhibited.

It is the duty of any person having in his possession or control any books, accounts, or papers of any company licensed under Articles 1 through 64 of this Chapter, to exhibit the same to the Commissioner or to any deputy, actuary, accountant, or persons acting with or for the Commissioner. Any person who shall refuse, on demand, to exhibit the books, accounts, or papers, as above provided, or who shall knowingly or willfully make any false statement in regard to the same, shall be subject to suspension or revocation of his license under Articles 1 through 64 of this Chapter; and shall be deemed guilty of a Class 1 misdemeanor. (1899, c. 54, s. 76; Rev., ss. 3494, 4697; 1907, c. 1000, s. 3; C.S., s. 6286; 1945, c. 383; 1985 (Reg. Sess., 1986), c. 1013, s. 6; 1991, c. 720, s. 4; 1993, c. 539, s. 445; 1994, Ex. Sess., c. 24, s. 14(c).)

§ 58-2-205. CPA audits of financial statements.

The Commissioner may adopt rules to provide for audits and opinions of insurers' financial statements by certified public accountants. These rules shall be substantially similar to the NAIC model rule that requires audited financial reports, as amended. The Commissioner may adopt, amend, or repeal provisions of these rules under G.S. 150B-21.1 in order to keep these rules current with the NAIC model rule. (1989, c. 485, s. 38; 1998-212, s. 26B(g).)

§ 58-2-210. Rules for mortgage insurance consolidations.

The Commissioner is authorized to adopt rules governing mortgage insurance consolidations and related rules concerning unfair rate discrimination. In the event the Commissioner adopts such rules, while such rules are in effect the unfair rate discrimination provisions of G.S. 58-58-35 and G.S. 58-63-15(7) will not apply to mortgage insurance consolidations to the extent those provisions are inconsistent with such rules. For purposes of this section, "mortgage insurance consolidation" means any transaction in which a mortgage loan servicer makes its premium collection services available to mortgage debtors in connection with an insurer's offer of mortgage insurance, which offer is made to debtors who, immediately prior to the offer, had mortgage insurance with another insurer and were paying premiums for that insurance with their monthly mortgage payments. (1989, c, 341, s. 1.)

§ 58-2-215. Consumer Protection Fund.

(a)   A special fund is created in the Office of the State Treasurer, to be known as the Department of Insurance Consumer Protection Fund. The Fund shall be placed in an interest bearing account and any interest or other income derived from the Fund shall be credited to the Fund. Moneys in the Fund shall only be spent pursuant to warrants drawn by the Commissioner on the Fund through the State Treasurer. The Fund shall be subject to the provisions of the Executive Budget Act; except that the provisions of Article 3C of Chapter 143 of the General Statutes do not apply to subdivision (b)(1) of this section.

(b)   All moneys credited to the Fund shall be used only to pay the following expenses incurred by the Department:

(1) For the purpose of retaining outside actuarial and economic consultants, legal counsel, and court reporting services in the review and analysis of rate filings and any other insurance regulatory matters, in conducting all hearings, and through any final adjudication.

(2) In connection with any delinquency proceeding under Article 30 of this Chapter, for the purpose of locating and recovering the assets of or any other obligations or liabilities owed to or due an insurer that has been placed under such proceeding.

(3) In connection with any civil litigation, other than under Chapter 150B of the General Statutes or any appeal from an order of the Commissioner or his deputies, that is commenced against the Commissioner or his deputies and that arises out of the performance of their official duties, for the purpose of retaining outside consultants, legal counsel, and court reporting services to defend such litigation.

(c) Moneys appropriated by the General Assembly shall be deposited in the Fund and shall become a part of the continuation budget of the Department of Insurance. Such continuation budget amount shall equal the actual expenditures drawn from the Fund during the prior fiscal year plus the official inflation rate designated by the Director of the Budget in the preparation of the State Budget for each ensuing fiscal year; provided that if interest income on the Fund exceeds the amount yielded by the application of the official inflation rate, such continuation budget amount shall be the actual expenditures drawn from the Fund. In the event the amount in the Fund exceeds two hundred fifty thousand dollars ($250,000) at the end of any fiscal year, such excess shall revert to the General Fund.

(d) Repealed by Session Laws 1996, c. 507, s. 11A(a), (b). (1989 (Reg. Sess., 1990), c. 1069, s. 22; 1993 (Reg. Sess., 1994), c. 769, s. 14.1; 1995, c. 507, s. 11A(a), (b), (c); 2005-215, s. 21; 2012-142, s. 20.2; 2013-360, s. 20.1.)

§ 58-2-220. Insurance Regulatory Information System and similar program test data not public records.

Except as provided in G.S. 58-4-25, financial test ratios, data, or information generated by the Commissioner pursuant to the NAIC Insurance Regulatory Information System, any successor program, or any similar program developed by the Commissioner, are not public records and are not subject to Chapter 132 of the General Statutes or G.S. 58-2-100. (1985 (Reg. Sess., 1986), c. 1013, s. 9; 1989 (Reg. Sess., 1990), c. 1021, s. 7; 1991, c. 681, s. 14.)

§ 58-2-225: Repealed by Session Laws 1995, c. 193, s. 8.

§ 58-2-230. Commissioner to share information with Department of Labor.

The Commissioner shall provide or cause to be provided to the Department of Labor, on an annual basis, the name and business address of every employer that is self-insured for workers' compensation. Information provided or caused to be provided by the Commissioner to the Department of Labor under this section is confidential and not open for public inspection under G.S. 132-6. (1991 (Reg. Sess., 1992), c. 894, s. 5.)

§ 58-2-235: Expired.

§ 58-2-240. Market conduct analysis, financial analysis, and related information not public record.

(a) Notwithstanding Chapter 132 of the General Statutes, all market analysis, documents arising from market conduct action, and financial statement analysis work papers are confidential, are not open for public inspection, and are not discoverable or admissible in evidence in a civil action brought by a party other than the Department against a person regulated by the Department, its directors, officers, or employees, unless the court finds that the interests of justice require that the documents be discoverable or admissible in evidence or except as provided in G.S. 58-2-128 and G.S. 58-2-132(g) through (j). The Commissioner, however, may use market analysis, documents arising from market conduct action, and financial statement analysis work papers in the furtherance of any regulatory or legal action brought as part of the Commissioner's official duties.

(b) As used in this Article:

(1) "Financial statement analysis" means a set of systems and procedures designed to provide relevant information derived from basic sources of data for the purpose of evaluating the risk of an insurer's insolvency.

(1a) "Financial statement analysis work papers" means:

a. Documents, programs, findings, and other information produced by persons employed or contracted by the Commissioner during and as part of the financial statement analysis of an insurer.

b. Documents, programs, findings, and other information disclosed by an entity to persons employed or contracted by the Commissioner in response to an inquiry from the Commissioner during and as part of the financial statement analysis of the insurer.

c. Documents, programs, findings, and other information obtained, during and as part of the financial statement analysis of an insurer, by persons employed or contracted by the Commissioner from or through any regulatory or law enforcement agency or the NAIC when the receipt of that information is conditioned upon the Commissioner maintaining the confidentiality of the information shared with the Commissioner.

"Financial statement analysis work papers" includes financial analysis programs and procedures; correspondence between persons employed or contracted by the Commissioner and the insurer during and as part of the financial statement analysis; memos, e-mails, and other correspondence, in any form, produced by persons employed or contracted by the Commissioner detailing findings or recommendations of the financial statement analysis; and the Actuarial Opinion Summary filed by an insurer as required by and in accordance with NAIC Annual Statement Instructions. "Financial statement analysis work papers" does not mean statements filed with the Commissioner under G.S. 58-2-165, CPA audit reports filed with the Commissioner under G.S. 58-2-205, or documents that constitute an initial filing and any supplemental filing necessary to complete a filing made by an insurer, independent of financial statement analysis.

(1b) "Market analysis" means work product arising from a process whereby persons employed or contracted by the Commissioner collect and analyze information from filed schedules, surveys, required reports other than periodic reports specifically required by statute, and other sources in order to develop a baseline understanding of the marketplace and to identify patterns or practices of insurers that deviate significantly from the norm or that may pose a potential risk to the insurance consumer.

(2) "Market conduct action" means any of the full range of activities, other than an examination that the Commissioner may initiate to assess and address the market practices of insurers, beginning with market analysis. Additional market conduct actions, including those taken subsequent to market analysis as a result of the findings of or indications from market analysis include: correspondence with an insurer; insurer interviews; information gathering; policy and procedure reviews; interrogatories; and review of insurer self-evaluation and compliance programs, including membership in a best-practice organization. The Commissioner's activities to resolve an individual consumer complaint or other report of a specific instance of misconduct are not market conduct actions for purposes of this section.

(c) For purposes of subdivisions (b)(1) and (b)(1a) of this section only, the term "insurer" has the same meaning as in G.S. 58-30-10(14) and includes a:

(1) Reciprocal that is or should be licensed under Article 15 of this Chapter.

(2) Local government risk pool that chooses to operate under Article 23 of this Chapter.

(3) Fraternal benefit society that is or should be licensed under Article 24 of this Chapter.

(4) Self-insurer that is or should be licensed under Article 5 of Chapter 97 of the General Statutes.

(d) Nothing in this section limits public access to financial or actuarial information or calculations filed by an insurer or other entity for rating purposes, including rate filings, deviation filings, and loss cost filings. (2005-206, s. 1; 2006-105, s. 2.4; 2007-127, s. 10.)

§ 58-2-245. Access to employer taxpayer identification numbers contained in public documents.

Notwithstanding G.S. 132-1.10(b)(5), the Department is not required to redact an employer taxpayer identification number on documents that may be made available to the general public. (2006-105, s. 2.5.)

§ 58-2-250. Electronic filings.

(a) As used in this section:

(1) "Commissioner's designee" includes the National Insurance Producer Registry of the NAIC.

(2) "License" includes any license, certificate, registration, or permit issued under this Chapter.

(3) "Licensee" means any person who holds a license.

(b) Notwithstanding any other provision of this Chapter, the Commissioner may adopt rules that require an applicant for a license or a licensee to file documents electronically with the Commissioner or the Commissioner's designee. The rules adopted under this section may contain procedures for the electronic payment of any fee required under this Chapter and the electronic filing of documents, including:

(1) Any document required as part of an application for a license under this Chapter.

(2) Any document required to be filed by an applicant for a license or a licensee to maintain the license in good standing.

(3) Any other document required or permitted to be filed.

(c) The Commissioner or the Commissioner's designee may charge an administrative fee for electronic filing. Fees charged for the processing of an electronic filing are in addition to any other fee imposed for the filing. Fees charged for an electronic filing are limited to the actual cost of the electronic transaction.

(d) This section does not supersede any other provision of law that requires the electronic filing of a document or requires an applicant for a license or a licensee to make any other filing electronically. (2009-383, s. 2.)

§ 58-2-255. Electronic insurance communications and records.

(a) Definitions. - As used in this section:

(1) "Communications" means notices, offers, disclosures, documents, forms, information, and correspondence required or permitted to be provided to a party in writing under the insurance laws of this State or that are otherwise provided by an insurer, including, but not limited to, notices pertaining to the cancellation, termination, or nonrenewal of insurance.

(2) "Delivered by electronic means" includes any of the following:

a. Delivery to an electronic mail address or an electronic account at which a party has consented to receive electronic communications.

b. Displaying information, or a link to information, as an essential step to completing the transaction to which such information relates.

c. Providing notice to a party at the electronic mail address or an electronic account at which the party has consented to receive notice of the posting of a communication on an electronic network or site.

(3) "Insurer" has the same meaning as in G.S. 58-1-5(3).

(4) "Party" means a recipient of any communications defined in this section. "Party" includes an applicant, policyholder, insured, claimant, member, provider, or beneficiary.

(b) When any insurance law of this State, except for cancellation, termination, or nonrenewal of workers' compensation policies pursuant to G.S. 58-36-105(b), requires a communication to be provided to a party in writing, signed by a party, provided by means of a specific delivery method, or retained by an insurer, those requirements are satisfied if the insurer complies with Article 40 of Chapter 66 of the General Statutes.

(c) Verification of communications delivered by electronic means shall constitute proof of mailing in civil and administrative proceedings and under the insurance laws of this State.

(d) Nothing in this section affects requirements related to the content or timing of any communication required under the insurance laws of this State.

(e) A recording of an oral communication between an insurer and a party that is reliably stored and reproduced by an insurer shall constitute an electronic communication or record. When a communication is required under the insurance laws of this State to be provided in writing, the communication provided in accordance with this subsection shall satisfy the requirement that the communication be in writing. When a communication is required under the insurance laws of this State to be signed, a recorded oral communication in which a party agrees to the terms stated in the oral communication shall satisfy the requirement. (2013-413, s. 13(b).)

Article 3.

General Regulations for Insurance.

§ 58-3-1. State law governs insurance contracts.

All contracts of insurance on property, lives, or interests in this State shall be deemed to be made therein, and all contracts of insurance the applications for which are taken within the State shall be deemed to have been made within this State and are subject to the laws thereof. (1899, c. 54, s. 2; 1901, c. 705, s. 1; Rev., s. 4806; C.S., s. 6287.)

§ 58-3-5. No insurance contracts except under Articles 1 through 64 of this Chapter.

Except as provided in G.S. 58-3-6, it is unlawful for any company to make any contract of insurance upon or concerning any property or interest or lives in this State, or with any resident thereof, or for any person as insurance agent or insurance broker to make, negotiate, solicit, or in any manner aid in the transaction of such insurance, unless and except as authorized under the provisions of Articles 1 though 64 of this Chapter. (1899, c. 54, s. 2; Rev., s. 4807; C.S., s. 6288; 1998-211, s. 1(a).)

§ 58-3-6. Charitable gift annuities.

(a) A charitable organization as described in section 501(c)(3) or section 170(c) of the Internal Revenue Code or an educational institution may receive a transfer of property from a donor in exchange for an annuity payable over one or two lives, under which the actuarial value of the annuity is less than the value of the property transferred and the difference in value constitutes a charitable deduction for federal tax purposes. The issuance of the annuity by a charitable organization does not constitute engaging in the business of insurance if the organization, when the annuity agreement is issued:

(1) Has a minimum of $100,000 in unrestricted cash, cash equivalents, or publicly-traded securities, exclusive of the assets contributed by the donor in return for the annuity agreement;

(2) Has been in active, continuous operation for at least three years or is a successor to or affiliate of a charitable organization that has been in active operation for at least three years; and

(3) Includes the following disclosure clause in each annuity agreement issued on or after November 1, 1998: "This annuity is not issued by an insurance company, is not subject to regulation by the State of North Carolina, and is not protected or otherwise guaranteed by any government agency or insurance guaranty fund."

Subdivisions (1) and (2) of this subsection do not apply to an educational institution that was issuing annuity agreements prior to October 30, 1998 nor to an organization formed solely to support an educational institution in active operation at least three years prior to October 30, 1998.

(b) A charitable organization or educational institution that issues a charitable annuity shall notify the Department by January 1, 1999, or within 90 days of issuing its first annuity, whichever is later. The notice shall be signed by an officer or director of the organization or educational institution, identify the organization or institution, and certify that the organization or institution is a charitable organization or educational institution and that its annuities are issued in compliance with the applicable provisions of subsection (a) of this section.

(c)   A charitable organization that issues charitable annuities must make available to the Commissioner, upon request, a copy of its Internal Revenue Service Form 990 or Form 990-EZ for the most recent fiscal year for which the due date has passed. If the organization was not required to file either form with the Internal Revenue Service for the preceding fiscal year, or was allowed to submit the form in abbreviated format, it shall make available to the Commissioner, upon request, the same information that would have been required to have been filed under the Form 990, in a similar format as specified by the Commissioner. A copy of the Form 990, or corresponding substitute information as authorized by the Commissioner, shall be made available to the prospective annuitant at the time of the initial solicitation of the contribution, and updated information shall be made available at the time of execution of the annuity agreement.

(d)   The Department may enforce performance of the requirements of this section by notifying the organization or institution and demanding that it comply with the requirements of this section. The Department may fine an organization or educational institution, up to $1,000 per annuity agreement, for failure to comply after notice and demand from the Commissioner.

(e)   A charitable gift annuity issued by a charitable organization or educational institution prior to October 30, 1998 does not constitute engaging in the business of insurance.

(f)   For purposes of this section, an "educational institution" means a public or private college, university, or community college that maintains a faculty to provide instruction to students. (1998-211, s. 1(b).)

§ 58-3-10. Statements in application not warranties.

All statements or descriptions in any application for a policy of insurance, or in the policy itself, shall be deemed representations and not warranties, and a representation, unless material or fraudulent, will not prevent a recovery on the policy. (1901, c. 705, s. 2; Rev., s. 4808; C.S., s. 6289.)

§ 58-3-15. Additional or coinsurance clause.

No insurance company or agent licensed to do business in this State may issue any policy or contract of insurance covering property in this State that contains any clause or provision requiring the insured to take or maintain a larger amount of insurance than that expressed in the policy, nor in any way provide that the insured shall be liable as a coinsurer with the company issuing the policy for any part of the loss or damage to the property described in the policy, and any such clause or provision shall be null and void, and of no effect: Provided, the coinsurance clause or provision may be written in or attached to a policy or policies issued when there is printed or stamped on the declarations page of the policy or on the form containing the clause the words "coinsurance contract," and the Commissioner may, in the Commissioner's discretion, determine the location of the words "coinsurance contract" and the size of the type to be used. If there is a difference in the rate for the insurance with and without the coinsurance clause, the rates for each shall be furnished the insured upon request. (1915, c. 109, s. 5; C.S., s. 6441; 1925, c. 70, s. 4; 1945, c. 377; 1947, c. 721; 1999-132, s. 7.1.)

§ 58-3-20. Group plans other than life, annuity or accident and health.

No policy of insurance other than life, annuity or accident and health may be written in North Carolina on a group plan which insures a group of individuals under a master policy at rates lower than those charged for individual policies covering similar risks. The master policy and certificates, if any, shall be first approved by the Commissioner and the rate, premiums or other essential information shall be shown on the certificate. (1945, c. 377.)

§ 58-3-25. Discriminatory practices prohibited.

(a)   No insurer shall after September 1, 1975, base any standard or rating plan for private passenger automobiles or motorcycles, in whole or in part, directly or indirectly, upon the age or sex of the persons insured.

(b) No insurer shall refuse to insure or refuse to continue to insure an individual, limit the amount, extent, or kind of coverage available to an individual, or charge an individual a different rate for the same coverage, solely because of blindness or partial blindness or deafness or partial deafness. With respect to all other physical conditions, including the underlying cause of the blindness or partial blindness or deafness or partial deafness, individuals who are blind or partially blind shall be subject to the same standards of sound actuarial principles or actual or reasonably anticipated experience as are sighted individuals or individuals whose hearing is not impaired. Refusal to insure or refusal to continue to insure includes denial by an insurer providing disability insurance on the grounds that the policy defines disability as being presumed in the event that the insured loses his eyesight or hearing: Provided that an insurer providing disability insurance may except disability coverage for blindness, partial blindness, deafness, or partial deafness when those conditions existed at the time the application was made for the disability insurance policy. The provisions of this subsection shall be construed to supplement the provisions of G.S. 58-63-15(7) and G.S. 168-10. This subsection shall apply only to the underwriting of life insurance, accident, health, or accident and health insurance under Articles 1 through 66 of this Chapter, and annuities.

(c) No insurer shall refuse to insure or refuse to continue to insure an individual; limit the amount, extent, or kind of coverage available to an individual; or charge an individual a different rate for the same coverage, because of the race, color, or national or ethnic origin of that individual. This subsection supplements the provisions of G.S. 58-3-120, 58-33-80, 58-58-35, and 58-63-15(7). (1975, c. 666, s. 1; 1985, c. 267, s. 1; 1989, c. 485, s. 22; 1991, c. 720, s. 67.)

§ 58-3-30. Meaning of terms "accident", "accidental injury", and "accidental means".

(a) This section applies to the provisions of all group life, group accident, group health, and group accident and health insurance policies and group annuities under Articles 1 through 64 of this Chapter that are issued on or after October 1, 1989, and preferred provider arrangements under Articles 1 through 64 of this Chapter that are entered into on or after October 1, 1989.

(b) "Accident", "accidental injury", and "accidental means" shall be defined to imply "result" language and shall not include words that establish an accidental means test. (1989, c. 485, s. 10.)

§ 58-3-33. Insurer conditionally required to provide information.

(a) A person who claims to have been physically injured or to have incurred property damage where such injury or damage is subject to a policy of nonfleet private passenger automobile insurance may request by certified mail directed to the insurance adjuster or to the insurance company (Attention Corporate Secretary) at its last known principal place of business that the insurance company provide information regarding the policy's limits of coverage under the applicable policy. Upon receipt of such a request, which shall include the policyholder's name, and, if available, policy number, the insurance company shall notify that person within 15 business days, on a form developed by the Department, that the insurer is required to provide this information prior to litigation only if the person seeking the information satisfies all of the following conditions:

(1) The person seeking the information submits to the insurer the person's written consent to all of the person's medical providers to release to the insurer the person's medical records for the three years prior to the date on which the claim arose, as well as all medical records pertaining to the claimed injury.

(2) The person seeking the information submits to the insurer the person's written consent to participate in mediation of the person's claim under G.S. 7A-38.3A.

(3) The person seeking the information submits to the insurer a copy of the accident report required under G.S. 20-166.1 and a description of the events at issue with sufficient particularity to permit the insurer to make an initial determination of the potential liability of its insured.

(b) Within 30 days of receiving the person's written documents required under subsection (a) of this section, the insurer shall provide the policy limits.

(c) Disclosure of the policy limits under this section shall not constitute an admission that the alleged injury or damage is subject to the policy.

(d) This section does not apply to claims seeking recovery for medical malpractice or claims for which an insurer intends to deny coverage under any policy of insurance. (2003-307, s. 1; 2004-199, s. 21.)

§ 58-3-35. Stipulations as to jurisdiction and limitation of actions.

(a) No insurer, self-insurer, service corporation, HMO, MEWA, continuing care provider, viatical settlement provider, or professional employer organization licensed under this Chapter shall make any condition or stipulation in its contracts concerning the court or jurisdiction in which any suit or action on the contract may be brought.

(b) No insurer, self-insurer, service corporation, HMO, MEWA, continuing care provider, viatical settlement provider, or professional employer organization licensed under this Chapter shall limit the time within which any suit or action referred to in subsection (a) of this section may be commenced to less than the period prescribed by law.

(c) All conditions and stipulations forbidden by this section are void. (1899, c. 54, ss. 23, 106; 1901, c. 391, s. 8; Rev., s. 4809; C.S., s. 6290; 2001-334, s. 1; 2007-298, s. 7.1; 2007-484, s. 43.5.)

§ 58-3-40. Proof of loss forms required to be furnished.

When any company under any insurance policy requires a written proof of loss after notice of such loss has been given by the insured or beneficiary, the company or its representative shall furnish a blank to be used for that purpose. If such forms are not so furnished within 15 days after the receipt of such notice the claimant shall be deemed to have complied with the requirements of this policy as to proof of loss, upon submitting within the time fixed in the policy for filing proofs of loss, written proof covering the occurrence, character, and extent of the loss for which claim is made. (1945, c. 377.)

§ 58-3-45. Insurance as security for a loan by the company.

Where an insurance company, as a condition for a loan by such company, of money upon mortgage or other security, requires that the borrower insure either his life or that of another, or his property, or the title to his property, with the company, and assign or cause to be assigned to it a policy of insurance as security for the loan, and agree to pay premiums thereon during the continuance of the loan, whether the premium is paid annually, semiannually, quarterly, or monthly, such premiums shall not be considered as interest on such loans, nor will any loan be rendered usurious by reason of any such requirements, where the rate of interest charged for the loan does not exceed the legal rate and where the premiums charged for the insurance do not exceed the premiums charged to other persons for similar policies who do not obtain loans. (1915, c. 8; 1917, c. 61; C.S., s. 6291.)

§ 58-3-50. Companies must do business in own name; emblems, insignias, etc.

Every insurance company or group of companies must conduct its business in the State in, and the policies and contracts of insurance issued by it shall be headed or entitled only by, its proper or corporate name or names. There shall not appear on the policy anything that would indicate that it is the obligation of any other than the company or companies responsible for the payment of losses under the policy, though it will be permissible to stamp or print on the policy, the name or names of the department or general agency issuing the same, and the group of companies with which the company is financially affiliated. The use of any emblem, insignia, or anything other than the true and proper corporate name of the company or group of companies shall be permitted only with the approval of the Commissioner. (1899, c. 54, s. 18; Rev., s. 4811; C.S., s. 6292; 1945, c. 377; 1951, c. 781, s. 10; 1995, c. 193, s. 9.)

§ 58-3-55. Must not pay death benefits in services.

No insurance company now doing business in this State or that may hereafter be authorized to do business in this State issuing contracts providing benefits in the event of death shall issue any contract providing for the payment of benefits in merchandise or service to be rendered to such policyholder or his beneficiary. (1945, c. 377.)

§ 58-3-60. Publication of assets and liabilities; penalty for failure.

When any company publishes its assets, it must in the same connection and with equal conspicuousness publish its liabilities computed on the basis allowed for its annual statements; and any publications purporting to show its capital must exhibit only the amount of such capital as has been actually paid in cash. Any company or agent thereof who violates this section shall be guilty of a Class 3 misdemeanor and, upon conviction, shall be punished only by a fine of not less than five hundred dollars ($500.00) nor more than one thousand dollars ($1,000). (1899, c. 54, ss. 18, 96; Rev., ss. 3492, 4812; C.S., s. 6293; 1985, c. 666, s. 14; 1993, c. 539, s. 446; 1994, Ex. Sess., c. 24, s. 14(c).)

§ 58-3-65. Publication of financial information.

Notwithstanding any other provision of the laws of this State an insurer may, subject to requirements set forth by regulation promulgated by the Commissioner, publish financial statements or information based on financial statements prepared on a basis which is in accordance with requirements of a competent authority and which differs from the basis of the statements which have been filed with the Commissioner. Such differing financial statements or information based on financial statements shall not be made the basis for the application of provisions of any laws of this State not relating solely to the publication of financial information unless such provisions specifically so require. (1973, c. 1130; 1991, c. 720, s. 5.)

§ 58-3-70: Repealed by Session Laws 1993, c. 452, s. 65.

§ 58-3-71. Unearned premium reserves.

(a)   Every insurance company, other than a life or real estate title insurance company, shall maintain reserves equal to the unearned portions of the gross premiums charged on unexpired or unterminated risks and policies.

(b) No deductions may be made from the gross premiums in force except for original premiums canceled on risks terminated or reduced before expiration, or except for premiums paid or credited for risks reinsured with other solvent assuming insurers authorized to transact business in this State.

(c) Premiums charged for bulk or portfolio reinsurance assumed from other insurers shall be included as premiums in force on the basis of the original premiums and original terms of the policies of the ceding insurer.

(d) Reinsurance ceded to an authorized assuming insurer may be deducted on the basis of original premiums and original terms, except in the case of excess loss or catastrophe reinsurance, which may be deducted only on the basis of actual reinsurance premiums and actual reinsurance terms.

(e) The reserve for unearned premiums shall be computed on an actual basis or may be computed on the monthly pro rata fractional basis if in the opinion of the Commissioner this method produces an adequate reserve.

(f) With respect to marine insurance, premiums on trip risks not terminated shall be deemed unearned; and the Commissioner may require a reserve to be carried thereon equal to one hundred percent (100%) of the premiums on trip risks written during the month ended as of the statement date.

(g) The Commissioner may adopt rules for the unearned premium reserve computation for premiums covering indefinite terms. (1993, c. 452, s. 1.)

§ 58-3-72. Premium deficiency reserves.

(a) In determining the financial condition of any casualty, fidelity, and surety company and any fire and marine company referred to in G.S. 58-7-75, and in any financial statement or report of the company, there shall be included in the liabilities of the company premium deficiency reserves at least equal to the amounts required under this section. The date as of which the determination, statement, or report is made is known as the "date of determination."

(b) For all recorded unearned premium reserves, a premium deficiency reserve shall be calculated to include the amount by which the anticipated losses, loss adjustment expenses, commissions and other acquisition costs, and maintenance costs exceed the sum of those unearned premium reserves and any related expected future installment premiums as of the date of determination.

(c)   Except as provided in subsection (f) of this section, commissions, other acquisition costs, and premium taxes do not have to be considered in the determination of the premium deficiency reserve, to the extent that they have previously been incurred.

(d)   Except as provided in subsection (f) of this section, no reduction shall be taken for anticipated investment income in the determination of the premium deficiency reserve.

(e)   For purposes of determining if a premium deficiency exists, insurance contracts shall be grouped in a manner consistent with the way in which such policies are marketed or serviced.

(f)   If the Commissioner determines that the premium deficiency reserves of any company that have been calculated in accordance with this section are inadequate or excessive, the Commissioner may prescribe any other basis that will produce adequate and reasonable reserves. (2001-223, s. 1.1.)

§ 58-3-75. Loss and loss expense reserves of fire and marine insurance companies.

In any determination of the financial condition of any fire or marine or fire and marine insurance company authorized to do business in this State, such company shall be charged, in addition to its unearned premium liability as prescribed in G.S. 58-3-71, with a liability for loss reserves in an amount equal to the aggregate of the estimated amounts payable on all outstanding claims reported to it which arose out of any contract of insurance or reinsurance made by it, and in addition thereto an amount fairly estimated as necessary to provide for unreported losses incurred on or prior to the date of such determination, as defined in G.S. 58-3-81(a), and including, both as to reported and unreported claims, an amount estimated as necessary to provide for the expense of adjusting such claims, and there shall be deducted, in determining such liability for loss reserves, the amount of reinsurance recoverable by such company, in respect to such claims, from assuming insurers in accordance with G.S. 58-7-21. Such loss and loss expense reserves shall be calculated in accordance with any method adopted or approved by the NAIC, unless the Commissioner determines that another more conservative method is appropriate. (1945, c. 377; 1993, c. 452, s. 2; 1993 (Reg. Sess., 1994), c. 678, s. 4.)

§ 58-3-80: Repealed by Session Laws 1993, c. 452, s. 65.

§ 58-3-81. Loss and loss expense reserves of casualty insurance and surety companies.

(a)   In determining the financial condition of any casualty insurance or surety company and in any financial statement or report of any such company, there shall be included in the liabilities of that company loss reserves and loss expense reserves at least equal to the amounts required under this section. The amount of those reserves shall be diminished by an allowance or credit for reinsurance recoverable from assuming reinsurers in accordance with G.S. 58-7-21 or G.S. 58-7-26. The date as of which the determination, statement, or report is made is known as the date of determination.

(b)   For all outstanding losses and loss expenses, the reserves shall be valued as of the date of determination and shall include the following:

(1)   The aggregate estimated amounts due for losses and loss adjustment expenses on account of all known claims.

(2)   The aggregate estimated amounts due for losses and loss adjustment expenses on account of all unknown, incurred but not reported claims.

(c)   Except as provided in subsection (e) of this section, the minimum loss and loss expense reserves for workers' compensation insurance shall be determined as follows:

(1)   In the case of indemnity benefits where tabular reserves are prescribed for the reporting of such benefits under the Workers' Compensation Statistical Plan (WCSP) of the National Council on Compensation Insurance, the minimum reserve shall be the result obtained by the application of the appropriate pension table in the WCSP, unless the reserve required by any method adopted or approved by the NAIC is greater, in which case that greater reserve shall be used.

(2)   In all other cases, including other indemnity benefits, medical benefits, and loss adjustment expense, the reserve shall be determined by subsection (b) of this section, unless the reserve required by any method adopted or approved by the NAIC is greater, in which case that greater reserve shall be used.

(d)   Repealed by Session Laws 2001-223, s. 1.2.

(e)   Whenever in the judgment of the Commissioner the loss and loss expense reserves of any casualty or surety company doing business in this State calculated in accordance with the foregoing provisions are inadequate or excessive, he may prescribe any other basis that will produce adequate and reasonable reserves.

(f)   Every casualty insurance and every surety company doing business in this State shall keep a complete and itemized record showing all losses and claims on which it has received notices, including all notices received by it of the occurrence of any event that may result in a loss. (1993, c. 452, s. 3; 2001-223, s. 1.2.)

§ 58-3-85. Corporation or association maintaining office in State required to qualify and secure license.

Any corporation or voluntary association, other than an association of companies, the members of which are licensed in this State, issuing contracts of insurance and maintaining a principal, branch, or other office within this State, whether soliciting business in this State or in foreign states, shall qualify under the insurance laws of this State applicable to the type of insurance written by such corporation or association and secure license from the Commissioner as provided under Articles 1 through 64 of this Chapter on insurance, as amended, and the officers and agents of any such corporation or association maintaining offices within this State and failing to qualify and secure license as herein provided shall be deemed guilty of a Class 1 misdemeanor. (1937, c. 39; 1991, c. 720, s. 4; 1993, c. 539, s. 447; 1994, Ex. Sess., c. 24, s. 14(c).)

§ 58-3-90: Repealed by Session Laws 2001-223, s. 2.1.

§ 58-3-95: Repealed by Session Laws 1991, c. 720, s. 71.

§ 58-3-100. Insurance company licensing provisions.

(a) The Commissioner may, after notice and opportunity for a hearing, revoke, suspend, or restrict the license of any insurer if:

(1) The insurer fails or refuses to comply with any law, order or rule applicable to the insurer.

(2) After considering the standards under G.S. 58-30-60(b), the Commissioner determines that the continued operation of the insurer is hazardous to its policyholders, to its creditors, or to the general public.

(3) The insurer has published or made to the Department or to the public any false statement or report.

(4) The insurer or any of the insurer's officers, directors, employees, or other representatives refuse to submit to any examination authorized by law or refuse to perform any legal obligation in relation to an examination.

(5) The insurer is found to make a practice of unduly engaging in litigation or of delaying the investigation of claims or the adjustment or payment of valid claims.

(b) Any suspension, revocation or refusal to renew an insurer's license under this section may also be made applicable to the license or registration of any individual regulated under this Chapter who is a party to any of the causes for licensing sanctions listed in subsection (a) of this section.

(c) The Commissioner may impose a civil penalty under G.S. 58-2-70 if an HMO, service corporation, MEWA, or insurer fails to acknowledge a claim within 30 days after receiving written or electronic notice of the claim, but only if the notice contains sufficient information for the insurer to identify the specific coverage involved. Acknowledgement of the claim shall be one of the following:

(1) A statement made to the claimant or to the claimant's legal representative advising that the claim is being investigated.

(2) Payment of the claim.

(3) A bona fide written offer of settlement.

(4) A written denial of the claim.

A claimant includes an insured, a beneficiary of a life or annuity contract, a health care provider, or a health care facility that is responsible for directly making the claim with an insurer, HMO, service corporation, or MEWA. With respect to a claim under an accident, health, or disability policy, if the acknowledgement sent to the claimant indicates that the claim remains under investigation, within 45 days after receipt by the insurer of the initial claim, the insurer shall send a claim status report to the insured and every 45 days thereafter until the claim is paid or denied. The report shall give details sufficient for the insured to understand why processing of the claim has not been completed and whether the insurer needs additional information to process the claim. If the claim acknowledgement includes information about why processing of the claim has not been completed and indicates whether additional information is needed, it may satisfy the requirement for the initial claim status report. This subsection does not apply to HMOs, service corporations, MEWAs or insurers subject to G.S. 58-3-225.

(d) If a foreign insurance company's license is suspended or revoked, the Commissioner shall cause written notification of the suspension or revocation to be given to all of the company's agents in this State. Until the Commissioner restores the company's license, the company shall not write any new business in this State.

(e) The Commissioner may, after considering the standards under G.S. 58-30-60(b), restrict an insurer's license by prohibiting or limiting the kind or amount of insurance written by that insurer. For a foreign insurer, this restriction relates to the insurer's business conducted in this State. The Commissioner shall remove any restriction under this subsection once the Commissioner determines that the operations of the insurer are no longer hazardous to the public or the insurer's policyholders or creditors. As used in this subsection, "insurer" includes an HMO, service corporation, and MEWA. (1899, c. 54, ss. 66, 75, 112; 1901, c. 391, s. 5; Rev., ss. 4703, 4705; C.S., s. 6297; 1947, c. 721; 1963, c. 1234; 1993, c. 409, s. 1; 1995, c. 193, s. 10; 1999-294, s. 9; 2000-

162, s. 4(b); 2001-223, s. 2.2; 2001-334, s. 15; 2003-212, s. 26(a); 2005-215, s. 2; 2005-223, s. 7.)

§ 58-3-102. Request for determination of coverage for transplants under health benefit payment mechanisms; required response time; penalties.

(a) As used in this section, "insurer" means any payer of health benefits that is subject to Articles 1 through 66 of this Chapter.

(b) When a person or that person's health care provider or representative requests that person's insurer to determine whether a transplant is eligible for benefits under that person's health benefit coverage, the insurer shall, within 10 business days after receipt of the request and medical documentation necessary to determine if there is coverage, inform the requesting person as to whether there is coverage; provided coverage exists at the time of the transplant. (1991, c. 644, s. 14.)

§ 58-3-105. Limitation of risk.

Except as otherwise provided in Articles 1 through 64 of this Chapter, no insurer doing business in this State shall expose itself to any loss on any one risk in an amount exceeding ten percent (10%) of its surplus to policyholders. Any risk or portion of any risk which shall have been reinsured shall be deducted in determining the limitation of risk prescribed in this section. This section shall not apply to (i) life insurance, (ii) accident and health insurance, (iii) the insurance of marine risks, or marine protection and indemnity risks, (iv) workers' compensation or employer's liability risks, and (v) certificates of title, guaranties of title or policies of title insurance. For the purpose of determining the limitation of risk under any provision of Articles 1 through 64 of this Chapter, "surplus to policyholders" shall

(1) Be deemed to include any voluntary reserves, or any part thereof, which are not required by or pursuant to law, and

(2) Be determined from the last sworn statement of such insurer on file with the Commissioner pursuant to law, or by the last report on examination filed by

the Commissioner, whichever is more recent at the time of assumption of such risk.

In applying the limitation of risk under any provision of Articles 1 through 64 of this Chapter to alien insurers, such provision shall be deemed to refer to the exposure to risk and to the surplus to policyholders of the United States branch of such alien insurer. (1945, c. 377; 1991, c. 636, s. 3; 2013-199, s. 1.)

§ 58-3-110. Limitation of liability assumed.

(a)   No company transacting fidelity or surety business in this State shall expose itself to any loss on any one fidelity or surety risk or hazard in an amount exceeding ten per centum (10%) of its policyholders' surplus, unless it shall be protected in excess of that amount by:

(1)   Reinsurance in such form as to enable the obligee or beneficiary to maintain an action thereon against the company reinsured jointly with such reinsurer and, upon recovering judgment against such reinsured, to have recovery against such reinsurer for payment to the extent in which it may be liable under such reinsurance and in discharge thereof; or

(2)   The cosuretyship of such a company similarly authorized; or

(3)   By deposit with it in pledge or conveyance to it in trust for its protection of property; or

(4)   By conveyance or mortgage for its protection; or

(5)   In case a suretyship obligation was made on behalf or on account of a fiduciary holding property in a trust capacity, by deposit or other disposition of a portion of the property so held in trust that no future sale, mortgage, pledge or other disposition can be made thereof without the consent of such company; except by decree or order of a court of competent jurisdiction;

(b)   Provided:

(1)   That such company may execute what are known as transportation or warehousing bonds for United States internal revenue taxes to an amount equal to fifty per centum (50%) of its policyholders' surplus;

(2) That, when the penalty of the suretyship obligation exceeds the amount of a judgment described therein as appealed from and thereby secured, or exceeds the amount of the subject matter in controversy or of the estate in the hands of the fiduciary for the performance of whose duties it is conditioned, the bond may be executed if the actual amount of the judgment or the subject matter in controversy or estate not subject to the supervision or control of the surety is not in excess of such limitation; and

(3) That, when the penalty of the suretyship obligation executed for the performance of a contract exceeds the contract price, the latter shall be taken as the basis for estimating the limit of risk within the meaning of this section.

(c) No such company shall, anything to the contrary in this section notwithstanding, execute suretyship obligations guaranteeing the deposits of any single financial institution in an aggregate amount in excess of ten per centum (10%) of the policyholders' surplus of such surety, unless it shall be protected in excess of that amount by credits in accordance with subdivisions (1), (2), (3) or (4) of subsection (a) of this section: Provided, nothing in this section shall be construed to make invalid any contract entered into by such company with another person, firm, corporation or municipal corporation, notwithstanding any provisions of this section. (1911, c. 28; C.S., s. 6382; 1931, c. 285; 1945, c. 377.)

§ 58-3-115. Twisting with respect to insurance policies; penalties.

No insurer shall make or issue, or cause to be issued, any written or oral statement that willfully misrepresents or willfully makes an incomplete comparison as to the terms, conditions, or benefits contained in any policy of insurance for the purpose of inducing or attempting to induce a policyholder in any way to terminate or surrender, exchange, or convert any insurance policy. Any person who violates this section is subject to the provisions of G.S. 58-2-70 or G.S. 58-3-100. (1961, c. 823; 1987, c. 629, s. 4; c. 787, s. 2; c. 864, ss. 3(a), 74; 1989, c. 485, s. 25; 1999-132, s. 1.3.)

§ 58-3-120. Discrimination forbidden.

(a)   No company doing the business of insurance as defined in G.S. 58-7-15 shall make any discrimination in favor of any person.

(b)   Discrimination between individuals of the same class in the amount of premiums or rates charged for any policy of insurance covered by Articles 50 through 55 of this Chapter, or in the benefits payable thereon, or in any of the terms or conditions of such policy, or in any other manner whatsoever, is prohibited. (1903, c. 488, s. 2; 1905, c. 170, s. 2; Rev., s. 4766; C.S., s. 6430; 1923, c. 4, s. 70; 1925, c. 70, s. 6; 1945, c. 458; 1987, c. 629, s. 5; 2001-297, s. 4.)

§ 58-3-121. Discrimination against coverage of certain bones and joints prohibited.

(a)   Discrimination against coverage of procedures involving bones or joints of the jaw, face, or head is prohibited in any health benefit plan. Whenever a health benefit plan provides coverage on a group or individual basis for diagnostic, therapeutic, or surgical procedures involving bones or joints of the human skeletal structure, that plan may not exclude or deny the same coverage for procedures involving any bone or joint of the jaw, face, or head, so long as the procedure is medically necessary to treat a condition which prevents normal functioning of the particular bone or joint involved and the condition is caused by congenital deformity, disease, or traumatic injury. The coverage required by this section involving bones or joints of the jaw, face, or head shall be subject to the same conditions and limitations as are applicable to coverage of procedures involving other bones and joints of the human skeletal structure.

(b)   For purposes of this section, in providing coverage for the treatment of conditions of the jaw (temporomandibular joint), authorized therapeutic procedures shall include splinting and use of intraoral prosthetic appliances to reposition the bones. Payment for these therapeutic procedures, and for procedures involved in any other nonsurgical treatment of temporomandibular joint dysfunction, may be subjected to a reasonable lifetime maximum dollar amount. Nothing in this subsection shall require a health benefit plan to cover orthodontic braces, crowns, bridges, dentures, treatment for periodontal disease, dental root form implants, or root canals.

(c)   For purposes of this section, "health benefit plan" means accident and health insurance policies or certificates; nonprofit hospital or medical service corporation contracts; health, hospital, or medical service corporation plan contracts; health maintenance (HMO) subscriber contracts; and plans provided by a MEWA or plans provided by other benefit arrangements, to the extent permitted by ERISA. (1995, c. 483, s. 1.)

§ 58-3-122. Anesthesia and hospital charges necessary for safe and effective administration of dental procedures for young children, persons with serious mental or physical conditions, and persons with significant behavioral problems; coverage in health benefit plans.

(a) All health benefit plans shall provide coverage for payment of anesthesia and hospital or facility charges for services performed in a hospital or ambulatory surgical facility in connection with dental procedures for children below the age of nine years, persons with serious mental or physical conditions, and persons with significant behavioral problems, where the provider treating the patient involved certifies that, because of the patient's age or condition or problem, hospitalization or general anesthesia is required in order to safely and effectively perform the procedures. The same deductibles, coinsurance, network requirements, medical necessity provisions, and other limitations as apply to physical illness benefits under the health benefit plan shall apply to coverage for anesthesia and hospital or facility charges required to be covered under this section.

(b) As used in this section, the term:

(1) "Health benefit plan" means an accident and health insurance policy or certificate; a nonprofit hospital or medical service corporation contract; a health maintenance organization subscriber contract; a plan provided by a multiple employer welfare arrangement; or a plan provided by another benefit arrangement, to the extent permitted by the Employee Retirement Income Security Act of 1974, as amended, or by any waiver of or other exception to that Act provided under federal law or regulation. "Health benefit plan" does not mean any plan implemented or administered by the North Carolina Department of Health and Human Services or the United States Department of Health and Human Services, or any successor agency, or its representatives. "Health benefit plan" also does not mean any of the following kinds of insurance:

a. Accident.

b. Credit.

c. Disability income.

d. Long-term care or nursing home care.

e. Medicare supplement.

f. Specified disease.

g. Dental or vision.

h. Coverage issued as a supplement to liability insurance.

i. Workers' compensation.

j. Medical payments under automobile or homeowners.

k. Hospital income or indemnity.

l. Insurance under which benefits are payable with or without regard to fault and that is statutorily required to be contained in any liability policy or equivalent self-insurance.

(2) "Insurer" includes an insurance company subject to this Chapter, a service corporation organized under Article 65 of this Chapter, a health maintenance organization organized under Article 67 of this Chapter, or a multiple employer welfare arrangement subject to Article 49 of this Chapter. (1999-134, s. 1.)

§ 58-3-125. Repealed by Session Laws 1999-132, s. 1.1.

§ 58-3-130. Agent, adjuster, etc., acting without a license or violating insurance law.

If any person shall assume to act either as principal, agent, broker, limited representative, adjuster or motor vehicle damage appraiser without license as is required by law or, pretending to be a principal, agent, broker, limited representative, adjuster or licensed motor vehicle damage appraiser, shall solicit, examine or inspect any risk, or shall examine into, adjust, or aid in adjusting any loss, investigate or advise relative to the nature and amount of damages to motor vehicles or the amount necessary to effect repairs thereto, or shall receive, collect, or transmit any premium of insurance, or shall do any other act in the soliciting, making or executing any contract of insurance of any kind otherwise than the law permits, or as principal or agent shall violate any provision of law contained in Articles 1 through 64 of this Chapter, the punishment for which is not elsewhere provided for, he shall be deemed guilty of a Class 1 misdemeanor. (1899, c. 54, s. 115; Rev., s. 3490; C.S., s. 6310; 1945, c. 458; 1949, c. 958, s. 1; 1951, c. 105, s. 1; 1971, c. 757, s. 7; 1985, c. 666, s. 20; 1987, c. 629, s. 9; 1993, c. 539, s. 448; 1994, Ex. Sess., c. 24, s. 14(c).)

§ 58-3-135. Certain insurance activities by lenders with customers prohibited.

No lender shall require the purchase of insurance from such lender or subsidiary or affiliate of such lender as a condition to the making, renewing or refinancing of any loan or to the establishing of any of the terms or conditions of such loan. Lenders shall not include organizations of the Farm Credit System. (1985, c. 679, s. 1.)

§ 58-3-140. Temporary contracts of insurance permitted.

A lender engaged in making or servicing real estate mortgage or deed of trust loans on one to four family residences shall accept as evidence of insurance a temporary written contract of insurance meeting the requirements of G.S. 58 44-20(4) and issued by any duly licensed insurance agent, broker, or insurance company.

Nothing herein prohibits the lender from refusing to accept a binder or from disapproving such insurer or agent provided such refusal or disapproval is reasonable.

Such lender need not accept a binder unless such binder:

(1)   Includes:

a. The name and address of the insured;

b. The name and address of the mortgagee;

c. A description of the insured collateral;

d. A provision that it may not be cancelled within a term of the binder except upon 10 days' written notice to the mortgagee; and

e. The amount of insurance bound.

(2) Is accompanied by a paid receipt for one year's premium, except in the case of the renewal of a policy subsequent to the closing of a loan; and

(3) Includes an undertaking of agent to use his best efforts to have the insurance company issue a policy.

The Department may require binders to contain any additional information to permit the binders to comply with the reasonable requirements of Fannie Mae, the Government National Mortgage Association, or the Federal Home Loan Mortgage Corporation for purchase of mortgage loans. (1989, c. 459, s. 1; 1991, c. 720, s. 4; 2001-487, s. 14(f).)

§ 58-3-145. Solicitation, negotiation or payment of premiums on insurance policies.

An insurer, agent, or broker may accept payment of an insurance premium by credit card or debit card if the insurer accepting payment by credit card or debit card meets the following conditions:

(1) The insurer complies with the prohibition against unfair discrimination contained in G.S. 58-63-15(7).

(2) The insurer pays the fees charged by the credit card company or debit card issuer for the payment of premiums by credit card or debit card. (1967, c. 1245; 1979, c. 528; 1991, c. 720, s. 7; 1999-365, s. 1; 2011-215, s. 1.)

§ 58-3-147. Credit card guaranty or collateral prohibited.

No insurer, representative of any insurer, or insurance broker shall enter into any arrangement that involves the sale of insurance or the pledging of existing insurance as guaranty or collateral for the issuance of any credit card. (1993, c. 226, s. 9, c. 504, s. 40.)

§ 58-3-150. Forms to be approved by Commissioner.

(a)   It is unlawful for any insurance company licensed and admitted to do business in this State to issue, sell, or dispose of any policy, contract, certificate, or certificate of insurance, or use applications in connection therewith, until the forms of the same have been submitted to and approved by the Commissioner, and copies filed in the Department. If a policy form filing is disapproved by the Commissioner, the Commissioner may return the filing to the filer. As used in this section, "policy form" includes endorsements, riders, or amendments to policies that have already been approved by the Commissioner.

(b)   With respect to group and blanket accident and health insurance, group life insurance, and group annuity policies issued and delivered to a trust or to an association outside of this State and covering persons resident in this State, the group certificates to be delivered or issued for delivery in this State shall be filed with and approved by the Commissioner pursuant to subsection (a) of this section.

(c)   If not submitted electronically, all contracts, literature, advertising materials, letters, and other documents submitted to the Department to comply with the filing requirements of this Chapter or an administrative rule adopted pursuant to this Chapter shall be submitted on paper eight and one-half inches by eleven inches. Brochures and pamphlets shall not be stapled or bound.

(d)   As used in this section, "certificate of insurance" means a document prepared or issued by an insurance company or producer that is used to verify or evidence the existence of property or casualty insurance coverage. "Certificate" or "certificate of insurance" shall not include a document prepared or issued by an insurance company or producer that is used to verify or evidence the existence of property insurance provided to a lender covering real or personal property which serves as the lender's security for commercial mortgages. For purposes of this section, "commercial mortgages" shall mean mortgages or other instruments given for the purpose of creating a lien encumbering office, multiunit residential, apartments, commercial, or industrial properties. Commercial mortgages shall not include a lien encumbering one- to four-family residential properties.

(e)   A certificate of insurance is not a policy of insurance and does not amend, extend, or alter the coverage afforded by the policy to which the certificate of insurance makes reference. A certificate of insurance shall not confer to a certificate of insurance holder new or additional rights beyond what the referenced policy of insurance expressly provides.

(f)   It is unlawful for any person to knowingly prepare, issue, request, or require a certificate of insurance that meets any of the following criteria:

(1)   Has not been filed with and approved by the Commissioner.

(2)   Contains any false or misleading information concerning the policy of insurance to which the certificate of insurance makes reference.

(3)   Purports to alter, amend, or extend the coverage provided by the policy of insurance to which the certificate of insurance makes reference.

(g)   A holder of a certificate of insurance shall have a legal right to notice of cancellation, nonrenewal, or any material change, or any similar notice concerning a policy of insurance, only if the holder is named within the policy or any endorsement and the policy or endorsement requires notice to be provided to the holder. The terms and conditions of the notice, including the required timing of the notice, are governed by the policy of insurance and cannot be altered by a certificate of insurance. (1907, c. 879; 1913, c. 139; C.S., s. 6312; 1945, c. 377; 1987, c. 752, s. 7; 1989, c. 485, s. 9; 1991, c. 720, ss. 5, 51; 1993, c. 506, s. 1; 1998-211, s. 37.3(a); 2003-290, s. 3; 2011-196, s. 3.)

§ 58-3-151. Deemer provisions.

No entity subject to the Commissioner's jurisdiction and regulation shall be fined or penalized by the Commissioner for using forms, contracts, schedules of premiums, or other documents required to be filed and approved under this Chapter or for executing contracts required to be filed and approved under this

Chapter if those forms, contracts, schedules of premiums, or other documents have been by law deemed to have been approved, and the entity has notified the Commissioner before using the filing or executing the contract that the law has deemed the filing or the contract to be approved. (2001-334, s. 14.)

§ 58-3-152. Excess liability policies; uninsured and underinsured motorist coverages.

With respect to policy forms that provide excess liability coverage, an insurer may limit or exclude coverage for uninsured motorists as provided in G.S. 20-279.21(b)(3) and for underinsured motorists as provided in G.S. 20-279.21(b)(4). (1997-396, s. 1.)

§ 58-3-155. Business transacted with insurer-controlled brokers.

(a)   As used in this section:

(1)   "Broker" means a person who, being a licensed agent, obtains insurance for another party through a duly authorized agent of an insurer that is licensed to do business in this State but for which the broker is not authorized to act as agent.

(2)   "Control" or "controlled" means the direct or indirect possession of the power to direct or cause the direction of the management and policies of a person, whether through the ownership of voting securities, by contract other than a commercial contract for goods or nonmanagement services, or otherwise, unless the power is the result of an official position with or a corporate office held by the person. Control is presumed to exist if any person directly or indirectly owns, controls, holds with the power to vote, or holds proxies representing ten percent (10%) or more of the voting securities of any other person.

(b)   The Commissioner may determine, after furnishing all persons in interest notice and opportunity to be heard and making specific findings of fact to support that determination, that control exists in fact, notwithstanding the absence of a presumption to that effect. The Commissioner may determine upon application that any person does not or will not upon the taking of some proposed action control another person. The Commissioner may prospectively revoke or modify that determination, after notice and opportunity to be heard whenever in the Commissioner's judgment revocation or modification is consistent with this section.

(c) No licensed property or casualty insurer that has control of a broker may accept insurance from the broker in any transaction in which the broker, when the insurance is placed, is acting as such on behalf of the insured for any compensation, commission, or thing of value unless the broker, before the effective date of the coverage, delivers written notice to the prospective insured disclosing the relationship between the insurer and broker. The disclosure must be signed by the insured and must be retained in the insurer's underwriting file until the completion and release of the examination report under G.S. 58-2-131 through G.S. 58-2-134 for the period in which the coverage is in effect. If the insurance is placed through a subbroker that is not a controlled broker, the controlling insurer shall retain in its records a signed commitment from the subbroker that the subbroker is aware of the relationship between the insurer and the broker and that the subbroker has notified or will notify the insured.

(d) This section does not affect the rights of policyholders, claimants, creditors, or other third parties. (1991, c. 681, s. 9; 1999-132, s. 11.1.)

§ 58-3-160. Sale of company or major reorganization; license to be restricted.

The Commissioner shall restrict the license by prohibiting new or renewal insurance business transacted in this State by any licensed insurer that, in anticipation of a sale of the insurer to new owners or a major reorganization of the business or management of the insurer, transfers all of its existing insurance business to another insurer through an assumption reinsurance agreement or does not write any new insurance business for over one year. The restriction shall remain in force until after the insurer has filed the following information with the Commissioner and the Commissioner has granted approval:

(1) Biographical information in a form acceptable to the Commissioner for each new owner, director, or management person;

(2) A detailed and complete plan of operation describing the kinds of insurance to be written and the method in which the reorganized insurer will perform its various functions;

(3) Financial projections of the anticipated operational results of the reorganized insurer for the succeeding three years based on the capitalization of the reorganized insurer and its plan of operation, which must be prepared by a properly qualified individual, be in sufficient detail for a complete analysis to be performed, and be accompanied by a list of the assumptions used in making the projections; and

(4) Any other information the Commissioner considers to be pertinent for a proper analysis of the reorganized insurer. (1991, c. 681, s. 10.)

§ 58-3-165. Business transacted with producer-controlled property or casualty insurers.

(a) As used in this section:

(1) "Accredited state" means a state in which the insurance department or regulatory agency has qualified as meeting the minimum financial regulatory standards promulgated and established from time to time by the NAIC.

(2) "Captive insurer" means an insurance company that is owned by another organization and whose exclusive purpose is to insure risks of the parent organization and affiliated companies. In the case of groups and associations, "captive insurer" means an insurance organization that is owned by the insureds, and whose exclusive purpose is to insure risks of member organizations or group members and their affiliates.

(3) "Control" and its cognates mean the direct or indirect possession of the power to direct or cause the direction of the management and policies of a person, whether through the ownership of voting securities, by contract other than a commercial contract for goods or nonmanagement services, or otherwise, unless the power is the result of an official position with or corporate office held by the person. Control is presumed to exist if any person directly or indirectly owns, controls, holds with the power to vote, or holds proxies representing ten percent (10%) or more of the voting securities of any other person.

(4) "Controlled insurer" means an insurer that is controlled, directly or indirectly, by a producer.

(5) "Controlling producer" means a producer who, directly or indirectly, controls an insurer.

(6) "Insurer" means any person licensed to write property or casualty insurance in this State. "Insurer" does not mean a risk retention group under Article 22 of this Chapter, residual market mechanism, joint underwriting authority, nor captive insurer.

(7) "Producer" means an insurance broker or brokers or any other person, when, for any compensation, commission, or other thing of value, that person acts or aids in any manner in soliciting, negotiating, or procuring the making of any insurance contract on behalf of an insured other than that person. "Producer" does not mean an exclusive agent or any independent agent acting on behalf of a controlled insurer, including any subagent or representative of the agent, who acts as such in the solicitation of, negotiation for, or procurement or making of an insurance contract, if the agent is not also acting in the capacity of an insurance broker in the transaction in question.

(b) The Commissioner may determine, after furnishing all persons in interest notice and opportunity to be heard and making specific findings of fact to support the determination, that control exists in fact, notwithstanding the absence of a presumption to that effect. The Commissioner may determine upon application that any person does not or will not upon the taking of some proposed action control another person. The Commissioner may prospectively revoke or modify that determination, after notice and opportunity to be heard, whenever in the Commissioner's judgment revocation or modification is consistent with this section.

(c) This section applies to insurers that are either domiciled in this State or domiciled in a state that is not an accredited state having in effect a substantially similar law. The provisions of Article 19 of this Chapter, to the extent they are not superseded by this section, apply to all parties within holding company systems subject to this section.

(d) The provisions of this section apply if, in any calendar year, the aggregate amount of gross written premiums on business placed with a controlled insurer by a controlling producer is equal to or greater than five percent (5%) of the admitted assets of the controlled insurer, as reported in the controlled insurer's most recent annual statement or its quarterly statement filed as of September 30 of the prior year. The provisions of this section do not apply if:

(1)   The controlling producer places insurance only with the controlled insurer, or only with the controlled insurer and a member or members of the controlled insurer's holding company system, or the controlled insurer's parent, affiliate, or subsidiary and receives no compensation based upon the amount of premiums written in connection with that insurance; and the controlling producer accepts insurance placements only from nonaffiliated subproducers, and not directly from insureds; and

(2)   The controlled insurer, except for insurance business written through a residual market mechanism, accepts insurance business only from a controlling producer, a producer controlled by the controlled insurer, or a producer that is a subsidiary of the controlled insurer.

(e)   A controlled insurer shall not accept business from a controlling producer and a controlling producer shall not place business with a controlled insurer unless there is a written contract between the producer and the insurer specifying the responsibilities of each party, and unless the contract has been approved by the board of directors of the insurer and contains all of "the following minimum provisions:

(1)   The insurer may terminate the contract for cause, upon written notice to the producer. The insurer shall suspend the producer's authority to write business during the pendency of any dispute regarding the cause for the termination.

(2)   The producer shall render accounts to the insurer detailing all material transactions, including information necessary to support all commissions, charges, and other fees received by, or owing to, the producer.

(3)   The producer shall remit all funds due under the contract terms to the insurer on at least a monthly basis. The due date shall be fixed so that premiums or installments of premiums collected shall be remitted no later than 90 days after the effective date of any policy placed with the insurer under this contract.

(4)   The producer shall hold all funds collected for the insurer's account in a fiduciary capacity, in one or more appropriately identified bank accounts in banks that are members of the Federal Reserve System, in accordance with the

provisions of this Chapter as applicable. Funds of a producer who is not required to be licensed in this State shall be maintained in compliance with the requirements of the producer's domiciliary jurisdiction.

(5)   The producer shall maintain separately identifiable records of business written for the insurer.

(6)   The producer shall not assign the contract in whole or in part.

(7)   The insurer shall provide the producer with its underwriting standards, rules and procedures, the manual setting forth the rates to be charged, and the conditions for the acceptance or rejection of risks. The producer shall adhere to the standards, rules, procedures, rates, and conditions. The standards, rules, procedures, rates, and conditions shall be the same as those applicable to comparable business placed with the insurer by a producer other than a controlling producer.

(8)   The rates and terms of the producer's commissions, charges, or other fees and the purposes for the charges or fees. The rates of the commissions, charges, and other fees shall be no greater than those applicable to comparable business placed with the insurer by producers other than controlling producers. For the purposes of this subdivision and subdivision (7) of this subsection, "comparable business" includes the same lines of insurance, same kinds of insurance, same kinds of risks, similar policy limits, and similar quality of business.

(9)   If the contract provides that the producer, on insurance business placed with the insurer, is to be compensated contingent upon the insurer's profits on that business, then the compensation shall not be determined and paid until at least five years after the premiums on liability insurance are earned and at least one year after the premiums are earned on any other insurance. In no event shall the commissions be paid until the adequacy of the insurer's reserves on remaining claims has been independently verified under subsection (g) of this section.

(10)   A limit on the producer's writings in relation to the insurer's surplus and total writings. The insurer may establish a different limit for each line or subline of business. The insurer shall notify the producer when the applicable limit is approached and shall not accept business from the producer if the limit is reached. The producer shall not place business with the insurer if it has been notified by the insurer that the limit has been reached.

(11) The producer may negotiate but shall not bind reinsurance on behalf of the insurer on business the producer places with the insurer; however, the producer may bind facultative reinsurance contracts under obligatory facultative agreements if the producer's contract with the insurer contains underwriting guidelines including, for both reinsurance assumed and ceded, a list of reinsurers with which the automatic agreements are in effect, the coverages and amounts or percentages that may be reinsured, and commission schedules.

(f) Every controlled insurer shall have an audit committee, consisting of independent directors, of the insurer's board of directors. The audit committee shall meet annually with the insurer's management, the insurer's independent certified public accountants, and an independent casualty actuary or another independent loss reserve specialist acceptable to the Commissioner, to review the adequacy of the insurer's loss reserves.

(g) In addition to any other required loss reserve certification, the controlled insurer shall, on or before April 1 of each year, file with the Commissioner an opinion of an independent casualty actuary or of another independent loss reserve specialist acceptable to the Commissioner, reporting loss ratios for each kind of insurance written and attesting to the adequacy of loss reserves established for losses incurred and outstanding and for incurred but not reported losses as of the end of the prior calendar year on business placed by the producer.

(h) The controlled insurer shall report annually to the Commissioner the amount of commissions paid to the controlling producer, the percentage that amount represents of the net premiums written, and comparable amounts and percentages paid to noncontrolling producers for placements of the same kinds of insurance.

(i) The controlling producer, before the effective date of any policy, shall deliver written notice to the prospective insured disclosing the relationship between the producer and the controlled insurer: However, if the business is placed through a subproducer who is not a controlling producer, the controlling producer shall retain in the controlling producer's records a signed commitment from the subproducer that the subproducer is aware of the relationship between the insurer and the producer and that the subproducer has or will notify the prospective insured.

(j)   If the Commissioner believes that a controlling producer or any other person has not materially complied with this section or with any rule adopted or order issued under this section, after notice and opportunity to be heard, the Commissioner may order the controlling producer to stop placing business with the controlled insurer. If it is found that, because of the material noncompliance, the controlled insurer or any policyholder of the controlled insurer has suffered any loss or damage, the Commissioner may maintain a civil action or intervene in an action brought by or on behalf of the insurer or policyholder for recovery of compensatory damages for the benefit of the insurer or policyholder or other appropriate relief.

(k)   If an order for liquidation or rehabilitation of the controlled insurer has been entered under Article 30 of this Chapter, and the receiver appointed under that order believes that the controlling producer or any other person has not materially complied with this section or any rule adopted or order issued under this section, and the insurer suffered any loss or damage therefrom, the receiver may maintain a civil action for recovery of damages or other appropriate sanctions for the benefit of the insurer.

(l)   In addition to any other remedies provided in this section, whenever the Commissioner believes that a person has not materially complied with this section, the Commissioner may institute a proceeding under G.S. 58-2-60 or under G.S. 58-2-70. In addition to the civil penalty or restitution proceedings provided for in G.S. 58-2-70, the Commissioner may issue a cease and desist order against the person.

(m)   This section does not affect the Commissioner's right to impose any other penalties provided for in this Chapter nor the rights of policyholders, claimants, creditors, or other third parties.

(n)   Controlled insurers and controlling producers who are not in compliance with subsection (e) of this section on October 1, 1991, have until December 1, 1991, to come into compliance and shall comply with subsection (i) of this section beginning with all policies written or renewed on or after December 1, 1991. (1991, c. 681, s. 28; c. 720, s. 92.)

§ 58-3-167. Applicability of acts of the General Assembly to health benefit plans.

(a) As used in this section:

(1) "Health benefit plan" means an accident and health insurance policy or certificate; a nonprofit hospital or medical service corporation contract; a health maintenance organization subscriber contract; a plan provided by a multiple employer welfare arrangement; or a plan provided by another benefit arrangement, to the extent permitted by the Employee Retirement Income Security Act of 1974, as amended, or by any waiver of or other exception to that act provided under federal law or regulation. "Health benefit plan" does not mean any plan implemented or administered by the North Carolina or United States Department of Health and Human Services, or any successor agency, or its representatives. "Health benefit plan" does not mean any plan consisting of one or more of any combination of benefits described in G.S. 58-68-25(b).

(2) "Insurer" includes an insurance company subject to this Chapter, a service corporation organized under Article 65 of this Chapter, a health maintenance organization organized under Article 67 of this Chapter, and a multiple employer welfare arrangement subject to Article 49 of this Chapter.

(b) Whenever a law is enacted by the General Assembly on or after October 1, 1999 that applies to a health benefit plan, the term "health benefit plan" shall be defined for purposes of that law as provided in subsection (a) of this section unless that law provides a different definition or otherwise expressly provides that the definition in this section is not applicable.

(c) Whenever a law is enacted by the General Assembly that applies to health benefit plans that are delivered, issued for delivery, or renewed on and after a certain date, the renewal of a health benefit plan is presumed to occur on each anniversary of the date on which coverage was first effective on the person or persons covered by the health benefit plan. (1999-294, s. 5; 1999-456, s. 16; 2007-298, s. 7.2; 2007-484, s. 43.5.)

§ 58-3-168. Coverage for postmastectomy inpatient care.

(a) Every entity providing a health benefit plan that provides coverage for mastectomy, including coverage for postmastectomy inpatient care, shall ensure that the decision whether to discharge the patient following mastectomy is made by the attending physician in consultation with the patient, and shall further ensure that the length of postmastectomy hospital stay is based on the unique characteristics of each patient taking into consideration the health and medical history of the patient.

(b) As used in this section, "health benefit plans" means accident and health insurance policies or certificates; nonprofit hospital or medical service corporation contracts; health, hospital, or medical service corporation plan contracts; health maintenance organization (HMO) subscriber contracts; and plans provided by a MEWA or plans provided by other benefit arrangements, to the extent permitted by ERISA.

(c) As used in this section, "mastectomy" means the surgical removal of all or part of a breast as a result of breast cancer or breast disease. (1997-440, s. 1.)

§ 58-3-169. Required coverage for minimum hospital stay following birth.

(a) Definitions. - As used in this section:

(1) "Attending providers" includes:

a. The obstetrician-gynecologists, pediatricians, family physicians, and other physicians primarily responsible for the care of a mother and newborn; and

b. The nurse midwives and nurse practitioners primarily responsible for the care of a mother and her newborn child in accordance with State licensure and certification laws.

(2) "Health benefit plan" means an accident and health insurance policy or certificate; a nonprofit hospital or medical service corporation contract; a health maintenance organization subscriber contract; a plan provided by a multiple employer welfare arrangement; or a plan provided by another benefit arrangement, to the extent permitted by the Employee Retirement Income Security Act of 1974, as amended, or by any waiver of or other exception to that Act provided under federal law or regulation. "Health benefit plan" does not mean any of the following kinds of insurance:

a. Accident,

b. Credit,

c. Disability income,

d. Long-term or nursing home care,

e. Medicare supplement,

f. Specified disease,

g. Dental or vision,

h. Coverage issued as a supplement to liability insurance,

i. Workers' compensation,

j. Medical payments under automobile or homeowners, and

k. Insurance under which benefits are payable with or without regard to fault and that is statutorily required to be contained in any liability policy or equivalent self-insurance.

l. Hospital income or indemnity.

(3) "Insurer" means an insurance company subject to this Chapter, a service corporation organized under Article 65 of this Chapter, a health maintenance organization organized under Article 67 of this Chapter, and a multiple employer welfare arrangement subject to Article 49 of this Chapter.

(b) In General. - Except as provided in subsection (c) of this section, an insurer that provides a health benefit plan that contains maternity benefits, including benefits for childbirth, shall ensure that coverage is provided with respect to a mother who is a participant, beneficiary, or policyholder under the plan and her newborn child for a minimum of 48 hours of inpatient length of stay following a normal vaginal delivery, and a minimum of 96 hours of inpatient length of stay following a cesarean section, without requiring the attending provider to obtain authorization from the insurer or its representative.

(c) Exception. - Notwithstanding subsection (b) of this section, an insurer is not required to provide coverage for postdelivery inpatient length of stay for a mother who is a participant, beneficiary, or policyholder under the insurer's health benefit plan and her newborn child for the period referred to in subsection (b) of this section if:

(1) A decision to discharge the mother and her newborn child before the expiration of the period is made by the attending provider in consultation with the mother; and

(2) The health benefit plan provides coverage for postdelivery follow-up care as described in subsections (d) and (e) of this section.

(d) Postdelivery Follow-Up Care. - In the case of a decision to discharge a mother and her newborn child from the inpatient setting before the expiration of 48 hours following a normal vaginal delivery or 96 hours following a cesarean section, the health benefit plan shall provide coverage for timely postdelivery care. This health care shall be provided to a mother and her newborn child by a registered nurse, physician, nurse practitioner, nurse midwife, or physician assistant experienced in maternal and child health in:

(1) The home, a provider's office, a hospital, a birthing center, an intermediate care facility, a federally qualified health center, a federally qualified rural health clinic, or a State health department maternity clinic; or

(2) Another setting determined appropriate under federal regulations promulgated under Title VI of Public Law 104-204.

The attending provider in consultation with the mother shall decide the most appropriate location for follow-up care.

(e) Timely Care. - As used in subsection (d) of this section, "timely postdelivery care" means health care that is provided:

(1) Following the discharge of a mother and her newborn child from the inpatient setting; and

(2) In a manner that meets the health care needs of the mother and her newborn child, that provides for the appropriate monitoring of the conditions of the mother and child, and that occurs not later than the 72-hour period immediately following discharge.

(f) Prohibitions. - An insurer shall not:

(1)   Deny enrollment, renewal, or continued coverage with respect to its health benefit plan to a mother and her newborn child who are participants, beneficiaries, or policyholders, based on compliance with this section;

(2)   Provide monetary payments or rebates to mothers to encourage the mothers to request less than the minimum coverage required under this section;

(3)   Penalize or otherwise reduce or limit the reimbursement of an attending provider because the provider provided treatment to an individual policyholder, participant, or beneficiary in accordance with this section; or

(4)   Provide monetary or other incentives to an attending provider to induce the provider to provide treatment to an individual policyholder, participant, or beneficiary in a manner inconsistent with this section.

(g)   Effect on Mother. - Nothing in this section requires that a mother who is a participant, beneficiary, or policyholder covered under this section:

(1)   Give birth in a hospital; or

(2)   Stay in the hospital for a fixed period of time following the birth of her child.

(h)   Level and Type of Reimbursements. - Nothing in this section prevents an insurer from negotiating the level and type of reimbursement with an attending provider for care provided in accordance with this section. (1997-259, s. 19.)

§ 58-3-170. Requirements for maternity coverage.

(a)   Every entity providing a health benefit plan that provides maternity coverage in this State shall provide benefits for the necessary care and treatment related to maternity that are no less favorable than benefits for physical illness generally.

(a1)   Repealed by Session Laws 1997-259, s. 20.

(b)   As used in this section, "health benefit plans" means accident and health insurance policies or certificates; nonprofit hospital or medical service corporation contracts; health, hospital, or medical service corporation plan contracts; health maintenance organization (HMO) subscriber contracts; and plans provided by a MEWA or plans provided by other benefit arrangements, to the extent permitted by ERISA. (1993, c. 506, s. 2; 1995, c. 517, s. 3.1; 1997-259, s. 20.)

§ 58-3-171. Uniform claim forms.

(a)   All claims submitted by health care providers to health benefit plans shall be submitted on a uniform form or format that shall be developed by the Department and approved by the Commissioner. Additional information beyond that contained on the uniform form or format may be collected subject to rules adopted by the Commissioner. This section applies to the submission of claims in writing and by electronic means.

(b)   After consultation with the North Carolina Industrial Commission, the Commissioner may include workers' compensation insurance policies as "health benefit plans" for the purpose of administering the provisions of this section.

(c)   For purposes of this section, "health benefit plans" means accident and health insurance policies or certificates; nonprofit hospital or medical service corporation contracts; health maintenance organization (HMO) subscriber contracts and other plans provided by managed-care organizations; plans provided by a MEWA or plans provided by other benefit arrangements, to the extent permitted by ERISA; the State Health Plan for Teachers and State Employees and any optional plans or programs operating under Part 2 of Article 3 of Chapter 135 of the General Statutes; and medical payment coverages under homeowners and automobile insurance policies. (1993, c. 529, s. 4.2; 2007-298, s. 8.2; 2007-323, s. 28.22A(o); 2007-345, s. 12.)

§ 58-3-172. Notice of claim denied.

(a)   For all claims denied for health care provider services under health benefit plans, written notification of the denied claim shall be given to the insured and to the health care provider submitting the claim if the health care provider would otherwise be eligible for payment. This subsection does not apply to insurers subject to G.S. 58-3-225.

(b) For purposes of this section, "health benefit plans" means accident and health insurance policies or certificates; nonprofit hospital or medical service corporation contracts; health, hospital, or medical service corporation plan contracts; health maintenance organization (HMO) subscriber contracts and other plans provided by managed-care organizations; plans provided by a MEWA or plans provided by other benefit arrangements, to the extent permitted by ERISA; and the State Health Plan for Teachers and State Employees and any optional plans or programs operating under Part 2 of Article 3 of Chapter 135 of the General Statutes. (1993, c. 529, s. 4.2; 1993 (Reg. Sess., 1994), c. 678, s. 6; 2000-162, s. 4(c); 2007-298, s. 8.3; 2007-323, s. 28.22A(o); 2007-345, s. 12.)

§ 58-3-173: Repealed by Session Laws 1997-259, s. 24.

§ 58-3-174. Coverage for bone mass measurement for diagnosis and evaluation of osteoporosis or low bone mass.

(a) Every entity providing a health benefit plan shall provide coverage for a qualified individual for scientifically proven and approved bone mass measurement for the diagnosis and evaluation of osteoporosis or low bone mass. The same deductibles, coinsurance, and other limitations as apply to similar services covered under the plan shall apply to coverage for bone mass measurement.

(b) A health benefit plan may provide that bone mass measurement will be covered if at least 23 months have elapsed since the last bone mass measurement was performed, except that a plan must provide coverage for follow-up bone mass measurement performed more frequently than every 23 months if the follow-up measurement is medically necessary. Conditions under which more frequent bone mass measurement coverage may be medically necessary include, but are not limited to:

(1) Monitoring beneficiaries on long-term glucocorticoid therapy of more than three months.

(2) Allowing for a central bone mass measurement to determine the effectiveness of adding an additional treatment regimen for a qualified individual who is proven to have low bone mass so long as the bone mass measurement is performed 12 to 18 months from the start date of the additional regimen.

(c) Nothing in this section shall be construed to require health benefit plans to cover screening for nonqualified individuals.

(d) As used in this section, the term:

(1) "Bone mass measurement" means a scientifically proven radiologic, radioisotopic, or other procedure performed on a qualified individual to identify bone mass or detect bone loss for the purpose of initiating or modifying treatment.

(2) "Health benefit plan" means an accident and health insurance policy or certificate; a nonprofit hospital or medical service corporation contract; a health maintenance organization subscriber contract; a plan provided by a multiple employer welfare arrangement; or a plan provided by another benefit arrangement, to the extent permitted by the Employee Retirement Income Security Act of 1974, as amended, or by any waiver of or other exception to that act provided under federal law or regulation. "Health benefit plan" does not mean any plan implemented or administered by the North Carolina Department of Health and Human Services or the United States Department of Health and Human Services, or any successor agency, or its representatives. "Health benefit plan" also does not mean any of the following kinds of insurance:

a. Accident

b. Credit

c. Disability income

d. Long-term care or nursing home care

e. Medicare supplement

f. Specified disease

g. Dental or vision

h. Short-term limited duration coverage

i. Coverage issued as a supplement to liability insurance

j. Workers' compensation

k. Medical payments under automobile or homeowners

l. Hospital income or indemnity

m. Insurance under which benefits are payable with or without regard to fault and that is statutorily required to be contained in any liability policy or equivalent self-insurance.

(3) "Insurer" includes an insurance company subject to this Chapter, a service corporation organized under Article 65 of this Chapter, a health maintenance organization organized under Article 67 of this Chapter, and a multiple employer welfare arrangement subject to Article 49 of this Chapter.

(4) "Qualified individual" means any one or more of the following:

a. An individual who is estrogen-deficient and at clinical risk of osteoporosis or low bone mass.

b. An individual with radiographic osteopenia anywhere in the skeleton.

c. An individual who is receiving long-term glucocorticoid (steroid) therapy.

d. An individual with primary hyperparathyroidism.

e. An individual who is being monitored to assess the response to or efficacy of commonly accepted osteoporosis drug therapies.

f. An individual who has a history of low-trauma fractures.

g. An individual with other conditions or on medical therapies known to cause osteoporosis or low bone mass. (1999-197, s. 1.)

§ 58-3-175. Direct payment to government agencies.

(a)   As used in this section, "health benefit plan" has the same meaning as in G.S. 58-50-110(11) and includes the State Health Plan for Teachers and State Employees and any optional plans or programs operating under Part 2 of Article 3 of Chapter 135 of the General Statutes.

(b)   Every entity providing or administering a health benefit plan covering persons in this State shall make payment for health care services covered by the health benefit plan that are provided by any State, county, or city agency, directly to the agency providing the services.

(c)   This section does not apply to the extent the agency providing the services has been paid for the services by or on behalf of the person receiving the services.

(d)   Nothing in this section shall require any entity providing or administering a health benefit plan covering persons in this State to pay any agency directly:

(1)   If the agency is outside of the health benefit plan's service area;

(2)   If the entity operates a program by which it only pays the health care provider directly upon the acceptance of certain rates and the agency does not accept said rates; or

(3)   If the entity operates a program by which it provides, authorizes, or arranges for a covered person to receive health care from a designated provider or refers the covered person to a designated provider, and the agency is not a designated provider. (1993, c. 41, s. 1; 2007-298, s. 8.4; 2007-323, s. 28.22A(o); 2007-345, s. 12.)

§ 58-3-176. Treatment discussions not limited.

(a)   An insurer shall not limit either of the following:

(1)   The participating plan provider's ability to discuss with an enrollee the clinical treatment options medically available, the risks associated with the treatments, or a recommended course of treatment.

(2) The participating plan provider's professional obligations to patients as specified under the provider's professional license.

(b) Nothing in this section shall be construed to expand or revise the scope of benefits covered by a health benefit plan.

(c) As used in this section:

(1) "Health benefit plan" means any of the following if written by an insurer: an accident and health insurance policy or certificate; a nonprofit hospital or medical service corporation contract; a health maintenance organization subscriber contract; or a plan provided by a multiple employer welfare arrangement. "Health benefit plan" does not mean any plan implemented or administered through the Department of Health and Human Services or its representatives. "Health benefit plan" also does not mean any of the following kinds of insurance:

a. Accident.

b. Credit.

c. Disability income.

d. Long-term or nursing home care.

e. Medicare supplement.

f. Specified disease.

g. Dental or vision.

h. Coverage issued as a supplement to liability insurance.

i. Workers' compensation.

j. Medical payments under automobile or homeowners insurance.

k. Hospital income or indemnity.

l. Insurance under which benefits are payable with or without regard to fault and that is statutorily required to be contained in any liability policy or equivalent self-insurance.

(2) "Insurer" means an entity that writes a health benefit plan and that is an insurance company subject to this Chapter, a service corporation under Article 65 of this Chapter, a health maintenance organization under Article 67 of this Chapter, or a multiple employer welfare arrangement under Article 49 of this Chapter. (1997-443, s. 11A.122; 1997-474, s. 1.)

§ 58-3-177. Uniform prescription drug identification cards.

(a) Every health benefit plan that provides coverage for prescription drugs or devices and that issues a prescription drug card, shall issue to its insureds a uniform prescription drug identification card. The uniform prescription drug identification card shall contain the information listed in subdivisions (1) through (7) of this subsection in the following order beginning at the top left margin of the card:

(1) The health benefit plan's name and/or logo.

(2) The American National Standards Institute assigned Issuer Identification Number.

(3) The processor control number.

(4) The insured's group number.

(5) The health benefit plan's card issuer identifier.

(6) The insured's identification number.

(7) The insured's name.

(b) In addition to the information required under subsection (a), the uniform prescription drug card shall contain, in one of the lower-most elements on the back side of the card, the following information:

(1) The health benefit plan's claims submission name and address.

(2) The health benefit plan's help desk telephone number and name.

Nothing in this section shall require a health benefit plan to violate a contractual agreement, service mark agreement, or trademark agreement.

(c) A new uniform prescription drug identification card as required under subsection (a) of this section shall be issued annually by a health benefit plan if there has been any change in the insured's coverage in the previous 12 months. A change in the insured's coverage shall include, but is not limited to, the addition or deletion of a dependent of the insured covered by a health benefit plan.

(d) Not later than January 1, 2003, the uniform prescription drug identification card provided under subsection (a) of this section shall contain one of the following mediums capable of the processing or adjudicating of a claim through electronic verification:

(1) A magnetic strip.

(2) A bar code.

(3) Any new technology available that is capable of processing or adjudicating a claim by electronic verification.

(e) As used in this section, "health benefit plan" means an accident and health insurance policy or certificate; a nonprofit hospital or medical service corporation contract; a health maintenance organization subscriber contract; a plan provided by a multiple employer welfare arrangement; or a plan provided by another benefit arrangement, to the extent permitted by the Employee Retirement Income Securlty Act of 1974, as amended, or by any waiver of or other exception to that Act provided under federal law or regulation. "Health benefit plan" does not mean any of the following kinds of insurance:

(1) Accident.

(2) Credit.

(3) Disability income.

(4) Long-term or nursing home care.

(5)   Medicare supplement.

(6)   Specified disease.

(7)   Dental or vision.

(8)   Coverage issued as a supplement to liability insurance.

(9)   Workers' compensation.

(10)   Medical payments under automobile or homeowners.

(11)   Insurance under which benefits are payable with or without regard to fault and that is statutorily required to be contained in any liability policy or equivalent self-insurance.

(12)   Hospital income or indemnity.

(f)   This section shall not apply to an entity that has its own facility and employs or contracts with physicians, pharmacists, nurses, and other health care personnel, to the extent that the entity dispenses prescription drugs or devices from its own pharmacies to its employees and to enrollees of its health benefit plan. This section does not apply to a health benefit plan that issues a single identification card to its insureds for all services covered under the plan. (1999-343, s. 1.)

§ 58-3-178. Coverage for prescription contraceptive drugs or devices and for outpatient contraceptive services; exemption for religious employers.

(a)   Except as provided in subsection (e) of this section, every insurer providing a health benefit plan that provides coverage for prescription drugs or devices shall provide coverage for prescription contraceptive drugs or devices. Coverage shall include coverage for the insertion or removal of and any medically necessary examination associated with the use of the prescribed contraceptive drug or device. Except as otherwise provided in this subsection, the same deductibles, coinsurance, and other limitations as apply to prescription drugs or devices covered under the health benefit plan shall apply to coverage for prescribed contraceptive drugs or devices. A health benefit plan may require that the total coinsurance, based on the useful life of the drug or device, be paid in advance for those drugs or devices that are inserted or prescribed and do not have to be refilled on a periodic basis.

(b) Every insurer providing a health benefit plan that provides coverage for outpatient services provided by a health care professional shall provide coverage for outpatient contraceptive services. The same deductibles, coinsurance, and other limitations as apply to outpatient services covered under the health benefit plan shall apply to coverage for outpatient contraceptive services.

(c) As used in this section, the term:

(1) "Health benefit plan" means an accident and health insurance policy or certificate; a nonprofit hospital or medical service corporation contract; a health maintenance organization subscriber contract; a plan provided by a multiple employer welfare arrangement; or a plan provided by another benefit arrangement, to the extent permitted by the Employee Retirement Income Security Act of 1974, as amended, or by any waiver of or other exception to that Act provided under federal law or regulation. "Health benefit plan" does not mean any plan implemented or administered by the North Carolina Department of Health and Human Services or the United States Department of Health and Human Services, or any successor agency, or its representatives. "Health benefit plan" also does not mean any of the following kinds of insurance:

a. Accident.

b. Credit.

c. Disability income.

d. Long-term care or nursing home care.

e. Medicare supplement.

f. Specified disease.

g. Dental or vision.

h. Coverage issued as a supplement to liability insurance.

i. Workers' compensation.

j. Medical payments under automobile or homeowners.

k. Hospital income or indemnity.

l. Insurance under which benefits are payable with or without regard to fault and that is statutorily required to be contained in any liability policy or equivalent self-insurance.

m. Short-term limited duration health insurance policies as defined in Part 144 of Title 45 of the Code of Federal Regulations.

(2) "Insurer" includes an insurance company subject to this Chapter, a service corporation organized under Article 65 of this Chapter, a health maintenance organization organized under Article 67 of this Chapter, and a multiple employer welfare arrangement subject to Article 49 of this Chapter.

(3) "Outpatient contraceptive services" means consultations, examinations, procedures, and medical services provided on an outpatient basis and related to the use of contraceptive methods to prevent pregnancy.

(4) "Prescribed contraceptive drugs or devices" means drugs or devices that prevent pregnancy and that are approved by the United States Food and Drug Administration for use as contraceptives and obtained under a prescription written by a health care provider authorized to prescribe medications under the laws of this State. Prescription drugs or devices required to be covered under this section shall not include:

a. The prescription drug known as "RU-486" or any "equivalent drug product" as defined in G.S. 90-85.27(1).

b. The prescription drug marketed under the name "Preven" or any "equivalent drug product" as defined in G.S. 90-85.27(1).

(d) A health benefit plan subject to this section shall not do any of the following:

(1) Deny eligibility or continued eligibility to enroll or to renew coverage under the terms of the health benefit plan, solely for the purpose of avoiding the requirements of this section.

(2) Provide monetary payments or rebates to an individual participant or beneficiary to encourage the individual participant or beneficiary to accept less than the minimum protections available under this section.

(3) Penalize or otherwise reduce or limit the reimbursement of an attending provider because the provider prescribed contraceptive drugs or devices, or provided contraceptive services in accordance with this section.

(4) Provide incentives, monetary or otherwise, to an attending provider to induce the provider to withhold from an individual participant or beneficiary contraceptive drugs, devices, or services.

(e) A religious employer may request an insurer providing a health benefit plan to provide to the religious employer a health benefit plan that excludes coverage for prescription contraceptive drugs or devices that are contrary to the employer's religious tenets. Upon request, the insurer shall provide the requested health benefit plan. An insurer providing a health benefit plan requested by a religious employer pursuant to this section shall provide written notice to each person covered under the health benefit plan that prescription contraceptive drugs or devices are excluded from coverage pursuant to this section at the request of the employer. The notice shall appear, in not less than 10-point type, in the health benefit plan, application, and sales brochure for the health benefit plan. Nothing in this subsection authorizes a health benefit plan to exclude coverage for prescription drugs ordered by a health care provider with prescriptive authority for reasons other than contraceptive purposes, or for prescription contraception that is necessary to preserve the life or health of a person covered under the plan. As used in this subsection, the term "religious employer" means an entity for which all of the following are true:

(1) The entity is organized and operated for religious purposes and is tax exempt under section 501(c)(3) of the U.S. Internal Revenue Code.

(2) The inculcation of religious values is one of the primary purposes of the entity.

(3) The entity employs primarily persons who share the religious tenets of the entity. (1999-231, s. 1; 1999-456, s. 15(a).)

§ 58-3-179. Coverage for colorectal cancer screening.

(a)   Every health benefit plan, as defined in G.S. 58-3-167, shall provide coverage for colorectal cancer examinations and laboratory tests for cancer, in accordance with the most recently published American Cancer Society guidelines or guidelines adopted by the North Carolina Advisory Committee on Cancer Coordination and Control for colorectal cancer screening, for any nonsymptomatic covered individual who is:

(1)   At least 50 years of age, or

(2)   Less than 50 years of age and at high risk for colorectal cancer according to the most recently published colorectal cancer screening guidelines of the American Cancer Society or guidelines adopted by the North Carolina Advisory Committee on Cancer Coordination and Control.

The same deductibles, coinsurance, and other limitations as apply to similar services covered under the plan apply to coverage for colorectal examinations and laboratory tests required to be covered under this section.

(b)   Reserved for future codification purposes. (2001-116, s. 1.)

§ 58-3-180. Motor vehicle repairs; selection by claimant.

(a)   A policy covering damage to a motor vehicle shall allow the claimant to select the repair service or source for the repair of the damage.

(b)   The amount determined by the insurer to be payable under a policy covering damage to a motor vehicle shall be paid regardless of the repair service or source selected by the claimant.

(b1)   No insurer or insurer representative shall recommend the use of a particular motor vehicle repair service without clearly informing the claimant that (i) the claimant is under no obligation to use the recommended repair service, (ii) the claimant may use the repair service of the claimant's choice, (iii) the amount determined by the insurer to be payable under the policy will be paid regardless of whether or not the claimant uses the recommended repair service, and (iv) that the insurer or insurer representative has, at the time the recommendations are made, a financial interest in the recommended motor vehicle repair service. No insurer shall require that the insured or claimant must have a damaged vehicle repaired at an insurer-owned motor vehicle repair service.

(b2) The provisions of subsection (b1) of this section shall be included in nonfleet private passenger motor vehicle insurance policy forms promulgated by the Bureau and approved by the Commissioner.

(c) Any person who violates this section is subject to the applicable provisions of G.S. 58-2-70 and G.S. 58-33-46, provided that the maximum civil penalty that can be assessed under G.S. 58-2-70(d) for a violation of this section is two thousand dollars ($2,000).

(d) As used in this section, "insurer representative" includes an insurance agent, limited representative, broker, adjuster, and appraiser. (1993, c. 525, s. 2; 2001-203, s. 26; 2001-451, s. 1; 2003-395, s. 1.)

§ 58-3-185. Lien created for payment of past-due child support obligations.

(a) In the event that the Department of Health and Human Services or any other obligee, as defined in G.S. 110-129, provides written notification to an insurance company authorized to issue policies of insurance pursuant to this Chapter that a claimant or beneficiary under a contract of insurance owes past-due child support and accompanies this information with a certified copy of the court order ordering support together with proof that the claimant or beneficiary is past due in meeting this obligation, there is created a lien upon any insurance proceeds in favor of the Department or obligee. This section shall apply only in those instances in which there is a nonrecurring payment of a lump-sum amount equal to or in excess of three thousand dollars ($3,000) or periodic payments with an aggregate amount that equals or exceeds three thousand dollars ($3,000).

(b) Liens arising under this section shall be subordinate to liens upon insurance proceeds for personal injuries arising under Article 9 of Chapter 44 of the General Statutes and valid health care provider claims covered by health benefit plans as defined in G.S. 58-3-172. As used in this section, the term health benefit plans does not include disability income insurance. (1995, c. 538, s. 6(a); 1995 (Reg. Sess., 1996), c. 674, ss. 1, 2; 1997-443, s. 11A.118(a).)

§ 58-3-190. Coverage required for emergency care.

(a)   Every insurer shall provide coverage for emergency services to the extent necessary to screen and to stabilize the person covered under the plan and shall not require prior authorization of the services if a prudent layperson acting reasonably would have believed that an emergency medical condition existed. Payment of claims for emergency services shall be based on the retrospective review of the presenting history and symptoms of the covered person.

(b)   With respect to emergency services provided by a health care provider who is not under contract with the insurer, the services shall be covered if:

(1)   A prudent layperson acting reasonably would have believed that a delay would worsen the emergency, or

(2)   The covered person did not seek services from a provider under contract with the insurer because of circumstances beyond the control of the covered person.

(c)   An insurer that has given prior authorization for emergency services shall cover the services and shall not retract the authorization after the services have been provided unless the authorization was based on a material misrepresentation about the covered person's health condition made by the provider of the emergency services or the covered person.

(d)   Coverage of emergency services shall be subject to coinsurance, co-payments, and deductibles applicable under the health benefit plan. An insurer shall not impose cost-sharing for emergency services provided under this section that differs from the cost-sharing that would have been imposed if the physician or provider furnishing the services were a provider contracting with the insurer.

(e)   Both the emergency department and the insurer shall make a good faith effort to communicate with each other in a timely fashion to expedite postevaluation or poststabilization services in order to avoid material deterioration of the covered person's condition within a reasonable clinical confidence, or with respect to a pregnant woman, to avoid material deterioration of the condition of the unborn child within a reasonable clinical confidence.

(f) Insurers shall provide information to their covered persons on all of the following:

(1) Coverage of emergency medical services.

(2) The appropriate use of emergency services, including the use of the "911" system and other telephone access systems utilized to access prehospital emergency services.

(3) Any cost-sharing provisions for emergency medical services.

(4) The process and procedures for obtaining emergency services, so that covered persons are familiar with the location of in-plan emergency departments and with the location and availability of other in-plan settings at which covered persons may receive medical care.

(g) As used in this section, the term:

(1) "Emergency medical condition" means a medical condition manifesting itself by acute symptoms of sufficient severity, including, but not limited to, severe pain, or by acute symptoms developing from a chronic medical condition that would lead a prudent layperson, possessing an average knowledge of health and medicine, to reasonably expect the absence of immediate medical attention to result in any of the following:

a. Placing the health of an individual, or with respect to a pregnant woman, the health of the woman or her unborn child, in serious jeopardy.

b. Serious impairment to bodily functions.

c. Serious dysfunction of any bodily organ or part.

(2) "Emergency services" means health care items and services furnished or required to screen for or treat an emergency medical condition until the condition is stabilized, including prehospital care and ancillary services routinely available to the emergency department.

(3) "Health benefit plan" means any of the following if written by an insurer: an accident and health insurance policy or certificate; a nonprofit hospital or medical service corporation contract; a health maintenance organization

subscriber contract; or a plan provided by a multiple employer welfare arrangement. "Health benefit plan" does not mean any plan implemented or administered through the Department of Health and Human Services or its representatives. "Health benefit plan" also does not mean any of the following kinds of insurance:

a. Accident.

b. Credit.

c. Disability income.

d. Long-term or nursing home care.

e. Medicare supplement.

f. Specified disease.

g. Dental or vision.

h. Coverage issued as a supplement to liability insurance.

i. Workers' compensation.

j. Medical payments under automobile or homeowners insurance.

k. Hospital income or indemnity.

l. Insurance under which benefits are payable with or without regard to fault and that is statutorily required to be contained in any liability policy or equivalent self-insurance.

(4) "Insurer" means an entity that writes a health benefit plan and that is an insurance company subject to this Chapter, a service corporation under Article 65 of this Chapter, a health maintenance organization under Article 67 of this Chapter, or a multiple employer welfare arrangement under Article 49 of this Chapter.

(5) "To stabilize" means to provide medical care that is appropriate to prevent a material deterioration of the person's condition, within reasonable medical probability, in accordance with the HCFA (Health Care Financing

Administration) interpretative guidelines, policies and regulations pertaining to responsibilities of hospitals in emergency cases (as provided under the Emergency Medical Treatment and Labor Act, section 1867 of the Social Security Act, 42 U.S.C.S. 1395dd), including medically necessary services and supplies to maintain stabilization until the person is transferred. (1997-443, s. 11A.122; 1997-474, s. 2.)

§ 58-3-191. Managed care reporting and disclosure requirements.

(a) Each health benefit plan shall annually, on or before the first day of May of each year, file in the office of the Commissioner the following information for the previous calendar year:

(1) The number of and reasons for grievances received from plan participants regarding medical treatment. The report shall include the number of covered lives, total number of grievances categorized by reason for the grievance, the number of grievances referred to the second level grievance review, the number of grievances resolved at each level and their resolution, and a description of the actions that are being taken to correct the problems that have been identified through grievances received. Every health benefit plan shall file with the Commissioner, as part of its annual grievance report, a certificate of compliance stating that the carrier has established and follows, for each of its lines of business, grievance procedures that comply with G.S. 58-50-62.

(2) The number of participants and groups who terminated coverage under the plan for any reason. The report shall include the number of participants who terminated coverage because the group contract under which they were covered was terminated, the number of participants who terminated coverage for reasons other than the termination of the group under which they were enrolled, and the number of group contracts terminated.

(3) The number of provider contracts that were terminated and the reasons for termination. This information shall include the number of providers leaving the plan and the number of new providers. The report shall show voluntary and involuntary terminations separately.

(4) Data relating to the utilization, quality, availability, and accessibility of services. The report shall include the following:

a. Information on the health benefit plan's program to determine the level of network availability, as measured by the numbers and types of network providers, required to provide covered services to covered persons. This information shall include the plan's methodology for:

1. Establishing performance targets for the numbers and types of providers by specialty, area of practice, or facility type, for each of the following categories: primary care physicians, specialty care physicians, nonphysician health care providers, hospitals, and nonhospital health care facilities.

2. Determining when changes in plan membership will necessitate changes in the provider network.

The report shall also include: the availability performance targets for the previous and current years; the numbers and types of providers currently participating in the health benefit plan's provider network; and an evaluation of actual plan performance against performance targets.

b. The health benefit plan's method for arranging or providing health care services from nonnetwork providers, both within and outside of its service area, when network providers are not available to provide covered services.

c. Information on the health benefit plan's program to determine the level of provider network accessibility necessary to serve its membership. This information shall include the health benefit plan's methodology for establishing performance targets for member access to covered services from primary care physicians, specialty care physicians, nonphysician health care providers, hospitals, and nonhospital health care facilities. The methodology shall establish targets for:

1. The proximity of network providers to members, as measured by member driving distance, to access primary care, specialty care, hospital-based services, and services of nonhospital facilities.

2. Expected waiting time for appointments for urgent care, acute care, specialty care, and routine services for prevention and wellness.

The report shall also include: the accessibility performance targets for the previous and current years; data on actual overall accessibility as measured by driving distance and average appointment waiting time; and an evaluation of actual plan performance against performance targets. Measures of actual accessibility may be developed using scientifically valid random sample techniques.

d. A statement of the health benefit plan's methods and standards for determining whether in-network services are reasonably available and accessible to a covered person, for the purpose of determining whether a covered person should receive the in-network level of coverage for services received from a nonnetwork provider.

e. A description of the health benefit plan's program to monitor the adequacy of its network availability and accessibility methodologies and performance targets, plan performance, and network provider performance.

f. A summary of the health benefit plan's utilization review program activities for the previous calendar year. The report shall include the number of: each type of utilization review performed, noncertifications for each type of review, each type of review appealed, and appeals settled in favor of covered persons. The report shall be accompanied by a certification from the carrier that it has established and follows procedures that comply with G.S. 58-50-61.

(5) Aggregate financial compensation data, including the percentage of providers paid under a capitation arrangement, discounted fee-for-service or salary, the services included in the capitation payment, and the range of compensation paid by withhold or incentive payments. This information shall be submitted on a form prescribed by the Commissioner.

The name, or group or institutional name, of an individual provider may not be disclosed pursuant to this subsection. No civil liability shall arise from compliance with the provisions of this subsection, provided that the acts or omissions are made in good faith and do not constitute gross negligence, willful or wanton misconduct, or intentional wrongdoing.

(b) Disclosure requirements. - Each health benefit plan shall provide the following applicable information to plan participants and bona fide prospective participants upon request:

(1) The evidence of coverage (G.S. 58-67-50), subscriber contract (G.S. 58-65-60, 58-65-140), health insurance policy (G.S. 58-51-80, 58-50-125, 58-50-126, 58-50-55), or the contract and benefit summary of any other type of health benefit plan;

(2) An explanation of the utilization review criteria and treatment protocol under which treatments are provided for conditions specified by the prospective participant. This explanation shall be in writing if so requested;

(3) If denied a recommended treatment, written reasons for the denial and an explanation of the utilization review criteria or treatment protocol upon which the denial was based;

(4) The plan's formularies, restricted access drugs or devices as defined in G.S. 58-3-221, or prior approval requirements for obtaining prescription drugs, whether a particular drug or therapeutic class of drugs is excluded from its formulary, and the circumstances under which a nonformulary drug may be covered; and

(5) The plan's procedures and medically based criteria for determining whether a specified procedure, test, or treatment is experimental.

(b1) Effective March 1, 1998, insurers shall make the reports that are required under subsection (a) of this section and that have been filed with the Commissioner available on their business premises and shall provide any insured access to them upon request.

(c) For purposes of this section, "health benefit plan" or "plan" means (i) health maintenance organization (HMO) subscriber contracts and (ii) insurance company or hospital and medical service corporation preferred provider benefit plans as defined in G.S. 58-50-56. (1997-480, s. 1; 1997-519, s. 1.1; 2001-334, s. 2.2; 2001-446, s. 2.1; 2006-154, s. 13; 2008-124, s. 10.1.)

§ 58-3-200. Miscellaneous insurance and managed care coverage and network provisions.

(a) Definitions. - As used in this section:

(1) "Health benefit plan" means any of the following if written by an insurer: an accident and health insurance policy or certificate; a nonprofit hospital or medical service corporation contract; a health maintenance organization subscriber contract; or a plan provided by a multiple employer welfare arrangement. "Health benefit plan" does not mean any plan implemented or

administered through the Department of Health and Human Services or its representatives. "Health benefit plan" also does not mean any of the following kinds of insurance:

a. Accident.

b. Credit.

c. Disability income.

d. Long-term or nursing home care.

e. Medicare supplement.

f. Specified disease.

g. Dental or vision.

h. Coverage issued as a supplement to liability insurance.

i. Workers' compensation.

j. Medical payments under automobile or homeowners insurance.

k. Hospital income or indemnity.

l. Insurance under which benefits are payable with or without regard to fault and that is statutorily required to be contained in any liability policy or equivalent self-insurance.

(2) "Insurer" means an entity that writes a health benefit plan and that is an insurance company subject to this Chapter, a service corporation under Article 65 of this Chapter, a health maintenance organization under Article 67 of this Chapter, or a multiple employer welfare arrangement under Article 49 of this Chapter.

(b) Medical Necessity. - An insurer that limits its health benefit plan coverage to medically necessary services and supplies shall define "medically necessary services or supplies" in its health benefit plan as those covered services or supplies that are:

(1) Provided for the diagnosis, treatment, cure, or relief of a health condition, illness, injury, or disease; and, except as allowed under G.S. 58-3-255, not for experimental, investigational, or cosmetic purposes.

(2) Necessary for and appropriate to the diagnosis, treatment, cure, or relief of a health condition, illness, injury, disease, or its symptoms.

(3) Within generally accepted standards of medical care in the community.

(4) Not solely for the convenience of the insured, the insured's family, or the provider.

For medically necessary services, nothing in this subsection precludes an insurer from comparing the cost-effectiveness of alternative services or supplies when determining which of the services or supplies will be covered.

(c) Coverage Determinations. - If an insurer or its authorized representative determines that services, supplies, or other items are covered under its health benefit plan, including any determination under G.S. 58-50-61, the insurer shall not subsequently retract its determination after the services, supplies, or other items have been provided, or reduce payments for a service, supply, or other item furnished in reliance on such a determination, unless the determination was based on a material misrepresentation about the insured's health condition that was knowingly made by the insured or the provider of the service, supply, or other item.

(d) Services Outside Provider Networks. - No insurer shall penalize an insured or subject an insured to the out-of-network benefit levels offered under the insured's approved health benefit plan, including an insured receiving an extended or standing referral under G.S. 58-3-223, unless contracting health care providers able to meet health needs of the insured are reasonably available to the insured without unreasonable delay.

(e) Nondiscrimination Against High-Risk Populations. - No insurer shall establish provider selection or contract renewal standards or procedures that are designed to avoid or otherwise have the effect of avoiding enrolling high-risk populations by excluding providers because they are located in geographic areas that contain high-risk populations or because they treat or specialize in treating populations that present a risk of higher-than-average claims or health care services utilization. This subsection does not prohibit an insurer from declining to select a provider or from not renewing a contract with a provider who fails to meet the insurer's selection criteria.

(f) Continuing Care Retirement Community Residents. - As used in this subsection, "Medicare benefits" means medical and health products, benefits, and services used in accordance with Title XVIII of the Social Security Act. If an insured with coverage for Medicare benefits or similar benefits under a plan for retired federal government employees is a resident of a continuing care retirement community regulated under Article 64 of this Chapter, and the insured's primary care physician determines that it is medically necessary for the insured to be referred to a skilled nursing facility upon discharge from an acute care facility, the insurer shall not require that the insured relocate to a skilled nursing facility outside the continuing care retirement community if the continuing care retirement community:

(1) Is a Medicare-certified skilled nursing facility.

(2) Agrees to be reimbursed at the insurer's contract rate negotiated with similar providers for the same services and supplies.

(3) Agrees not to bill the insured for fees over and above the insurer's contract rate.

(4) Meets all guidelines established by the insurer related to quality of care, including:

a. Quality assurance programs that promote continuous quality improvement.

b. Standards for performance measurement for measuring and reporting the quality of health care services provided to insureds.

c. Utilization review, including compliance with utilization management procedures.

d. Confidentiality of medical information.

e. Insured grievances and appeals from adverse treatment decisions.

f. Nondiscrimination.

(5) Agrees to comply with the insurer's procedures for referral authorization, risk assumption, use of insurer services, and other criteria applicable to providers under contract for the same services and supplies.

A continuing care retirement community that satisfies subdivisions (1) through (5) of this subsection shall not be obligated to accept, as a skilled nursing facility, any patient other than a resident of the continuing care retirement community, and neither the insurer nor the retirement community shall be allowed to list or otherwise advertise the skilled nursing facility as a participating network provider for Medicare benefits for anyone other than residents of the continuing care retirement community. (1997-443, s. 11A.122; 1997-519, s. 2.1; 2001-446, ss. 5(b), 1.2A.)

§ 58-3-215. Genetic information in health insurance.

(a) Definitions. - As used in this section:

(1) "Genetic information" means information about genes, gene products, or inherited characteristics that may derive from an individual or a family member. "Genetic information" does not include the results of routine physical measurements, blood chemistries, blood counts, urine analyses, tests for abuse of drugs, and tests for the presence of human immunodeficiency virus.

(2) "Health benefit plan" means an accident and health insurance policy or certificate; a nonprofit hospital or medical service corporation contract; a health maintenance organization subscriber contract; a plan provided by a multiple employer welfare arrangement; or a plan provided by another benefit arrangement, to the extent permitted by the Employee Retirement Income Security Act of 1974, as amended, or by any waiver of or other exception to that Act provided under federal law or regulation. "Health benefit plan" does not mean any plan implemented or administered through the Department of Health and Human Services or its representatives. "Health benefit plan" also does not mean any of the following kinds of insurance:

a. Accident

b. Credit

c. Disability income

d. Long-term or nursing home care

e. Medicare supplement

f. Specified disease

g. Dental or vision

h. Coverage issued as a supplement to liability insurance

i. Workers' compensation

j. Medical payments under automobile or homeowners

k. Hospital income or indemnity

l. Insurance under which benefits are payable with or without regard to fault and that is statutorily required to be contained in any liability policy or equivalent self-insurance

m. Blanket accident and sickness.

(3) "Insurer" means an insurance company subject to this Chapter; a service corporation organized under Article 65 of this Chapter; a health maintenance organization organized under Article 67 of this Chapter; or a multiple employer welfare arrangement subject to Article 49 of this Chapter.

(b) For the purpose of this section, routine physical measurements, blood chemistries, blood counts, urine analyses, tests for abuse of drugs, and tests for the presence of human immunodeficiency virus are not to be considered genetic tests.

(c) No insurer shall:

(1) Raise the premium or contribution rates paid by a group for a group health benefit plan on the basis of genetic information obtained about an individual member of the group.

(2) Refuse to issue or deliver a health benefit plan because of genetic information obtained about any person to be insured by the health benefit plan.

(3) Charge a higher premium rate or charge for a health benefit plan because of genetic information obtained about any person to be insured by the health benefit plan.

(d) Notwithstanding any other provision of this section, a health benefit plan, as defined in G.S. 58-3-167, and insurers, as defined in G.S. 58-3-167, shall comply with all applicable standards of Public Law 110-233, known as the Genetic Information Nondiscrimination Act of 2008, as amended by Public Law 110-343, and as further amended. (1997-350, s. 1; 1997-443, s. 11A.118(b); 2009-382, s. 18.)

§ 58-3-220. Mental illness benefits coverage.

(a) Mental Health Equity Requirement. - Except as provided in subsection (b), an insurer shall provide in each group health benefit plan benefits for the necessary care and treatment of mental illnesses that are no less favorable than benefits for physical illness generally, including application of the same limits. For purposes of this subsection, mental illnesses are as diagnosed and defined in the Diagnostic and Statistical Manual of Mental Disorders, DSM-IV, or a subsequent edition published by the American Psychiatric Association, except those mental disorders coded in the DSM-IV or subsequent edition as substance-related disorders (291.0 through 292.2 and 303.0 through 305.9), those coded as sexual dysfunctions not due to organic disease (302.70 through 302.79), and those coded as "V" codes. For purposes of this subsection, "limits" includes deductibles, coinsurance factors, co-payments, maximum out-of-pocket limits, annual and lifetime dollar limits, and any other dollar limits or fees for covered services.

(b) Minimum Required Benefits. - Except as provided in subsection (c), a group health benefit plan may apply durational limits to mental illnesses that differ from durational limits that apply to physical illnesses. A group health benefit plan shall provide at least the following minimum number of office visits and combined inpatient and outpatient days for all mental illnesses and disorders not listed in subsection (c), as diagnosed and defined in the Diagnostic and Statistical Manual of Mental Disorders, DSM-IV, or a subsequent edition published by the American Psychiatric Association, except those mental disorders coded in the DSM-IV or subsequent edition as substance-related disorders (291.0 through 292.2 and 303.0 through 305.9), those coded as sexual dysfunctions not due to organic disease (302.70 through 302.79), and those coded as "V" codes:

(1) Thirty combined inpatient and outpatient days per year.

(2) Thirty office visits per year.

(c) Durational limits for the following mental illnesses shall be subject to the same limits as benefits for physical illness generally:

(1) Bipolar Disorder.

(2) Major Depressive Disorder.

(3) Obsessive Compulsive Disorder.

(4) Paranoid and Other Psychotic Disorder.

(5) Schizoaffective Disorder.

(6) Schizophrenia.

(7) Post-Traumatic Stress Disorder.

(8) Anorexia Nervosa.

(9) Bulimia.

(d) Nothing in this section prevents an insurer from offering a group health benefit plan that provides greater than the minimum required benefits, as set forth in subsection (b).

(e) Nothing in this section requires an insurer to cover treatment or studies leading to or in connection with sex changes or modifications and related care.

(f) Weighted Average. - If a group health benefit plan contains annual limits, lifetime limits, co-payments, deductibles, or coinsurance only on selected physical illness and injury benefits, and these benefits do not represent substantially all of the physical illness and injury benefits under the group health benefit plan, then the insurer may impose limits on the mental health benefits based on a weighted average of the respective annual, lifetime, co-payment, deductible, or coinsurance limits on the selected physical illness and injury benefits. The weighted average shall be calculated in accordance with rules adopted by the Commissioner.

(g) Nothing in this section prevents an insurer from applying utilization review criteria to determine medical necessity as defined in G.S. 58-50-61 as long as it does so in accordance with all requirements for utilization review programs and medical necessity determinations specified in that section, including the offering of an insurer appeal process and, where applicable, health benefit plan external review as provided for in Part 4 of Article 50 of Chapter 58 of the General Statutes.

(h) Definitions. - As used in this section:

(1) "Health benefit plan" has the same meaning as in G.S. 58-3-167.

(2) "Insurer" has the same meaning as in G.S. 58-3-167.

(3) "Mental illness" has the same meaning as in G.S. 122C-3(21), with a mental disorder defined in the Diagnostic and Statistical Manual of Mental Disorders, DSM-IV, or subsequent editions published by the American Psychiatric Association, except those mental disorders coded in the DSM-IV or subsequent editions as substance-related disorders (291.0 through 292.9 and 303.0 through 305.9), those coded as sexual dysfunctions not due to organic disease (302.70 through 302.79), and those coded as "V" codes.

(i) Notwithstanding any other provisions of this section, a group health benefit plan that covers both medical and surgical benefits and mental health benefits shall, with respect to the mental health benefits, comply with all applicable standards of Subtitle B of Title V of Public Law 110-343, known as the Paul Wellstone and Pete Domenici Mental Health Parity and Addiction Equity Act of 2008.

(j) Subsection (i) of this section applies only to a group health benefit plan covering a large employer as defined in G.S. 58-68-25(a)(10). (2007-268, s. 2; 2009-382, s. 19.)

§ 58-3-221. Access to nonformulary and restricted access prescription drugs.

(a) If an insurer maintains one or more closed formularies for or restricts access to covered prescription drugs or devices, then the insurer shall do all of the following:

(1) Develop the formulary or formularies and any restrictions on access to covered prescription drugs or devices in consultation with and with the approval of a pharmacy and therapeutics committee, which shall include participating physicians who are licensed to practice medicine in this State.

(2) Make available to participating providers, pharmacists, and enrollees the complete drugs or devices formulary or formularies maintained by the insurer including a list of the devices and prescription drugs on the formulary by major therapeutic category that specifies whether a particular drug or device is preferred over other drugs or devices.

(3) Establish and maintain an expeditious process or procedure that allows an enrollee or the enrollee's physician acting on behalf of the enrollee to obtain, without penalty or additional cost-sharing beyond that provided for in the health benefit plan, coverage for a specific nonformulary drug or device determined to be medically necessary and appropriate by the enrollee's participating physician without prior approval from the insurer, after the enrollee's participating physician notifies the insurer that:

a. Either (i) the formulary alternatives have been ineffective in the treatment of the enrollee's disease or condition, or (ii) the formulary alternatives cause or are reasonably expected by the physician to cause a harmful or adverse clinical reaction in the enrollee; and

b. Either (i) the drug is prescribed in accordance with any applicable clinical protocol of the insurer for the prescribing of the drug, or (ii) the drug has been approved as an exception to the clinical protocol pursuant to the insurer's exception procedure.

(4) Provide coverage for a restricted access drug or device to an enrollee without requiring prior approval or use of a nonrestricted formulary drug if an enrollee's physician certifies in writing that the enrollee has previously used an alternative nonrestricted access drug or device and the alternative drug or device has been detrimental to the enrollee's health or has been ineffective in treating the same condition and, in the opinion of the prescribing physician, is likely to be detrimental to the enrollee's health or ineffective in treating the condition again.

(b) An insurer may not void a contract or refuse to renew a contract between the insurer and a prescribing provider because the prescribing provider has prescribed a medically necessary and appropriate nonformulary or restricted access drug or device as provided in this section.

(c) As used in this section:

(1) "Closed formulary" means a list of prescription drugs and devices reimbursed by the insurer that excludes coverage for drugs and devices not listed.

(1a) "Health benefit plan" has definition provided in G.S. 58-3-167.

(2) "Insurer" has the meaning provided in G.S. 58-3-167.

(3) "Restricted access drug or device" means those covered prescription drugs or devices for which reimbursement by the insurer is conditioned on the insurer's prior approval to prescribe the drug or device or on the provider prescribing one or more alternative drugs or devices before prescribing the drug or device in question.

(d) Nothing in this section requires an insurer to pay for drugs or devices or classes of drugs or devices related to a benefit that is specifically excluded from coverage by the insurer. (1999-178, s. 1; 1999-294, s. 14(a), (b); 2001-446, s. 1.5.)

§ 58-3-223. Managed care access to specialist care.

(a) Each insurer offering a health benefit plan that does not allow direct access to all in-plan specialists shall develop and maintain written policies and procedures by which an insured may receive an extended or standing referral to an in-plan specialist. The insurer shall provide for an extended or standing referral to a specialist if the insured has a serious or chronic degenerative, disabling, or life-threatening disease or condition, which in the opinion of the insured's primary care physician, in consultation with the specialist, requires ongoing specialty care. The extended or standing referral shall be for a period not to exceed 12 months and shall be made under a treatment plan coordinated with the insurer in consultation with the primary care physician, the specialist, and the insured or the insured's designee.

(b) As used in this section:

(1) "Health benefit plan" has the meaning applied in G.S. 58-3-167.

(2) "Insurer" has the meaning applied in G.S. 58-3-167.

(3) "Serious or chronic degenerative, disabling, or life-threatening disease or condition" means a disease or condition, which in the opinion of the patient's treating primary care physician and specialist, requires frequent and periodic monitoring and consultation with the specialist on an ongoing basis.

(4) "Specialist" includes a subspecialist. (1999-168, s. 1; 2001-446, s. 1.2.)

§ 58-3-225. Prompt claim payments under health benefit plans.

(a) As used in this section:

(1) "Claimant" includes a health care provider or facility that is responsible or permitted under contract with the insurer or by valid assignment of benefits for directly making the claim with an insurer.

(2) "Health benefit plan" means an accident and health insurance policy or certificate; a nonprofit hospital or medical service corporation contract; a health maintenance organization subscriber contract; a plan provided by a multiple employer welfare arrangement; or a plan provided by another benefit arrangement, to the extent permitted by the Employee Retirement Income Security Act of 1974, as amended, or by any waiver of or other exception to that act provided under federal law or regulation. "Health benefit plan" does not mean any plan implemented or administered by the North Carolina or United States Department of Health and Human Services, or any successor agency, or its representatives. "Health benefit plan" also does not mean any of the following kinds of insurance:

a. Credit.

b. Disability income.

c. Coverage issued as a supplement to liability insurance.

d. Hospital income or indemnity.

e. Insurance under which benefits are payable with or without regard to fault and that is statutorily required to be contained in any liability policy or equivalent self-insurance.

f. Long-term or nursing home care.

g. Medical payments under motor vehicle or homeowners' insurance policies.

h. Medicare supplement.

i. Short-term limited duration health insurance policies as defined in Part 144 of Title 45 of the Code of Federal Regulations.

j. Workers' compensation.

(3) "Health care facility" means a facility that is licensed under Chapter 131E or Chapter 122C of the General Statutes or is owned or operated by the State of North Carolina in which health care services are provided to patients.

(4) "Health care provider" means an individual who is licensed, certified, or otherwise authorized under Chapter 90 or 90B of the General Statutes or under the laws of another state to provide health care services in the ordinary course of business or practice of a profession or in an approved education or training program.

(5) "Insurer" includes an insurance company subject to this Chapter, a service corporation organized under Article 65 of this Chapter, a health maintenance organization organized under Article 67 of this Chapter, or a multiple employer welfare arrangement subject to Article 49 of this Chapter, that writes a health benefit plan.

(b) An insurer shall, within 30 calendar days after receipt of a claim, send by electronic or paper mail to the claimant:

(1) Payment of the claim.

(2) Notice of denial of the claim.

(3) Notice that the proof of loss is inadequate or incomplete.

(4) Notice that the claim is not submitted on the form required by the health benefit plan, by the contract between the insurer and health care provider or health care facility, or by applicable law.

(5) Notice that coordination of benefits information is needed in order to pay the claim.

(6) Notice that the claim is pending based on nonpayment of fees or premiums.

For purposes of this section, an insurer is presumed to have received a written claim five business days after the claim has been placed first-class postage prepaid in the United States mail addressed to the insurer or an electronic claim transmitted to the insurer or a designated clearinghouse on the day the claim is electronically transmitted. The presumption may be rebutted by sufficient evidence that the claim was received on another day or not received at all.

(c) If the claim is denied, the notice shall include all of the specific good faith reason or reasons for the denial, including, without limitation, coordination of benefits, lack of eligibility, or lack of coverage for the services provided. If the claim is contested or cannot be paid because the proof of loss is inadequate or incomplete, or not paid pending receipt of requested coordination of benefits information, the notice shall contain the specific good faith reason or reasons why the claim has not been paid and an itemization or description of all of the information needed by the insurer to complete the processing of the claim. If all or part of the claim is contested or cannot be paid because of the application of a specific utilization management or medical necessity standard is not satisfied, the notice shall contain the specific clinical rationale for that decision or shall refer to specific provisions in documents that are made readily available through the insurer which provide the specific clinical rationale for that decision; however, if a notice of noncertification has already been provided under G.S. 58-50-61(h), then the specific clinical rationale for the decision is not required under this subsection. If the claim is contested or cannot be paid because of nonpayment of premiums, the notice shall contain a statement advising the claimant of the nonpayment of premiums. If a claim is not paid pending receipt of requested coordination of benefits information, the notice shall so specify. If a claim is denied or contested in part, the insurer shall pay the undisputed portion of the claim within 30 calendar days after receipt of the claim and send the notice of the denial or contested status within 30 days after receipt of the claim. If a claim is contested or cannot be paid because the claim was not submitted on the required form, the notice shall contain the required form, if the form is other than a UB or HCFA form, and instructions to complete that form. Upon receipt of additional information requested in its notice to the claimant, the insurer shall continue processing the claim and pay or deny the claim within 30 days after receiving the additional information.

(d)   If an insurer requests additional information under subsection (c) of this section and the insurer does not receive the additional information within 90 days after the request was made, the insurer shall deny the claim and send the notice of denial to the claimant in accordance with subsection (c) of this section. The insurer shall include the specific reason or reasons for denial in the notice, including the fact that information that was requested was not provided. The insurer shall inform the claimant in the notice that the claim will be reopened if the information previously requested is submitted to the insurer within one year after the date of the denial notice closing the claim.

(e)   Health benefit plan claim payments that are not made in accordance with this section shall bear interest at the annual percentage rate of eighteen percent (18%) beginning on the date following the day on which the claim should have been paid. If additional information was requested by the insurer under subsection (b) of this section, interest on health benefit claim payments shall begin to accrue on the 31st day after the insurer received the additional information. A payment is considered made on the date upon which a check, draft, or other valid negotiable instrument is placed in the United States Postal Service in a properly addressed, postpaid envelope, or, if not mailed, on the date of the electronic transfer or other delivery of the payment to the claimant. This subsection does not apply to claims for benefits that are not covered by the health benefit plan; nor does this subsection apply to deductibles, co-payments, or other amounts for which the insurer is not liable.

(f)   Insurers may require that claims be submitted within 180 days after the date of the provision of care to the patient by the health care provider and, in the case of health care provider facility claims, within 180 days after the date of the patient's discharge from the facility. However, an insurer may not limit the time in which claims may be submitted to fewer than 180 days. Unless otherwise agreed to by the insurer and the claimant, failure to submit a claim within the time required does not invalidate or reduce any claim if it was not reasonably possible for the claimant to file the claim within that time, provided that the claim is submitted as soon as reasonably possible and in no event, except in the absence of legal capacity of the insured, later than one year from the time submittal of the claim is otherwise required.

(g)   If a claim for which the claimant is a health care provider or health care facility has not been paid or denied within 60 days after receipt of the initial claim, the insurer shall send a claim status report to the insured. Provided, however, that the claims status report is not required during the time an insurer is awaiting information requested under subsection (c) of this section. The report shall indicate that the claim is under review and the insurer is communicating with the health care provider or health care facility to resolve the matter. While a claim remains unresolved, the insurer shall send a claim status report to the insured with a copy to the provider 30 days after the previous report was sent.

(h)   Subject to the time lines required under this section, the insurer may recover overpayments made to the health care provider or health care facility by making demands for refunds and by offsetting future payments. Any such recoveries may also include related interest payments that were made under the requirements of this section. Not less than 30 calendar days before an insurer seeks overpayment recovery or offsets future payments, the insurer shall give written notice to the health care provider or health care facility, which notice shall be accompanied by adequate specific information to identify the specific claim and the specific reason for the recovery. The recovery of overpayments or offsetting of future payments shall be made within the two years after the date of the original claim payment unless the insurer has reasonable belief of fraud or other intentional misconduct by the health care provider or health care facility or its agents, or the claim involves a health care provider or health care facility receiving payment for the same service from a government payor. The health care provider or health care facility may recover underpayments or nonpayments by the insurer by making demands for refunds. Any such recoveries by the health care provider or health care facility of underpayments or nonpayment by the insurer may include applicable interest under this section. The recovery of underpayments or nonpayments shall be made within the two years after the date of the original claim adjudication, unless the claim involves a health provider or health care facility receiving payment for the same service from a government payor.

(i)   Every insurer shall maintain written or electronic records of its activities under this section, including records of when each claim was received, paid, denied, or pended, and the insurer's review and handling of each claim under this section, sufficient to demonstrate compliance with this section.

(j)   A violation of this section by an insurer subjects the insurer to the sanctions in G.S. 58-2-70. The authority of the Commissioner under this subsection does not impair the right of a claimant to pursue any other action or remedy available under law. With respect to a specific claim, an insurer paying statutory interest in good faith under this section is not subject to sanctions for that claim under this subsection.

(k)   An insurer is not in violation of this section nor subject to interest payments under this section if its failure to comply with this section is caused in material part by (i) the person submitting the claim, or (ii) by matters beyond the insurer's reasonable control, including an act of God, insurrection, strike, fire, or power outages. In addition, an insurer is not in violation of this section or subject to interest payments to the claimant under this section if the insurer has a reasonable basis to believe that the claim was submitted fraudulently and notifies the claimant of the alleged fraud.

(l)   Expired January 1, 2003.

(m)   Nothing in this section limits or impairs the patient's liability under existing law for payment of medical expenses. (2000-162, s. 4(a); 2001-417, s. 1; 2007-362, s. 1; 2009-382, s. 16.)

§ 58-3-227. Health plans fee schedules.

(a)   Definitions. - As used in this section, the following terms mean:

(1)   Claim submission policy. - The procedure adopted by an insurer and used by a provider or facility to submit to the insurer claims for services rendered and to seek reimbursement for those services.

(2)   Health care facility or facility. - A facility that is licensed under Chapter 131E or Chapter 122C of the General Statutes or is owned or operated by the State of North Carolina in which health care services are provided to patients.

(3)   Health care provider or provider. - An individual who is licensed, certified, or otherwise authorized under Chapter 90 or Chapter 90B of the

General Statutes or under the laws of another state to provide health care services in the ordinary course of business or practice of a profession or in an approved education or training program.

(4) Insurer. - An entity that writes a health benefit plan and that is an insurance company subject to this Chapter, a service corporation under Article 65 of this Chapter, a health maintenance organization under Article 67 of this Chapter, or a multiple employer welfare arrangement under Article 49 of this Chapter, except it does not include an entity that writes stand alone dental insurance.

(5) Reimbursement policy. - Information relating to payment of providers and facilities including policies on the following:

a. Claims bundling and other claims editing processes.

b. Recognition or nonrecognition of CPT code modifiers.

c. Downcoding of services or procedures.

d. The definition of global surgery periods.

e. Multiple surgical procedures.

f. Payment based on the relationship of procedure code to diagnosis code.

(6) Schedule of fees. - CPT, HCPCS, ICD-9-CM codes, ASA codes, modifiers, and other applicable codes for the procedures billed for that class of provider.

(b) Purpose. - The purpose of this section is to establish the minimum required provisions for the disclosure and notification of an insurer's schedule of fees, claims submission, and reimbursement policies to health care providers and health care facilities. Nothing in this section shall supercede (i) the schedule of fees, claim submission, and reimbursement policy terms in an insurer's contract with a provider or facility that exceed the minimum requirements of this section nor (ii) any contractual requirement for mutual written consent of changes to reimbursement policies, claims submission policies, or fees. Nothing in this section shall prevent an insurer from requiring that providers and facilities keep confidential, and not disclose to third parties, the information that an insurer must provide under this section.

(c) Disclosure of Fee Schedules. - An insurer shall make available to contracted providers the following information:

(1) The insurer's schedule of fees associated with the top 30 services or procedures most commonly billed by that class of provider, and, upon request, the full schedule of fees for services or procedures billed by that class of provider, in accordance with subdivision (3) of this subsection.

(2) In the case of a contract incorporating multiple classes of providers, the insurer's schedule of fees associated with the top 30 services or procedures most commonly billed for each class of provider, and, upon request, the full schedule of fees for services or procedures billed for each class of provider, in accordance with subdivision (3) of this subsection.

(3) If a provider requests fees for more than 30 services and procedures, the insurer may require the provider to specify the additional requested services and procedures and may limit the provider's access to the additional schedule of fees to those associated with services and procedures performed by or reasonably expected to be performed by the provider. The insurer may also limit the frequency of requests for the additional codes by each provider, provided that such additional codes will be made available upon request at least annually and at any time there are changes for which notification is required pursuant to subsection (f) of this section.

(d) Disclosure of Policies. - An insurer shall make available to contracted providers and facilities a description of the insurer's claim submission and reimbursement policies.

(e) Availability of Information. - Insurers shall notify contracted providers and facilities in writing of the availability of information required or authorized to be provided under this section. An insurer may satisfy this requirement by indicating in the contract with the provider the availability of this information or by providing notice in a manner authorized under subsection (f) of this section for notification of changes.

(f) Notification of Changes. - Insurers shall provide advance notice to providers and facilities of changes to the information that insurers are required to provide under this section. The notice period for a change in the schedule of fees, reimbursement policies, or submission of claims policies shall be the contractual notice period, but in no event shall the notices be given less than 30 days prior to the change. An insurer is not required to provide advance notice of changes to the information required under this section if the change has the effect of increasing fees, expanding health benefit plan coverage, or is made for patient safety considerations, in which case, notification of the changes may be made concurrent with the implementation of the changes. Information and notice of changes may be provided in the medium selected by the insurer, including an electronic medium. However, the insurer must inform the affected contracted provider or facility of the notification method to be used by the insurer and, if the insurer uses an electronic medium to provide notice of changes required under this section, the insurer shall provide clear instructions regarding how the provider or facility may access the information contained in the notice.

(g)   Reference Information. - If an insurer references source information that is the basis for a schedule of fees, reimbursement policy, or claim submission policy, and the source information is developed independently of the insurer, the insurer may satisfy the requirements of this section by providing clear instructions regarding how the provider or facility may readily access the source information or by providing for actual access if agreed to in the contract between the insurer and the provider.

(h)   Contract Negotiations. - When an insurer offers a contract to a provider, the insurer shall also make available its schedule of fees associated with the top 30 services or procedures most commonly billed by that class of provider. Upon the request of a provider, the insurer shall also make available the full schedule of fees for services or procedures billed by that class of provider or for each class of provider in the case of a contract incorporating multiple classes of providers. If a provider requests fees for more than 30 services and procedures, the insurer may require the provider to specify the additional requested services and procedures and may limit the provider's access to the additional schedule of fees to those associated with services and procedures performed by or reasonably expected to be performed by the provider.

(i)   Expired pursuant to Session Laws 2003-364, s.3, effective January 1, 2005. (2003-369, s. 1.)

§ 58-3-228. Coverage for extra prescriptions during a state of emergency or disaster.

(a) All health benefit plans as defined in G.S. 58-3-167, the State Health Plan for Teachers and State Employees, and any optional plans or programs operating under Part 2 of Article 3 of Chapter 135 of the General Statutes, and other stand-alone prescription medication plans issued by entities that are licensed by the Department shall have, when an event described in subdivision (b)(1) of this section occurs and the requirements of subdivisions (b)(2) and (b)(3) of this section are satisfied, a procedure in place to waive time restrictions on filling or refilling prescriptions for medication if requested by the covered person or subscriber. The procedure shall include waiver or override of electronic "refill too soon" edits to pharmacies and shall include provision for payment to the pharmacy in accordance with the prescription benefit plan and applicable pharmacy provider agreement. The procedure shall enable covered persons or subscribers to:

(1) Obtain one refill on a prescription if there are authorized refills remaining, or

(2) Fill one replacement prescription for one that was recently filled, as prescribed or approved by the prescriber of the prescription that is being replaced and not contrary to the dispensing authority of the dispensing pharmacy.

(b) All entities subject to this section shall authorize payment to pharmacies for any prescription dispensed in accordance with subsection (a) of this section regardless of the date upon which the prescription had most recently been filled by a pharmacist, if all of the following conditions apply:

(1) The Commissioner issues a Bulletin Advisory notifying all insurance carriers licensed in this State of a declared state of disaster or state of emergency in North Carolina. The Department shall provide a copy of the Bulletin to the North Carolina Board of Pharmacy.

(2) The covered person requesting coverage of the refill or replacement prescription resides in a county that:

a. Is covered under a state of emergency issued by the Governor or General Assembly under G.S. 166A-19.20, or a declaration of major disaster issued by the President of the United States under the Robert T. Stafford Disaster Relief and Emergency Assistance Act, 42 U.S.C. § 5121, et seq., as amended; or

b. Repealed by Session Laws 2012-12, s. 2(k), effective October 1, 2012.

(3) The prescription medication is requested within 29 days after the origination date of the conditions stated in subdivision (b)(1) of this section.

(c) The time period for the waiver of prescription medication refills may be extended in 30-day increments by an order issued by the Commissioner. Additional refills still remaining on a prescription shall be covered by the insurer as long as consistent with the orders of the prescriber or authority of the dispensing pharmacy.

(d) This section does not excuse or exempt an insured or subscriber from any other terms of the policy or certificate providing coverage for prescription medications.

(e) Quantity limitations shall be consistent with the original prescription and the extra or replacement fill may recognize proportionate dosage use prior to the disaster.

(f) No requirements additional to those under the pharmacy provider agreement or the prescription benefit plan may be placed upon the provider for coverage of the replacement fill or extra fill.

(g) Nothing in this section is intended to affect the respective authority or scope of practice of prescribers or pharmacies. (2007-133, s. 1; 2007-323, s. 28.22A(o); 2007-345, s. 12; 2012-12, s. 2(k).)

§ 58-3-230. Uniform provider credentialing.

(a) An insurer that provides a health benefit plan and that credentials providers for its networks shall maintain a process to assess and verify the qualifications of a licensed health care practitioner within 60 days of receipt of a completed provider credentialing application form approved by the Commissioner. If the insurer has not approved or denied the provider credentialing application form within 60 days of receipt of the completed application, upon receipt of a written request from the applicant and within five business days of its receipt, the insurer shall issue a temporary credential to the applicant if the applicant has a valid North Carolina professional or occupational license to provide the health care services to which the credential would apply.

The insurer shall not issue a temporary credential if the applicant has reported on the application a history of medical malpractice claims, a history of substance abuse or mental health issues, or a history of Medical Board disciplinary action. The temporary credential shall be effective upon issuance and shall remain in effect until the provider's credentialing application is approved or denied by the insurer. When a health care practitioner joins a practice that is under contract with an insurer to participate in a health benefit plan, the effective date of the health care practitioner's participation in the health benefit plan network shall be the date the insurer approves the practitioner's credentialing application.

(b)   The Commissioner shall by rule adopt a uniform provider credentialing application form that will provide health benefit plans with the information necessary to adequately assess and verify the qualifications of an applicant. The Commissioner may update the uniform provider credentialing application form, as necessary. No insurer that provides a health benefit plan may require an applicant to submit information that is not required by the uniform provider credentialing application form.

(c)   As used in this section, the terms "health benefit plan" and "insurer" shall have the meaning provided under G.S. 58-3-167. (2001-172, s. 1; 2002-126, s. 6.9(a); 2005-223, s. 9; 2009-487, s. 1.)

§ 58-3-231. Payment under locum tenens arrangements.

(a)   As used in this section, the following definitions apply:

(1)   Covered visit services. - All office visits, emergency visits, and any related service performed by a physician that is covered by the insurer.

(2)   Insurer. - Defined in G.S. 58-3-167(a).

(3)   Locum tenens agency. - A company authorized to conduct business in North Carolina that provides, through contract, locum tenens placement and administrative services for regular physicians, locum tenens physicians, medical groups, and hospitals.

(4)   Locum tenens physician. - A physician who substitutes for a regular physician on a temporary basis and is not an employee of the regular physician.

(5) Regular physician. - The physician that is normally scheduled to see a patient, including physician specialists and a physician who has left a group practice for whom a locum tenens physician is retained.

(b) An insurer that provides a health benefit plan shall establish and maintain a process to allow a patient's regular physician to submit a claim and, if the claim is accepted, receive payment for covered visit services that the regular physician or a locum tenens agency arranges to be provided by a locum tenens physician, provided the following are true:

(1) The regular physician is unavailable to provide the covered visit services or the locum tenens physician is assisting the regular physician in providing covered visit services.

(2) The insured patient has arranged or seeks to receive the covered visit services from the regular physician.

(3) The locum tenens physician does not provide the covered visit services to insured patients of a single regular physician for more than 90 consecutive days.

(4) The regular physician identifies the covered visit services as locum tenens physician services meeting the requirements of this section by entering the proper code required by the insurer after the procedure code.

(5) The regular physician pays for the locum tenens physician's covered visit services on a per diem or similar fee-for-time basis.

(6) The regular physician maintains a record of each covered visit service provided by the locum tenens physician and makes this record available to the insurer upon request.

(c) A medical group or hospital may submit claims for the covered visit services of a locum tenens physician substituting for a regular physician who is a member of the group or an employee of the hospital if the requirements of subsection (b) of this section are met. For purposes of these requirements, per diem or similar fee-for-time compensation that the group or hospital pays for the locum tenens physician is considered paid by the regular physician. A physician who has left the group and for whom the group has engaged a locum tenens physician as a temporary replacement may bill for the temporary physician for up to 90 consecutive days.

(d) An insurer shall allow a locum tenens physician credentialed with that insurer to substitute for a regular physician in accordance with this section without a statement of supervision if (i) the regular physician is a solo practitioner or (ii) there is not otherwise a regular physician who is able to provide a statement of supervision.

(e) Locum tenens agencies may contract with regular physicians, medical groups, hospitals, and locum tenens physicians to provide placement and administrative services related to the locum tenens substitution, provided the following are true:

(1) The locum tenens agency charges fees that are reasonably related to the value of the services that the locum tenens agency provides.

(2) The locum tenens agency does not interfere with or attempt to influence the clinical judgment of a physician providing locum tenens services. (2011-315, s. 1.)

§ 58-3-235. Selection of specialist as primary care provider.

(a) Each insurer that offers a health benefit plan shall have a procedure by which an insured diagnosed with a serious or chronic degenerative, disabling, or life-threatening disease or condition, either of which requires specialized medical care may select as his or her primary care physician a specialist with expertise in treating the disease or condition who shall be responsible for and capable of providing and coordinating the insured's primary and specialty care. If the insurer determines that the insured's care would not be appropriately coordinated by that specialist, the insurer may deny access to that specialist as a primary care provider.

(b) The selection of the specialist shall be made under a treatment plan approved by the insurer, in consultation with the specialist and the insured or the insured's designee and after notice to the insured's primary care provider, if any. The specialist may provide ongoing care to the insured and may authorize such referrals, procedures, tests, and other medical services as the insured's primary care provider would otherwise be allowed to provide or authorize, subject to the terms of the treatment plan. Services provided by a specialist who is providing and coordinating primary and specialty care remain subject to utilization review and other requirements of the insurer, including its requirements for primary care providers. (2001-446, s. 1.3.)

§ 58-3-240. Direct access to pediatrician for minors.

Each insurer offering a health benefit plan that uses a network of contracting health care providers shall allow an insured to choose a contracting pediatrician in the network as the primary care provider for the insured's children under the age of 18 and covered under the policy. (2001-446, s. 1.4.)

§ 58-3-245. Provider directories; cost tools for insured.

(a) Every health benefit plan utilizing a provider network shall maintain a provider directory that includes a listing of network providers available to insureds and shall update the listing no less frequently than once a year. In addition, every health benefit plan shall maintain a telephone system and may maintain an electronic or on-line system through which insureds can access up-to-date network information. The health benefit plan shall ensure that a patient is provided accurate and current information on each provider's network status through the telephone system and any electronic or online system. If the health benefit plan produces printed directories, the directories shall contain language disclosing the date of publication, frequency of updates, that the directory listing may not contain the latest network information, and contact information for accessing up-to-date network information.

(b) Each directory listing shall include the following network information:

(1) The provider's name, address, telephone number, and, if applicable, area of specialty.

(2) Whether the provider may be selected as a primary care provider.

(3) To the extent known to the health benefit plan, an indication of whether the provider:

a. Is or is not currently accepting new patients.

b. Has any other restrictions that would limit an insured's access to that provider.

(c) The directory listing shall include all of the types of participating providers. Upon a participating provider's written request, the insurer shall also list in the directory, as part of the participating provider's listing, the names of any allied health professionals who provide primary care services under the supervision of the participating provider and whose services are covered by virtue of the insurer's contract with the supervising participating provider and whose credentials have been verified by the supervising participating provider. These allied health professionals shall be listed as a part of the directory listing for the participating provider upon receipt of a certification by the supervising participating provider that the credentials of the allied health professional have been verified consistent with the requirements for the type of information required to be verified under G.S. 58-3-230.

(d) A health care provider shall provide to a patient or prospective patient, upon request, information on that provider's network status with a particular health benefit plan. (2001-446, s. 2.2; 2013-382, s. 13.4.)

§ 58-3-247. Insurance identification card.

(a) Every insurer offering a health benefit plan as defined under G.S. 58-3-167, including the State Health Plan, shall provide the health benefit plan subscriber or members with an insurance identification card. The card shall contain at a minimum:

(1) The subscriber's name and identification number.

(2) The member's name and identification number, if applicable and different from the subscriber's name and identification number.

(3) The group number.

(4) The name of the organization issuing the policy, the name of the organization administering the policy, and the name of the network, whichever applies.

(5) The effective date of health benefits plan coverage or the date the card is issued if it is after the effective date.

(6) The address where claims are to be filed and, if applicable, the electronic claims filing payor identification number.

(7) The policyholder's obligations with regard to co-payments, if applicable, for at least the following:

a. Primary care office visit.

b. Specialty care office visit.

c. Urgent care visit.

d. Emergency room visit.

(8) The phone number or Web site address whereby the subscriber, member, or service provider, in compliance with privacy rules under the Health Insurance Portability and Accountability Act may readily obtain the following:

a. Confirmation of eligibility.

b. Benefits verification in order to estimate patient financial responsibility.

c. Prior authorization for services and procedures.

d. The list of participating providers in the network.

e. The employer group number.

f. Special mental health medical benefits under the health plan, if applicable.

(b) The insurance identification card must be designed such that if the card is photocopied or electronically scanned, the resulting image is clearly legible. The identification card must present the information in a readily identifiable manner or, alternatively, the information may be embedded on the card and available through magnetic stripe or smart card. The information may also be provided through other electronic technology. (2007-362, s. 2.)

§ 58-3-250. Payment obligations for covered services.

(a) If an insurer calculates a benefit amount for a covered service under a health benefit plan through a method other than a fixed dollar co-payment, the insurer shall clearly explain in its evidence of coverage and plan summaries how it determines its payment obligations and the payment obligations of the insured. The explanation shall include:

(1) An example of the steps the insurer would take in calculating the benefit amount and the payment obligations of each party.

(2) Whether the insurer has obtained the agreement of health care providers not to bill an insured for any amounts by which a provider's charge exceeds the insurer's recognized charge for a covered service and whether the insured may be liable for paying any excess amount.

(3) Which party is responsible for filing a claim or bill with the insurer.

(b) If an insured is liable for an amount that differs from a stated fixed dollar co-payment or may differ from a stated coinsurance percentage because the coinsurance amount is based on a plan allowance or other such amount rather than the actual charges and providers are permitted to balance bill the insured, the evidence of coverage, plan summaries, and marketing and advertising materials that include information on benefit levels shall contain the following statement: "NOTICE: Your actual expenses for covered services may exceed the stated [coinsurance percentage or co-payment amount] because actual provider charges may not be used to determine [plan/insurer or similar term] and [insured/member/enrollee or similar term] payment obligations." (2001-446, s. 2.3.)

§ 58-3-255. Coverage of clinical trials.

(a) As used in this section:

(1) "Covered clinical trials" means phase II, phase III, and phase IV patient research studies designed to evaluate new treatments, including prescription drugs, and that: (i) involve the treatment of life-threatening medical conditions,

(ii) are medically indicated and preferable for that patient compared to available noninvestigational treatment alternatives, and (iii) have clinical and preclinical data that shows the trial will likely be more effective for that patient than available noninvestigational alternatives. Covered clinical trials must also meet the following requirements:

a. Must involve determinations by treating physicians, relevant scientific data, and opinions of experts in relevant medical specialties.

b. Must be trials approved by centers or cooperative groups that are funded by the National Institutes of Health, the Food and Drug Administration, the Centers for Disease Control, the Agency for Health Care Research and Quality, the Department of Defense, or the Department of Veterans Affairs. The health benefit plan may also cover clinical trials sponsored by other entities.

c. Must be conducted in a setting and by personnel that maintain a high level of expertise because of their training, experience, and volume of patients.

(2) "Health benefit plan" is defined by G.S. 58-3-167.

(3) "Insurer" is defined by G.S. 58-3-167.

(b) Each health benefit plan shall provide coverage for participation in phase II, phase III, and phase IV covered clinical trials by its insureds or enrollees who meet protocol requirements of the trials and provide informed consent.

(c) Only medically necessary costs of health care services, as defined in G.S. 58-50-61, associated with participation in a covered clinical trial, including those related to health care services typically provided absent a clinical trial, the diagnosis and treatment of complications, and medically necessary monitoring, are required to be covered by the health benefit plan and only to the extent that such costs have not been or are not funded by national agencies, commercial manufacturers, distributors, or other research sponsors of participants in clinical trials. Nothing in this section shall be construed to require a health benefit plan to pay or reimburse for non-FDA approved drugs provided or made available to a patient who received the drug during a covered clinical trial after the clinical trial has been discontinued.

(d) Clinical trial costs not required to be covered by a health benefit plan include the costs of services that are not health care services, those provided solely to satisfy data collection and analysis needs, those related to investigational drugs and devices, and those that are not provided for the direct clinical management of the patient. In the event a claim contains charges related to services for which coverage is required under this section, and those charges have not been or cannot be separated from costs related to services for which coverage is not required under this section, the health benefit plan may deny the claim. (2001-446, s. 3.1.)

§ 58-3-260. Insurance coverage for newborn hearing screening mandated.

(a) As used in this section, the terms "health benefit plan" and "insurer" have the meanings applied under G.S. 58-3-167.

(b) Each health benefit plan shall provide coverage for newborn hearing screening ordered by the attending physician pursuant to G.S. 130A-125. The same deductibles, coinsurance, reimbursement methodologies, and other limitations and administrative procedures as apply to similar services covered under the health benefit plan shall apply to coverage for newborn hearing screening. (2001-446, s. 3.2.)

§ 58-3-265. Prohibition on managed care provider incentives.

An insurer offering a health benefit plan may not offer or pay any type of material inducement, bonus, or other financial incentive to a participating provider to deny, reduce, withhold, limit, or delay specific medically necessary and appropriate health care services covered under the health benefit plan to a specific insured or enrollee. This section does not prohibit insurers from paying a provider on a capitated basis or withholding payment or paying a bonus based on the aggregate services rendered by the provider or the insurer's financial performance. (2001-446, s. 1.8.)

§ 58-3-270. Coverage for surveillance tests for women at risk for ovarian cancer.

(a) Every health benefit plan, as defined in G.S. 58-3-167, shall provide coverage for surveillance tests for women age 25 and older at risk for ovarian cancer. As used in this section:

(1) "At risk for ovarian cancer" means either:

a. Having a family history:

1. With at least one first-degree relative with ovarian cancer; and

2. A second relative, either first-degree or second-degree, with breast, ovarian, or nonpolyposis colorectal cancer; or

b. Testing positive for a hereditary ovarian cancer syndrome.

(2) "Surveillance tests" mean annual screening using:

a. Transvaginal ultrasound; and

b. Rectovaginal pelvic examination.

(b) The same deductibles, coinsurance, and other limitations as apply to similar services covered under the plan apply to coverage for transvaginal ultrasound and rectovaginal pelvic examinations required to be covered under this section. (2003-223, s. 1.)

§ 58-3-275. Closure of a block of business.

(a) An insurer that determines to create a closed block of business in this State shall no later than 60 days prior to the closure date:

(1) Notify the Commissioner in writing of the insurer's decision to cease sales of the policy form(s) and provide a reasonable estimate, based on sound actuarial principles, of the expected impact on future premiums of ceasing sales of the policy form(s). If the insurer's qualified actuary estimates that the expected impact on future annual premiums of ceasing sales of the policy form(s) exceeds five percent (5%) per annum, then the insurer shall comply with the requirements of subdivision (3) of this subsection. If each subsequent annual premium rate filing results in an approved annual premium rate increase

no greater than the last premium rate increase approved when the block of insurance was open, plus five percent (5%) per annum, then the insurer shall not be required to comply with the requirements of subdivision (3) of this subsection. If any subsequent annual premium rate filing results in an approved premium rate increase in excess of five percent (5%) per annum more than the last premium rate increase approved while the block of insurance was open, then the insurer shall comply with the requirements of subdivision (3) of this subsection at the time the filing is approved, unless the insurer can demonstrate to the satisfaction of the Commissioner that the portion of the increase that is due to the closing of the block is not more than five percent (5%) per annum.

(2) Inform each agent and broker selling the product of the decision and the date of closure.

(3) If required pursuant to subdivision (1) of this subsection, notify all affected policyholders of the determination and provide a statement of the general effect that might be expected to result from the closure of the block. Notice shall comply with any rules adopted pursuant to subsection (b) of this section.

(b) The Commissioner may adopt rules to carry out the purposes and provisions of this section, including rules establishing the language, content, format, and methods of distribution of the notices required by this section.

(c) As used in this section, the term:

(1) "Accident and health insurance" means insurance against death or injury resulting from accident or from accidental means and insurance against disablement, disease, or sickness of the insured. This includes Medicare supplemental insurance, long-term care, nursing home, or home health care insurance, or any combination thereof, specified disease or illness insurance, hospital indemnity or other fixed indemnity insurance, short-term limited duration health insurance, dental insurance, vision insurance, and medical, hospital, or surgical expense insurance or any combination thereof.

(2) "Block of business" means a particular policy form or contract of individual accident and health insurance issued by an insurer.

(3) "Closed block of business" means a block of business for which an insurer ceases to actively market, sell, and issue new contracts under a particular policy form in this State.

(4)   "Closure date" means the effective date that no new insureds will be issued coverage of the particular policy form(s).

(5)   "Insurer" includes an insurance company subject to this Chapter, a service corporation organized under Article 65 of this Chapter, a health maintenance organization organized under Article 67 of this Chapter, or a multiple employer welfare arrangement subject to Article 49 of this Chapter.

(6)   "Policyholders" includes those applicants for the particular policy form that is being closed and for which the policy is not yet issued.

(d)   This section does not apply when an insurer makes a decision to discontinue a particular policy form or contract of accident and health insurance coverage subject to Article 68 of this Chapter, cancels or nonrenews the coverage, and offers replacement coverage pursuant to G.S. 58-68-65(c)(1). (2005-412, s. 2.)

§ 58-3-276: Repealed by Session Laws 2013-410, s. 28.5(e), effective August 23, 2013.

§ 58-3-280. Coverage for the diagnosis and treatment of lymphedema.

(a)   Every health benefit plan, as defined in G.S. 58-3-167, shall provide coverage for the diagnosis, evaluation, and treatment of lymphedema. The coverage required by this section shall include benefits for equipment, supplies, complex decongestive therapy, gradient compression garments, and self-management training and education, if the treatment is determined to be medically necessary and is provided by a licensed occupational or physical therapist or licensed nurse that has experience providing this treatment, or other licensed health care professional whose treatment of lymphedema is within the professional's scope of practice.

(b)   The same deductibles, coinsurance, and other limitations as apply to similar services covered under the health benefit plan apply to coverage for the diagnosis, evaluation, and treatment of lymphedema required to be covered under this section. Nothing in this section requires a health benefit plan to provide a separate set of benefit limitations or maximums for the diagnosis, evaluation, or treatment of lymphedema.

(c)   As used in this section, gradient compression garments:

(1)   Require a prescription;

(2)   Are custom-fit for the covered individual; and

(3)   Do not include disposable medical supplies such as over-the-counter compression or elastic knee-high or other stocking products. (2009-313, s. 1.)

§ 58-3-285. Coverage for hearing aids.

(a)   Every health benefit plan, including the State Health Plan for Teachers and State Employees, shall provide coverage for one hearing aid per hearing-impaired ear up to two thousand five hundred dollars ($2,500) per hearing aid every 36 months for covered individuals under the age of 22 years subject to subsection (b) of this section. The coverage shall include all medically necessary hearing aids and services that are ordered by a physician or an audiologist licensed in this State. Only those persons authorized by law to fit hearing aids, including individuals licensed under Chapter 93D of the General Statutes, are eligible to fit a hearing aid under this section. Coverage shall be as follows:

(1)   Initial hearing aids and replacement hearing aids not more frequently than every 36 months.

(2)   A new hearing aid when alterations to the existing hearing aid cannot adequately meet the needs of the covered individual.

(3)   Services, including the initial hearing aid evaluation, fitting, and adjustments, and supplies, including ear molds.

(b)   The same deductibles, coinsurance, and other limitations as apply to similar services covered under the health benefit plan apply to hearing aids and related services and supplies required to be covered under this section.

(c) Nothing in this section prevents an insurer from applying utilization review criteria to determine medical necessity as defined by G.S. 58-50-61 as long as it does so in accordance with all requirements for utilization review programs and medical necessity determinations specified in that section, including the offering of an insurer appeal process and where applicable, health benefit plans external review as provided in Part 4 of Article 50 of Chapter 58 of the General Statutes. (2010-2, s. 1; 2010-97, s. 7.)

§ 58-3-290. Nondependent child coverage defined; open enrollment.

(a) As used in this section, the following definitions apply:

(1) "Health benefit plan" has the same meaning as G.S. 58-3-167(a)(1).

(2) "Individual market" has the same meaning as G.S. 58-68-25(a)(9).

(3) "Insurer" has the same meaning as G.S. 58-3-167(a)(2).

(4) "Nondependent child coverage" or "nondependent child policy" means an individual health benefit plan which provides coverage to an individual under age 19. This shall not include health benefit plans that cover children under age 19 as dependents.

(5) "Open enrollment" means, with respect to "nondependent child coverage," the period of time during which any individual under age 19 has the opportunity to apply for coverage under a health benefit plan offered by an insurer and shall not be denied eligibility for coverage under the plan due to factors relating to the individual's health status.

(b) An insurer who offers nondependent child coverage shall offer open enrollment either continuously throughout the year or for the months of January and July of each year. Coverage issued under this section shall be issued without any riders based on the health status of the child. Nothing in this section shall require an insurer to offer nondependent child coverage or maternity coverage within an offer of nondependent child coverage.

(c) The Commissioner shall adopt rules as necessary or proper to implement the provisions of this section.

(d) Nothing in this section shall prohibit an insurer from adjusting the initial premium charged an individual afforded coverage under this section based upon medical underwriting to the extent that such an adjustment is in compliance with the applicable product's current rate filing approved by the Commissioner. (2011-196, s. 5.)

§ 58-3-295: Reserved for future codification purposes.

§ 58-3-300. Health insurance issuers subject to certain requirements of federal law.

Pursuant to the authority granted to the states under 42 U.S.C. § 300gg-22(a)(1), health insurance issuers that issue, sell, renew, or offer health benefit plans, as defined in G.S. 58-3-167(a)(1), in the State in the individual or group market shall meet the requirements of Part A of Subchapter XXV of Chapter 6A of Title 42 of the United States Code and regulations issued thereunder. (2013-199, s. 24.)

Article 4.

NAIC Filing Requirements.

§ 58-4-1. Scope.

The provisions of this Article shall apply to all domestic, foreign, and alien insurers who are authorized to transact business in this State. (1985, c. 305, s. 1.)

§ 58-4-5. Filing requirements.

(a) Each domestic, foreign, and alien insurer that is authorized to transact insurance in this State shall file with the NAIC a copy of its financial statements required by G.S. 58-2-165, applicable rules, and legal directives and bulletins issued by the Department. The statements shall, in the Commissioner's discretion, be filed annually, semiannually, quarterly, or monthly and shall be filed in a form or format prescribed or permitted by the Commissioner. The Commissioner may require the statements to be filed in a format that can be read by electronic data processing equipment. Any amendments and addenda to the financial statement that are subsequently filed with the Commissioner shall also be filed with the NAIC.

(b) Foreign insurers that are domiciled in a state that has a law or regulation substantially similar to this Article shall be deemed to be in compliance with this section. (1985, c. 305, s. 1; 1991, c. 681, s. 11; 1993, c. 504, s. 2.)

§ 58-4-10. Immunity.

In the absence of actual malice, or gross negligence, members of the NAIC, their duly authorized committees, subcommittees, and task forces, their delegates, NAIC employees, and all others charged with the responsibility of collecting, reviewing, analyzing, and disseminating the information developed from the filings made pursuant to G.S. 58-4-10 shall be acting as agents of the Commissioner under the authority of this Article and shall not be subject to civil liability for libel, slander, or any other cause of action by virtue of their collection, review, and analysis or dissemination of the data and information collected from the filings required under this Article. (1985, c. 305, s. 1.)

§ 58-4-15. Revocation or suspension of license.

The Commissioner may suspend or revoke the license of any insurer failing to file its financial statement when due or within any extension of time that the Commissioner, for good cause, may have granted. (1985, c. 305, s. 1; 1991, c. 681, s. 12; 1999-132, s. 9.1; 2003-212, s. 26(b).)

§ 58-4-20: Recodified as § 58-2-220 pursuant to Session Laws 1989 (Regular Session, 1990), c. 0121, s. 7.

§ 58-4-25. Insurance Regulatory Information System and similar program test data records.

Financial test ratios, data, or information generated by the NAIC Insurance Regulatory Information System, any successor program, or any similar program shall be disseminated by the Commissioner consistent with procedures established by the NAIC. (1991, c. 681, s. 13.)

Article 5.

Deposits and Bonds by Insurance Companies.

§ 58-5-1. Deposits; use of master trust.

Notwithstanding any other provision of law, the Commissioner is authorized to select a bank or trust company as master trustee to hold cash or securities to be pledged to the State when deposited with him pursuant to statute. Securities may be held by the master trustee in any form which, in fact, perfects the security interest of the State in the securities. The Commissioner shall by rule establish the manner in which the master trust shall operate. The master trustee may charge the person making the deposit reasonable fees for services rendered in connection with the operation of the trust. (1985, c. 666, s. 55; 1987, c. 864, s. 23.)

§ 58-5-5. Amount of deposits required of foreign or alien fire and/or marine insurance companies.

Unless otherwise provided in this Article, every fire, marine, or fire and marine insurance company chartered by any other state or foreign government shall make and maintain deposits of securities with the Commissioner in the amount of one hundred thousand dollars ($100,000) market value. (1909, c. 923, s. 1; 1911, c. 164, s. 1; Ex. Sess. 1913, c. 62, ss. 1, 2, 3; 1915, c. 166, s. 6; C.S., s. 6442; 1933, c. 60; 1945, c. 384; 1991, c. 681, s. 15; 2003-212, s. 1.)

§ 58-5-10. Amount of deposits required of foreign or alien fidelity, surety and casualty insurance companies.

Unless otherwise provided in this Article, every fidelity, surety or casualty insurance company chartered by any other state or foreign government shall make and maintain deposits of securities with the Commissioner in the amount of two hundred thousand dollars ($200,000) market value. (1945, c. 384; 1991, c. 681, s. 16; 2003-212, s. 2.)

§ 58-5-15. Minimum deposit required upon admission.

Upon admission to do business in the State of North Carolina every foreign or alien fire, marine, or fire and marine, fidelity, surety or casualty company shall deposit with the Commissioner securities in the amounts required under G.S. 58-5-5 and G.S. 58-5-10. (1945, c. 384; 1991, c. 681, s. 17; 2001-487, s. 18.)

§ 58-5-20. Type of deposits.

The deposits required to be made under G.S. 58-5-5, 58-5-10, and 58-5-50 shall be composed of:

(a)   Interest-bearing bonds of the United States of America;

(b)   Interest-bearing bonds of the State of North Carolina, or of its cities or counties; or

(c)   Certificates of deposit issued by any solvent bank domesticated in the State of North Carolina. (1945, c. 384; 1989, c. 485, s. 34; 1991, c. 681, s. 18.)

§ 58-5-25. Replacements upon depreciation of securities.

Whenever any of the securities deposited by companies under the provisions of G.S. 58-5-5, 58-5-10, and 58-5-50 shall be depreciated or reduced in value, such company shall forthwith increase the deposit in order to maintain the required deposit in accordance with the amounts required by the said sections. (1945, c. 384; 1989, c. 485, s. 34.)

§ 58-5-30. Power of attorney.

With the securities deposited in accordance with G.S. 58-5-5, 58-5-10, and 58-5-50 the company shall at the same time deliver to the Commissioner a power of attorney executed by its president and secretary or other proper officers authorizing the sale or transfer of said securities or any part thereof for the purpose of paying any of the liabilities provided for in this Article. (1945, c. 384; 1989, c. 485, s. 34; 1991, c. 720, s. 4.)

§ 58-5-35. Securities held by Treasurer; faith of State pledged therefor; nontaxable.

Unless a master trustee is selected by the Commissioner pursuant to G.S. 58-5-1, the securities required to be deposited by each insurance company in this Article shall be delivered for safekeeping by the Commissioner to the Treasurer of the State who shall receipt him therefor. For the securities so deposited the faith of the State is pledged that they shall be returned to the companies entitled to receive them or disposed of as herein provided for. The securities deposited by any company under this Article shall not, on account of such securities being in this State, be subjected to taxation but shall be held exclusively and solely for the protection of contract holders. (1945, c. 384; 1985, c. 666, s. 56.)

§ 58-5-40. Authority to increase deposit.

When, in the Commissioner's opinion, it is necessary for the protection of the public interest to increase the amount of deposits specified in G.S. 58-5-5, 58-5-10, 58-5-50, and 58-5-55, the companies described in those sections shall, upon demand, make additional deposits in such sums as the Commissioner may require, and those additional deposits shall be held in accordance with and for the purposes set out in this Article, and shall comprise:

(a)   Interest-bearing bonds of the United States of America;

(b)   Interest-bearing bonds of the State of North Carolina or of its cities or counties;

(c)   Certificates of deposit issued by any solvent bank domesticated in the State of North Carolina;

(d)   Interest-bearing AA or better rated corporate bonds and classified as investment grade in the latest NAIC Securities Valuation Manual; or

(e)   Other interest-bearing bonds or notes considered to be acceptable by the Commissioner on a case by case basis. (1945, c. 384; 1989, c. 485, s. 34; 1991, c. 681, s. 19.)

§ 58-5-45: Repealed by Session Laws 1991, c. 681, s. 21.

§ 58-5-50. Deposits of foreign life insurance companies.

In addition to other requirements of this Chapter, all foreign life insurance companies shall deposit securities, as specified in G.S. 58-5-20, that have a market value of four hundred thousand dollars ($400,000) as a prerequisite of doing business in this State. All foreign life insurance companies shall deposit an additional two hundred thousand dollars ($200,000) where such companies cannot show three years of net income before being licensed in this State. (1989, c. 485, s. 35; 2003-212, s. 3; 2005-215, s. 3; 2008-124, s. 2.1.)

§ 58-5-55. Deposits of capital and surplus by domestic insurance companies.

(a)   In addition to other requirements of Articles 1 through 64 of this Chapter, all domestic stock insurance companies shall deposit their required statutory capital with the Commissioner. Such deposits shall be under the exclusive control of the Commissioner for the protection of policyholders.

(b)   In addition to other requirements of Articles 1 through 64 of this Chapter, all domestic mutual insurance companies shall deposit at least fifty percent (50%) of their minimum required surplus with the Commissioner, with the amount of the deposit to be determined by the Commissioner. Such deposits shall be under the exclusive control of the Commissioner for the protection of policyholders.

(c)   Deposits fulfilling the requirements of this section shall comprise:

(1)   Interest-bearing bonds of the United States of America;

(2)   Interest-bearing bonds of the State of North Carolina or of its cities or counties; or

(3)   Certificates of deposit issued by any solvent bank domesticated in the State of North Carolina. (1989, c. 485, s. 35; 1991, c. 681, s. 20; 1993, c. 504, s. 3; 2008-124, s. 2.5.)

§ 58-5-60: Repealed by Session Laws 1995, c. 193, s. 8.

§ 58-5-63. Interest; liquidation of deposits for liabilities.

(a)   All insurance companies making deposits under this Article are entitled to interest on those deposits. The right to interest is subject to a company paying its insurance policy liabilities. If any company fails to pay those liabilities, interest accruing after the failure is payable to the Commissioner for the payment of those liabilities under subsection (b) of this section.

(b)   If any company fails to pay its insurance policy liabilities after those liabilities have been established by settlement or final adjudication, the Commissioner may liquidate the amount of the company's deposit and accrued interest specified in subsection (a) of this section that will satisfy the company's policy liabilities and make payment to the person to whom the liability is owed. After payment has been made, the Commissioner may require the company to deposit the amount paid out under this subsection. As used in this section, "insurance policy" includes a policy written by a surety bondsman under Article 71 of this Chapter.

(c) Notwithstanding the provisions of G.S. 58-5-70, if any company that is or has been the subject of supervision or rehabilitation proceedings fails to pay its liabilities for temporary disability payments or emergency medical expenses under policies of workers' compensation insurance, the Commissioner shall liquidate the company's deposits and accrued interest and shall use the proceeds to pay such liabilities until that company becomes the subject of a final order of liquidation with a finding of insolvency that has not been stayed or been the subject of a writ of supersedeas or other comparable order. The Commissioner also may enter into one or more contracts to handle the administration of the identification and payment of such liabilities, and to the extent such a contract is entered into, the contractor and its employees, agents, and attorneys, shall have immunity of the same scope and extent as an employee of the State acting in the course and scope of the public duties of such employment. After an order of liquidation with a finding of insolvency has been entered by a court of competent jurisdiction that has not been stayed or been the subject of a writ of supersedeas or other comparable order, then the balance of the proceeds, if any, shall be delivered to the North Carolina Insurance Guaranty Association in accordance with G.S. 58-48-95. To the extent that any payment made hereunder reduces the ratable amount payable to policyholders under G.S. 58-5-70, the liens obtained by the North Carolina Insurance Guaranty Association pursuant to Article 48 of this Chapter shall be reduced to such extent as necessary to permit the policyholders to be paid the ratable share that would have been due but for such payments. (1995, c. 193, s. 11; 1999-294, s. 8; 2001-223, s. 23.2; 2002-185, s. 8.)

Articles 1 through 64 of this Chapter may be cited and shall be known as the Insurance Law. (1899, c. 54; Rev., s. 4677; C.S., s. 6260.)

§ 58-5-65: Repealed by Session Laws 1995, c. 193, s. 8.

§ 58-5-70. Lien of policyholders; action to enforce.

Upon the securities deposited with the Commissioner by any foreign or alien insurance company, the holders of all contracts of the company who are citizens or residents of this State at the time, or who hold policies issued upon property in the State, shall have a lien for amounts in excess of fifty dollars ($50.00) due them, respectively, under or in consequence of the contracts for losses, equitable values, return premiums, or otherwise, and shall be entitled to be paid ratably out of the proceeds of the securities, if the proceeds are not sufficient to pay all of the contract holders. When any foreign or alien insurance company depositing securities under this Article becomes insolvent or bankrupt or makes an assignment for the benefit of its creditors, any holder of the contract may begin an action in the Superior Court of the County of Wake to enforce the lien for the benefit of all the holders of the contracts. The Commissioner shall be a party to the suit, and the funds shall be distributed by the court, but the cost of the action shall not be adjudged against the Commissioner. (1909, c. 923, s. 4; C.S., s. 6445; 1991, c. 720, s. 4; 1995, c. 193, s. 12; 2001-223, s. 24.1; 2001-487, s. 103(a).)

§ 58-5-71. Liens of policyholders; subordination.

Liens against the deposit of a foreign insurer under G.S. 58-5-70 shall be subordinated to the reasonable and necessary expenses of the Commissioner in liquidating the deposit and paying the special deposit claims. "Special deposit claims" has the same meaning set forth in G.S. 58-30-10(19). (1993 (Reg. Sess., 1994), c. 678, s. 7; 2008-124, s. 2.4.)

§ 58-5-75. Substitution for securities paid.

Where the principal of any of the securities so deposited is paid to the Commissioner, he shall notify the company or its agent in this State, and pay the money so received to the company upon receiving other securities of the character named in this Article to an equal amount, or, upon the failure of the company for 30 days after receiving notice to deliver such securities to an equal amount to the Commissioner, he may invest the money in any such securities and hold the same as he held those which were paid. (1909, c. 923, s. 5; C.S., s. 6446; 1991, c. 720, s. 4.)

§ 58-5-80. Return of deposits.

If such company ceases to do business in this State and its liabilities, whether fixed or contingent upon its contracts, to persons residing in this State or having policies upon property situated in this State have been satisfied or have been terminated, or have been fully reinsured, with the approval of the Commissioner, in a solvent company licensed to do an insurance business in North Carolina approved by the Commissioner, upon satisfactory evidence of this fact to the Commissioner the State Treasurer or the trustee selected pursuant to G.S. 58-5-1 shall deliver to such company, upon the order of the Commissioner, the securities in his possession belonging to it, or such of them as remain after paying the liabilities aforesaid. (1909, c. 923, s. 6; C.S., s. 6447; 1951, c. 781, s. 1; 1985, c. 666, s. 57; 1991, c. 720, s. 4.)

§ 58-5-85: Repealed by Session Laws 1991, c. 681, s. 21.

§ 58-5-90. Deposits held in trust by Commissioner or Treasurer.

(a) Deposits by Domestic Company. - The Commissioner or the Treasurer, in that officer's official capacity, shall take and hold in trust deposits made by any domestic insurance company for the benefit of all of the insurer's policyholders and for the purpose of complying with the laws of any other state to enable the company to do business in that state. The company making the deposits is entitled to the income thereof, and may, from time to time, with the consent of the Commissioner or Treasurer, and when not forbidden by the law under which the deposit was made, change in whole or in part the securities which compose the deposit for other solvent securities of equal par value. Upon request of any domestic insurance company the Commissioner or the Treasurer may return to the company the whole or any portion of the securities of the company held by the officer on deposit, when the officer is satisfied that the deposits are subject to no liability and are no longer required to be held by any provision of law or purpose of the original deposit.

(b) Deposits by Foreign or Alien Company. - The Commissioner or Treasurer, in that respective officer's official capacity, shall take and hold in trust deposits made by any foreign or alien insurance company for the benefit of the holders of all insurance contracts of the company who are citizens or residents of this State or who hold policies issued upon property in this State in accordance with G.S. 58-5-70. The Commissioner or Treasurer may return to the trustees or other representatives authorized for that purpose any deposit made by a foreign or alien insurance company, when it appears that the company has ceased to do business in the State and is under no obligation to policyholders or other persons in the State for whose benefit the deposit was made.

(c) Action to Enforce or Terminate the Trust. - An insurance company which has made a deposit in this State pursuant to Articles 1 through 64 of this Chapter, or its trustees or resident managers in the United States, or the Commissioner, or any creditor of the company, may at any time bring an action in the Superior Court of Wake County against the State and other parties properly joined therein, to enforce, administer, or terminate the trust created by the deposit. The process in this action shall be served on the officer of the State having the deposit, who shall appear and answer in behalf of the State and perform such orders and judgments as the court may make in such action. (1899, c. 54, s. 17; 1901, c. 391, s. 2; 1903, c. 438, s. 1; c. 536, s. 4; Rev., s. 4709; C.S., s. 6313; 1945, c. 384; 1991, c. 720, s. 4; 2005-215, s. 4.)

§ 58-5-95. Deposits subject to approval and control of Commissioner.

The deposits of securities required to be made by any insurance company of this State shall be approved by the Commissioner of the State, and he may examine them at all times, and may order all or any part thereof changed for better security, and no change or transfer of the same may be made without his assent. (1903, c. 536, s. 5; Rev., s. 4710; C.S., s. 6314; 1945, c. 384; 1991, c. 720, s. 4.)

§ 58-5-100. Deposits by alien companies required and regulated.

An alien company, other than life, shall not be admitted to do business in this State until, in addition to complying with the conditions by law prescribed for the licensing and admission of such companies to do business in this State, it has made a deposit with the Treasurer or Commissioner, or with the financial officer of some other state of the United States, of a sum not less than the capital required of like companies under Articles 1 through 64 of this Chapter. This deposit must be in exclusive trust for the benefit and security of all the company's policyholders and creditors in the United States, and may be made in the securities, but subject to the limitations, specified in Articles 1 through 64 of this Chapter with regard to the investment of the capital of domestic companies formed and organized under the provisions of Articles 1 through 64 of this Chapter. The deposit shall be deemed for all purposes of the insurance law the capital of the company making it. (1899, c. 54, s. 64; 1903, c. 438, s. 6; Rev., s. 4711; C.S., s. 6315; 1945, c. 384; 1991, c. 720, s. 52.)

§ 58-5-105. Deposits by life companies not chartered in United States.

Every alien life insurance company organized under the laws of any other country than the United States must have and keep on deposit with some state insurance department or in the hands of trustees, in exclusive trust for the security of its contracts with policyholders in the United States, funds of an amount equal to the net value of all its policies in the United States and not less than three hundred thousand dollars ($300,000). (1899, c. 54, s. 56; Rev., s. 4712; C.S., s. 6316; 1945, c. 384.)

§ 58-5-110. Registration of bonds deposited in name of Treasurer or Commissioner.

The Commissioner is hereby empowered, upon the written consent of any insurance company depositing with the Commissioner or the State Treasurer under any law of this State, any state, county, city, or town bonds or notes which are payable to bearer, to cause such bonds or notes to be registered as to the principal thereof in lawful books of registry kept by or in behalf of the issuing state, county, city or town, such registration to be in the name of the Treasurer of North Carolina or the Commissioner in trust for the company depositing the notes or bonds and the State of North Carolina, as their respective interest may appear, and is further empowered to require of any and all such companies the filing of written consent to such registration as a condition precedent to the right of making any such deposit or right to continue any such deposit heretofore made. (1925, c. 145, s. 2; 1945, c. 384; 1985, c. 666, s. 58; 1991, c. 720, s. 4.)

§ 58-5-115. Notation of registration; release.

Bonds or notes so registered shall bear notation of such registration on the reverse thereof, signed by the registering officer or agent, and may be released from such registration and may be transferred on such books of registry by the signature of the State Treasurer or Commissioner. (1925, c. 145, s. 3; 1945, c. 384; 1985, c. 666, s. 59.)

§ 58-5-120. Expenses of registration.

The necessary expenses of procuring such registration and any transfer thereof shall be paid by the company making the deposits. (1925, c. 145, s. 4; 1945, c. 384.)

§ 58-5-125: Repealed by Session Laws 1991, c. 681, s. 21.

Article 6.

License Fees and Taxes.

§ 58-6-1. Commissioner to report taxes and fees and pay monthly.

On or before the 10th day of each month the Commissioner shall furnish to the Auditor a statement in detail of the taxes and fees received during the previous month, and shall pay the amounts received to the Treasurer. Except as otherwise provided, the amounts shall be credited to the General Fund. The Auditor may examine the accounts of the Commissioner and check them up with said statement. (1899, c. 54, s. 82; 1901, c. 391, s. 7; 1905, c. 430, s. 4; Rev., s. 4714; C.S., s. 6317; 1991, c. 720, s. 4; 1991 (Reg. Sess., 1992), c. 1014, s. 4; 1998-215, s. 83(b).)

§ 58-6-5. Schedule of fees and charges.

The Commissioner shall collect and pay into the State treasury fees and charges as follows:

(1) For filing and examining an insurance company application for admission, a nonrefundable fee of one thousand dollars ($1,000), to be submitted with the filing; for each certification or confirmation of an insurance company deposit held by the Commissioner pursuant to this Chapter, twenty-five dollars ($25.00).

(2) Repealed by Session Laws 1977, c. 376, s. 2.

(3) The Commissioner shall receive for copy of any record or paper in his office fifty cents (50¢) per copy sheet.

(4) He shall collect all other fees and charges due and payable into the State treasury by any company, association, order, or individual under his Department.

(5) Repealed by Session Laws 1999-435, s. 1. (1899, c. 54, ss. 50, 68, 80, 81, 82, 87, 90, 92; 1901, c. 391, s. 7; c. 706, s. 2; 1903, c. 438, ss. 7, 8; c. 536, s. 4; cc. 680, 774; 1905, c. 588, s. 68; Rev., s. 4715; 1913, c. 140, s. 1; 1919, c. 186, s. 6; C.S., s. 6318; 1921, c. 218; 1935, c. 334; 1939, c. 158, s. 208; 1945, c. 386; 1947, c. 721; 1957, cc. 133, 1047; 1959, c. 911; 1963, c. 692; 1977, c. 376, s. 2; c. 802, s. 50; 1983, c. 790, s. 6; 1989 (Reg. Sess., 1990), c. 1069, s. 2; 1991, c. 720, s. 4; 1995, c. 360, s. 2(f); c. 507, s. 11A(c); 1999-435, s. 1; 2005-424, s. 1.1; 2009-451, s. 21.11(a).)

§ 58-6-7. Licenses; perpetual licensing; annual license continuation fees for insurance companies.

(a) In order to do business in this State, an insurance company shall apply for and obtain a license from the Commissioner. The license shall be perpetual and shall continue in full force and effect, subject to timely payment of the annual license continuation fee in accordance with this Chapter and subject to any other applicable provision of the insurance laws of this State. The insurance company shall pay a fee for each year the license is in effect, as follows:

For each domestic farmer's mutual assessment fire insurance company......
$.. 25.00

For each fraternal order..
.... 500.00

For each of all other insurance companies, except mutual burial associations taxed under G.S.105-121.1..
....
2,500.00

The fees levied in this subsection are in addition to those specified in G.S. 58-6-5.

(b)   Repealed by Session Laws 2005-424, s. 1.2, effective January 1, 2006, and applicable to applications filed, licenses issued, and licenses continued on or after that date.

(c)   Upon payment of the fee specified above and the fees and taxes elsewhere specified, each insurance company, exchange, bureau, or agency, shall be entitled to do the types of business specified in Chapter 58, of the General Statutes of North Carolina as amended, to the extent authorized therein. All fees and charges collected by the Commissioner under this Chapter are nonrefundable.

(d)   Any rating bureau established by action of the General Assembly of North Carolina shall be exempt from the fees in this section. (1945, c. 752, s. 2; 1947, c. 501, s. 8; 1955, c. 179, s. 5; 1989 (Reg. Sess., 1990), c. 1069, s. 4; 1993, c. 495, s. 4; 1993 (Reg. Sess., 1994), c. 745, s. 12; 1995, c. 193, s. 65; c. 360, s. 1(c); c. 507, s. 11A(c); 1999-435, s. 2; 2003-212, s. 26(c); 2005-424, s. 1.2; 2009-451, s. 21.11(b).)

§ 58-6-10. Repealed by Session Laws 1999-132, s 1.1.

§ 58-6-15. Annual license continuation fee definition; requirements.

For purposes of this Chapter only, "annual license continuation fee" means the fee specified in G.S. 58-6-7 submitted to the Commissioner for each year the license is in effect after the company's year of initial licensing. The annual license continuation fee must be submitted annually on or before the first day of March for as long as the license is to remain in effect. If the Commissioner is satisfied that the company has met all requirements of law and appears to be financially solvent, the Commissioner shall not revoke or suspend the license of the company, and the company shall be authorized to do business in this State, subject to all other applicable provisions of the insurance laws of this State. Nothing contained in this section shall be interpreted as applying to licenses issued to individual representatives of insurance companies. (1899, c. 54, s. 78; Rev., s. 4718; C.S., s. 6321; 1955, c. 179, s. 1; 1987, c. 629, s. 16; 1989 (Reg. Sess., 1990), c. 1069, s. 3; 1995, c. 507, s. 11A(c); 2003-212, s. 26(d); 2005-215, s. 5.)

§ 58-6-20. Policyholders to furnish information.

Every corporation, firm, or individual doing business in the State shall, upon request of the Commissioner, furnish the Commissioner any information the Commissioner considers necessary to enable the Commissioner to enforce the payment of a tax levied in this Chapter. (1899, c. 54, s. 79; 1901, c. 391, s. 7; 1903, c. 438, s. 8; Rev., s. 4720; C.S., s. 6323; 1987, c. 864, s. 38; 1991, c. 720, s. 4; 1995 (Reg. Sess., 1996), c. 747, s. 11.)

§ 58-6-25. Insurance regulatory charge.

(a) Charge Levied. - There is levied on each insurance company, other than a captive insurance company, an annual charge for the purposes stated in subsection (d) of this section. The charge levied in this section is in addition to all other fees and taxes. The percentage rate of the charge is established pursuant to subsection (b) of this section and is applied to the company's premium tax liability for the taxable year. In determining an insurance company's premium tax liability for a taxable year, the following shall be disregarded:

(1) Additional taxes imposed by G.S. 105-228.8.

(2) Repealed by Session Laws 2008-134, s. 67(a), as amended by Session Laws 2009-445, s. 44, effective for taxable years beginning on or after January 1, 2008.

(3) Any tax credits for guaranty or solvency fund assessments under G.S. 105-228.5A or G.S. 97-133(a).

(4) Any tax credits allowed under Chapter 105 of the General Statutes other than tax payments made by or on behalf of the taxpayer.

(b) Rates. - The rate of the charge for each taxable year shall be the percentage rate established by the General Assembly. When the Department prepares its budget request for each upcoming fiscal year, the Department shall propose a percentage rate of the charge levied in this section. The Governor shall submit that proposed rate to the General Assembly each fiscal year. The General Assembly shall set by law the percentage rate of the charge levied in this section. The percentage rate may not exceed the rate necessary to generate funds sufficient to defray the estimated cost of the operations of the Department for each upcoming fiscal year, including a reasonable margin for a reserve fund. The amount of the reserve may not exceed one-third of the estimated cost of operating the Department for each upcoming fiscal year. In calculating the amount of the reserve, the General Assembly shall consider all relevant factors that may affect the cost of operating the Department or a possible unanticipated increase or decrease in North Carolina premiums or other charge revenue.

(c) Returns; When Payable. - The charge levied on each insurance company is payable at the time the insurance company remits its premium tax. If the insurance company is required to remit installment payments of premiums tax under G.S. 105-228.5 for a taxable year, it shall also remit installment payments of the charge levied in this section for that taxable year at the same time and on the same basis as the premium tax installment payments. Each installment payment shall be equal to at least thirty-three and one-third percent (33.3%) of the insurance company's regulatory charge liability incurred in the immediately preceding taxable year.

Every insurance company shall, on or before the date the charge levied in this section is due, file a return on a form prescribed by the Secretary of Revenue. The return shall state the company's total North Carolina premiums or presumed premiums for the taxable year and shall be accompanied by any supporting documentation that the Secretary of Revenue may by rule require.

(d) Use of Proceeds. - The Insurance Regulatory Fund is created in the State treasury, under the control of the Office of State Budget and Management. The proceeds of the charge levied in this section and all fees collected under Articles 69 through 71 of this Chapter and under Articles 9 and 9C of Chapter 143 of the General Statutes shall be credited to the Fund. The Fund shall be placed in an interest-bearing account and any interest or other income derived from the Fund shall be credited to the Fund. Moneys in the Fund may be spent only pursuant to appropriation by the General Assembly and in accordance with the line item budget enacted by the General Assembly. The Fund is subject to the provisions of the Executive Budget Act, except that no unexpended surplus of the Fund shall revert to the General Fund. All money credited to the Fund shall be used to reimburse the General Fund for the following:

(1) Money appropriated to the Department of Insurance to pay its expenses incurred in regulating the insurance industry, including the captive insurance industry, and other industries in this State.

(2) Money appropriated to State agencies to pay the expenses incurred in regulating the insurance industry, in certifying statewide data processors under Article 11A of Chapter 131E of the General Statutes, and in purchasing reports of patient data from statewide data processors certified under that Article.

(3) Money appropriated to the Department of Revenue to pay the expenses incurred in collecting and administering the taxes on insurance companies levied in Article 8B of Chapter 105 of the General Statutes.

(4) Money appropriated for the office of Health Insurance Smart NC under G.S. 143-730 to pay the actual costs of administering the program.

(5) Money appropriated to the Department of Insurance for the implementation and administration of independent external review procedures required by Part 4 of Article 50 of this Chapter.

(6) Money appropriated to the Department of Justice to pay its expenses incurred in representing the Department of Insurance in its regulation of the insurance industry and other related programs and industries in this State that fall under the jurisdiction of the Department of Insurance.

(7) Money appropriated to the Department of Insurance to pay its expenses incurred in connection with providing staff support for State boards and

commissions, including the North Carolina Manufactured Housing Board, State Fire and Rescue Commission, North Carolina Building Code Council, North Carolina Code Officials Qualification Board, Public Officers and Employees Liability Insurance Commission, North Carolina Home Inspector Licensure Board, and the Volunteer Safety Workers' Compensation Board.

(8) Money appropriated to the Department of Insurance to pay its expenses incurred in connection with continuing education programs under Article 33 of this Chapter and in connection with the purchase and sale of copies of the North Carolina State Building Code.

(9) Money appropriated to the Department of Insurance for the regulation of the professional employer organization industry pursuant to Article 89A of Chapter 58 of the General Statutes.

(10) Money appropriated to the Department of Insurance to pay its expenses incurred in promoting North Carolina's captive insurance industry.

(e) Definitions. - The following definitions apply in this section:

(1) Repealed by Session Laws 2003-284, s. 43.2, effective for taxable years beginning on or after January 1, 2004.

(1a) Captive insurance company. - Defined in G.S. 105-228.3.

(2) Insurance company. - A company that pays the gross premiums tax levied in G.S. 105-228.5 and G.S. 105-228.8.

(3) Insurer. - Defined in G.S. 105-228.3. (1991, c. 689, s. 289; 1991 (Reg. Sess., 1992), c. 812, s. 6(e); 1995, c. 360, ss. 1(i), 3(a); c. 517, s. 39(f), (g); 1995 (Reg. Sess., 1996), c. 646, s. 19; c. 747, s. 3; 1997-443, s. 26.1; 1997-475, s. 2.2; 1998-212, s. 29A.7(b); 1999-413, s. 4; 2000-140, s. 93.1(a); 2001-424, ss. 12.2(b), 14E.1(a), 34.22(b), 34.22(c); 2001-489, s. 2(d); 2002-72, s. 9(a); 2002-126, s. 15.5; 2002-144, s. 1; 2002-159, s. 66.5; 2003-284, ss. 22.2, 43.2; 2004-124, s. 21.1; 2005-124, s. 7; 2005-276, s. 38.4(b); 2008-134, s. 67(a); 2009-445, s. 44; 2013-116, s. 7; 2013-199, s. 12.)

Article 7.

General Domestic Companies.

§ 58-7-1. Application of this Chapter and general laws.

The general provisions of law relative to the powers, duties, and liabilities of corporations apply to all incorporated domestic insurance companies where pertinent and not in conflict with other provisions of law relative to such companies or with their charters. All insurance companies of this State shall be governed by this Chapter, notwithstanding anything in their special charters to the contrary, provided notice of the acceptance of this Chapter is filed with the Commissioner. (1899, c. 54, s. 19; Rev., s. 4721; C.S., s. 6324; 1991, c. 720, s. 4; 2006-105, s. 1.2.)

§ 58-7-5. Extension of existing charters.

Domestic insurance companies incorporated by special acts, whose charters are subject to limitation of time, shall, after the limitation expires, and upon filing statement and paying the taxes and fees required for an amendment of the charter, continue to be bodies corporate, subject to all general laws applicable to such companies. (1899, c. 54, s. 20; Rev., s. 4722; C.S., s. 6325.)

§ 58-7-10. Certificate required before issuing policies.

No domestic insurance company may issue policies until upon examination of the Commissioner, his deputy or examiner, it is found to have complied with the laws of the State, and until it has obtained from the Commissioner a certificate setting forth that fact and authorizing it to issue policies. The issuing of policies in violation of this section renders the company liable to the forfeiture prescribed by law, but such policies are binding upon the company. (1899, c. 54, ss. 21, 99; 1903, c. 438, s. 10; Rev., s. 4723; C.S., s. 6326; 1991, c. 720, s. 4.)

§ 58-7-15. Kinds of insurance authorized.

The kinds of insurance that may be authorized in this State, subject to the other provisions of Articles 1 through 64 of this Chapter, are set forth in this section. Except to the extent an insurer participates in a risk sharing plan under Article 42 of this Chapter, nothing in this section requires any insurer to insure every kind of risk that it is authorized to insure. Except to the extent an insurer participates in a risk sharing plan under Article 42 of this Chapter, no insurer may transact any other business than that specified in its charter and articles of association or incorporation. The power to do any kind of insurance against loss of or damage to property includes the power to insure all lawful interests in the property and to insure against loss of use and occupancy and rents and profits resulting therefrom; but no kind of insurance includes life insurance or insurance against legal liability for personal injury or death unless specified in this section. In addition to any power to engage in any other kind of business than an insurance business that is specifically conferred by the provisions of Articles 1 through 64 of this Chapter, any insurer authorized to do business in this State may engage in such other kinds of business to the extent necessarily or properly incidental to the kinds of insurance business that it is authorized to do in this State. Each of the following indicates the scope of the kind of insurance business specified:

(1) "Life insurance", meaning every insurance upon the lives of human beings and every insurance appertaining thereto. The business of life insurance includes the granting of endowment benefits; additional benefits in the event of death by accident or accidental means; additional benefits operating to safeguard the contract from lapse, or to provide a special surrender value, in the event of total and permanent disability of the insured, including industrial sick benefit; and optional modes of settlement of proceeds.

(2) "Annuities", meaning all agreements to make periodical payments, whether in fixed or variable dollar amounts, or both, at specified intervals.

(3) "Accident and health insurance", meaning:

a. Insurance against death or personal injury by accident or by any specified kinds of accident and insurance against sickness, ailment or bodily injury except as specified in paragraph b following; and

b. "Noncancelable disability insurance," meaning insurance against disability resulting from sickness, ailment or bodily injury (but not including insurance solely against accidental injury), under any contract that does not give the insurer the option to cancel or otherwise terminate the contract at or after one year from its effective date or renewal date.

(4) "Fire insurance", meaning insurance against loss of or damage to any property resulting from fire, including loss or damage incident to the extinguishment of a fire or to the salvaging of property in connection therewith.

(5) "Miscellaneous property insurance", meaning loss of or damage to property resulting from:

a. Lightning, smoke or smudge, windstorm, tornado, cyclone, earthquake, volcanic eruption, rain, hail, frost and freeze, weather or climatic conditions, excess or deficiency of moisture, flood, the rising of the waters of the ocean or its tributaries, or

b. Insects, or blights, or from disease of such property other than animals, or

c. Electrical disturbance causing or concomitant with a fire or an explosion in public service or public utility property, or

d. Bombardment, invasion, insurrection, riot, civil war or commotion, military or usurped power, any order of a civil authority made to prevent the spread of a conflagration, epidemic or catastrophe, vandalism or malicious mischief, strike or lockout, or explosion; but not including any kind of insurance specified in subdivision (9), except insurance against loss or damage to property resulting from:

1. Explosion of pressure vessels (except steam boilers of more than 15 pounds pressure) in buildings designed and used solely for residential purposes by not more than four famIlIIes,

2. Explosion of any kind originating outside of the insured building or outside of the building containing the property insured,

3. Explosion of pressure vessels that do not contain steam or that are not operated with steam coils or steam jackets,

4. Electrical disturbance causing or concomitant with an explosion in public service or public utility property.

(6) "Water damage insurance," meaning insurance against loss or damage by water or other fluid or substance to any property resulting from the breakage or leakage of sprinklers, pumps, or other apparatus erected for extinguishing fires or of water pipes or other conduits or containers; or resulting from casual water entering through leaks or openings in buildings or by seepage through building walls; but not including loss or damage resulting from flood or the rising of the waters of the ocean or its tributaries; and including insurance against accidental injury of such sprinklers, pumps, fire apparatus, conduits, or containers.

(7) "Burglary and theft insurance," meaning:

a. Insurance against loss of or damage to any property resulting from burglary, theft, larceny, robbery, forgery, fraud, vandalism, malicious mischief, confiscation, or wrongful conversion, disposal or concealment by any person or persons, or from any attempt at any of the foregoing, and

b. Insurance against loss of or damage to moneys, coins, bullion, securities, notes, drafts, acceptances, or any other valuable papers or documents, resulting from any cause, except while in the custody or possession of and being transported by any carrier for hire or in the mail.

(8) "Glass insurance," meaning insurance against loss of or damage to glass and its appurtenances resulting from any cause.

(9) "Boiler and machinery insurance," meaning insurance against loss of or damage to any property of the insured, resulting from the explosion of or injury to:

a. Any boiler, heater or other fired pressure vessel;

b. Any unfired pressure vessel;

c. Pipes or containers connected with any of said boilers or vessels;

d. Any engine, turbine, compressor, pump or wheel;

e. Any apparatus generating, transmitting or using electricity;

f. Any other machinery or apparatus connected with or operated by any of the previously named boilers, vessels or machines;

and including the incidental power to make inspections of and to issue certificates of inspection upon, any such boilers, apparatus, and machinery, whether insured or otherwise.

(10) "Elevator insurance," meaning insurance against loss of or damage to any property of the insured, resulting from the ownership, maintenance or use of elevators, except loss or damage by fire.

(11) "Animal insurance," meaning insurance against loss of or damage to any domesticated or wild animal resulting from any cause.

(12) "Collision insurance," meaning insurance against loss of or damage to any property of the insured resulting from collision of any other object with the property, but not including collision to or by elevators or to or by vessels, craft, piers or other instrumentalities of ocean or inland navigation.

(13) "Personal injury liability insurance," meaning insurance against legal liability of the insured, and against loss, damage, or expense incident to a claim of such liability; including personal excess liability or personal "umbrella" insurance; and including an obligation of the insurer to pay medical, hospital, surgical, or funeral benefits; and in the case of motor vehicle liability insurance including also disability and death benefits to injured persons, irrespective of legal liability of the insured, arising out of the death or injury of any person, or arising out of injury to the economic interests of any person as a result of negligence in rendering expert, fiduciary, or professional service; but not including any kind of insurance specified in subdivision (15) of this section.

(14) "Property damage liability insurance," meaning insurance against legal liability of the insured, and against loss, damage or expense incident to a claim of such liability, arising out of the loss or destruction of, or damage to, the property of any other person, but not including any kind of insurance specified in subdivision (13) or (15).

(15) "Workers' compensation and employer's liability insurance," meaning insurance against the legal liability, whether imposed by common law or by statute or assumed by contract, of any employer for the death or disablement of, or injury to, the employer's employee.

(16) "Fidelity and surety insurance," meaning:

a. Guaranteeing the fidelity of persons holding positions of public or private trust;

b. Becoming surety on, or guaranteeing the performance of, any lawful contract except the following:

1. A contract of indebtedness secured by title to, or mortgage upon, or interest in, real or personal property;

2. Any insurance contract except reinsurance;

c. Becoming surety on, or guaranteeing the performance of, bonds and undertakings required or permitted in all judicial proceedings or otherwise by law allowed, including surety bonds accepted by states and municipal authorities in lieu of deposits as security for the performance of insurance contracts;

d. Guaranteeing contracts of indebtedness secured by any title to, or interest in, real property, only to the extent required for the purpose of refunding, extending, refinancing, liquidating or salvaging obligations heretofore lawfully made and guaranteed;

e. Indemnifying banks, bankers, brokers, financial or moneyed corporations or associations against loss resulting from any cause of bills of exchange, notes, bonds, securities, evidences of debts, deeds, mortgages, warehouse receipts, or other valuable papers, documents, money, precious metals and articles made therefrom, jewelry, watches, necklaces, bracelets, gems, precious and semiprecious stones, including any loss while the same are being transported in armored motor vehicles, or by messenger; but not including any other risks of transportation or navigation; also against loss or damage to such an insured's premises, or to the insured's furnishings, fixtures, equipment, safes and vaults therein, caused by burglary, robbery, theft, vandalism or malicious mischief, or any attempt thereat.

(17) "Credit insurance," meaning indemnifying merchants or other persons extending credit against loss or damage resulting from the nonpayment of debts owed to them; and including the incidental power to acquire and dispose of debts so insured, and to collect any debts owed to the insurer or to any person so insured by the insurer; and also including insurance where the debt is secured by either (a) a junior lien on real estate or (b) a first lien on real estate as long as (i) the purpose of the debt being insured is not for the purchase of the real estate and the insurance is limited to twenty-five percent (25%) of the

insurer's aggregate insured risk outstanding, before reinsurance ceded or assumed or (ii) the insurance is not included within the definition of mortgage guaranty insurance.

(18)   "Title insurance," meaning insuring the owners of real property and chattels real and other persons lawfully interested therein against loss by reason of defective titles and encumbrances thereon and insuring the correctness of searches for all instruments, liens or charges affecting the title to that property, including the power to procure and furnish information relative thereto, and other incidental powers that are specifically granted in Articles 1 through 64 of this Chapter.

(19)   "Motor vehicle or aircraft insurance," meaning insurance against loss of or damage resulting from any cause to motor vehicles or aircraft and their equipment, and against legal liability of the insured for loss or damage to another's property resulting from the ownership, maintenance or use of motor vehicles or aircraft and against loss, damage or expense incident to a claim of such liability. This subdivision does not apply to commercial aircraft as defined in G.S. 58-1-5.

(20)   "Marine insurance," meaning insurance against any and all kinds of loss or damage to:

a.   Vessels, craft, aircraft, cars, automobiles and vehicles of every kind, as well as all goods, freights, cargoes, merchandise, effects, disbursements, profits, moneys, bullion, precious stones, securities, choses in action, evidences of debt, valuable papers, bottomry and respondentia interests and all other kinds of property and interests therein, in respect to, appertaining to or in connection with any and all risks or perils of navigation, transit, or transportation, including war risks, on or under any seas or other waters, on land or in the air, or while being assembled, packed, crated, baled, compressed or similarly prepared for shipment or while awaiting the same or during any delays, storage, transshipment, or reshipment incident thereto, including marine builder's risks and all personal property floater risks, and

b.   Person or to property in connection with or appertaining to a marine, inland marine, transit or transportation insurance, including liability for loss of or damage to either, arising out of or in connection with the construction, repair, operation, maintenance or use of the subject matter of the insurance (but not including life insurance or surety bonds nor insurance against loss because of bodily injury to the person arising out of the ownership, maintenance or use of automobiles), and

c. Precious stones, jewels, jewelry, gold, silver and other precious metals, whether used in business or trade or otherwise and whether the same be in course of transportation or otherwise, and

d. Bridges, tunnels and other instrumentalities of transportation and communication (excluding buildings, their furniture and furnishings, fixed contents and supplies held in storage) unless fire, tornado, sprinkler leakage, hail, explosion, earthquake, riot and/or civil commotion are the only hazards to be covered; piers, wharves, docks and slips, excluding the risks of fire, tornado, sprinkler leakage, hail, explosion, earthquake, riot and/or civil commotion; other aids to navigation and transportation, including dry docks and marine railways against all risks.

(21) "Marine protection and indemnity insurance," meaning insurance against, or against legal liability of the insured for, loss, damage or expense arising out of, or incident to, the ownership, operation, chartering, maintenance, use, repair or construction of any vessel, craft or instrumentality in use in ocean or inland waterways, including liability of the insured for personal injury, illness or death or for loss of or damage to the property of another person.

(22) "Miscellaneous insurance," meaning insurance against any other casualty authorized by the charter of the company, not included in this section, which is a proper subject of insurance.

(23) "Mortgage guaranty insurance," meaning insurance against financial loss by reason of nonpayment of principal, interest, or other sums agreed to be paid under the terms of any note or bond or other evidence of indebtedness which constitutes, or is equivalent to, a first lien or charge on the real estate, provided the improvement on the real estate is a residential building or a condominium unit or buildings designed for occupancy by not more than four families. (1899, c. 54, ss. 24, 26; 1903, c. 438, s. 1; Rev., s. 4726; 1911, c. 111, s. 1; C.S., s. 6327; 1945, c. 386; 1947, c. 721; 1953, c. 992; 1967, c. 624, s. 1; 1969, c. 616, s. 1; 1979, c. 714, s. 2; 1986, Ex. Sess., c. 7, ss. 2, 3; 1987, c. 731, s. 1, c. 864, ss. 39, 40; 1991, c. 644, s. 7; 1999-219, s. 5.1; 2001-236, s. 3; 2001-423, s. 3; 2007-127, ss. 1-3; 2008-124, s. 2.3.)

§ 58-7-16. Funding agreements authorized.

(a) As used in this section, "funding agreement" means an agreement that authorizes a licensed life insurer to accept funds and that provides for an accumulation of funds for the purpose of making one or more payments at future dates in amounts that are not based on mortality or morbidity contingencies. A "funding agreement" is not an "annuity" as defined in G.S. 58-7-15; and is not a "security" as defined in G.S. 78A-2.

(b) Any insurer that is licensed to write life insurance or annuities in this State may deliver, or issue for delivery, funding agreements in this State.

(c) Funding agreements may be issued to persons authorized by a state or foreign country to engage in an insurance business or to their affiliates, including affiliates of the issuer. Issuance to an affiliate of an issuer is not subject to the provisions of Article 19 of this Chapter. Funding agreements may be issued to persons other than those licensed to write life insurance and annuities or their affiliates in order to fund one or more of the following:

(1) Benefits under any employee benefit plan as defined in the federal Employee Retirement Income Security Act of 1974, 29 U.S.C. § 1001 et seq., maintained in the United States or in a foreign country.

(2) The activities of an organization exempt from taxation under section 501(c) of the Internal Revenue Code or of any similar organization in a foreign country.

(3) A program of the government of the United States, the government of a state, foreign country, or political subdivision, agency, or instrumentality thereof.

(4) An agreement providing for one or more payments in satisfaction of a claim or liability.

(5) A program of an institution that has assets in excess of twenty-five million dollars ($25,000,000).

(d) Amounts shall not be guaranteed or credited under a funding agreement except upon reasonable assumptions as to investment income and expenses and on a basis equitable to all holders of funding agreements of a given class.

(e) Amounts paid to the insurer and proceeds applied under optional modes of settlement under funding agreements may be allocated by the insurer to one or more separate accounts pursuant to G.S. 58-7-95.

(f) The Commissioner has sole authority to regulate the issuance and sale of funding agreements on behalf of insurers. In addition to the authority in G.S. 58-2-40, the Commissioner may adopt rules relating to:

(1) Standards to be followed in the approval of forms of funding agreements.

(2) Reserves to be maintained by and valuation rules for insurers issuing funding agreements.

(3) Accounting and reporting of funds credited under funding agreements.

(4) Disclosure of information to be given to holders and prospective holders of funding agreements.

(5) Qualification and compensation of persons selling funding agreements on behalf of insurers.

In determining minimum valuation reserves to be maintained by and valuation rules for insurers issuing funding agreements, the Commissioner may use any relevant actuarial guideline, regulation, interpretation, or paper published by the Society of Actuaries or the American Academy of Actuaries that the Commissioner considers reasonable. (1993 (Reg. Sess., 1994), c. 600, s. 1; 1998-212, s. 26B(e); 2001-334, s. 17.2.)

§ 58-7-20: Repealed by Session Laws 1991, c. 681, s. 23.

§ 58-7-21. Credit allowed a domestic ceding insurer.

(a) The purpose of this section and G.S. 58-7-26 is to protect the interest of insureds, claimants, ceding insurers, assuming insurers, and the public generally. The General Assembly declares its intent is to ensure adequate regulation of insurers and reinsurers and adequate protection for those to whom they owe obligations. In furtherance of that interest, the General Assembly provides a mandate that upon the insolvency of an alien insurer or reinsurer that provides security to fund its United States obligations in accordance with this section and G.S. 58-7-26, the assets representing the security shall be maintained in the United States and claims shall be filed with and valued by the state insurance commissioner with regulatory oversight, and the assets shall be distributed, in accordance with the insurance laws of the state in which the trust is domiciled that are applicable to the liquidation of domestic United States insurance companies. The General Assembly declares that the matters contained in this section and G.S. 58-7-26 are fundamental to the business of insurance in accordance with 15 U.S.C. §§ 1011-1012.

(b) Credit for reinsurance shall be allowed a domestic ceding insurer as either an asset or a reduction from liability on account of reinsurance ceded only when the reinsurer meets the requirements of subdivisions (1), (2), (3), (4), or (5) of this subsection. Credit shall be allowed under subdivision (1), (2), or (3) of this subsection only with regard to cessions of those kinds or classes of business in which the assuming insurer is licensed or otherwise permitted to write or assume in its state of domicile or, in the case of a United States branch of an alien assuming insurer, in the state through which it is entered and licensed to transact insurance or reinsurance. Credit shall be allowed under subdivision (3) or (4) of this subsection only if the applicable requirements of subdivision (6) of this section have been satisfied.

(1) Credit shall be allowed when the reinsurance is ceded to an assuming insurer that is licensed to transact insurance or reinsurance in this State.

(2) Credit shall be allowed when the reinsurance is ceded to an assuming insurer that is accredited as a reinsurer in this State. An accredited reinsurer is one that:

a. Files with the Commissioner evidence of its submission to this State's jurisdiction;

b. Submits to this State's authority to examine its books and records;

c. Is licensed to transact insurance or reinsurance in at least one state, or in the case of a United States branch of an alien assuming insurer is entered through and licensed to transact insurance or reinsurance in at least one state;

d. Files annually with the Commissioner a copy of its annual statement filed with the insurance regulator of its state of domicile, a copy of its most recent audited financial statement, and a fee of seven hundred fifty dollars ($750.00) and either

1. Maintains a policyholders' surplus in an amount that is not less than twenty million dollars ($20,000,000) and whose accreditation has not been denied by the Commissioner within 90 days after its submission; or

2. Maintains a policyholders' surplus in an amount less than twenty million dollars ($20,000,000) and whose accreditation has been approved by the Commissioner.

Credit shall not be allowed a domestic ceding insurer if the assuming insurer's accreditation has been revoked by the Commissioner after notice and opportunity for a hearing.

(3) Credit shall be allowed when the reinsurance is ceded to an assuming insurer that is domiciled in, or in the case of a United States branch of an alien assuming insurer is entered through, a state that uses standards regarding credit for reinsurance substantially similar to those applicable under this section and the assuming insurer or United States branch of an alien assuming insurer:

a. Maintains a policyholders' surplus in an amount not less than twenty million dollars ($20,000,000); and

b. Submits to the authority of this State to examine its books and records.

The requirement in sub-subdivision (3)a. of this subsection does not apply to reinsurance ceded and assumed under pooling arrangements among insurers in the same holding company system.

(4) a. Credit shall be allowed when the reinsurance is ceded to an assuming insurer that maintains a trust fund in a qualified United States financial institution, as defined in G.S. 58-7-26(b), for the payment of the valid claims of its United States ceding insurers, their assigns and successors in interest. The assuming insurer shall report annually to the Commissioner information substantially the same as that required to be reported on the NAIC Annual Statement form by licensed insurers to enable the Commissioner to determine the sufficiency of the trust fund. The assuming insurer shall submit to

examination of its books and records by the Commissioner and bear the expense of examination.

b. Repealed by Session Laws 2001-223, s. 3.1. For applicability, see note.

b1. Credit for reinsurance shall not be granted under this subdivision unless the form of the trust and any amendments to the trust have been approved by:

1. The insurance regulator of the state where the trust is domiciled; or

2. The insurance regulator of another state who, pursuant to the terms of the trust instrument, has accepted principal regulatory oversight of the trust.

b2. The form of the trust and any trust amendments also shall be filed with the insurance regulator of every state in which the ceding insurer beneficiaries of the trust are domiciled. The trust instrument shall provide that contested claims shall be valid and enforceable upon the final order of any court of competent jurisdiction in the United States. The trust shall vest legal title to its assets in its trustees for the benefit of the assuming insurer's United States ceding insurers, their assigns, and successors in interest. The trust and the assuming insurer shall be subject to examination as determined by the Commissioner.

b3. The trust shall remain in effect for as long as the assuming insurer has outstanding obligations due under the reinsurance agreements subject to the trust. No later than February 28 of each year, the trustees of the trust shall report to the Commissioner in writing the balance of the trust, shall list the trust's investments at the end of the preceding year, and shall certify the date of termination of the trust, if so planned, or shall certify that the trust will not expire before the following December 31.

c. The following requirements apply to the following categories of assuming insurer:

1. The trust fund for a single assuming insurer shall consist of funds in trust in an amount not less than the assuming insurer's liabilities attributable to reinsurance ceded by United States ceding insurers, and, in addition, the assuming insurer shall maintain a surplus in trust of not less than twenty million dollars ($20,000,000).

2. In the case of a group including incorporated and individual unincorporated underwriters:

I. For reinsurance ceded under reinsurance agreements with an inception, amendment, or renewal date on or after August 1, 1995, the trust shall consist of an account in trust in an amount not less than the group's several liabilities attributable to business ceded by United States domiciled ceding insurers to any member of the group.

II. For reinsurance ceded under reinsurance agreements with an inception date on or before July 31, 1995, and not amended or renewed after that date, notwithstanding the other provisions of this section and G.S. 58-7-26, the trust shall consist of an account in trust in an amount not less than the group's several insurance and reinsurance liabilities attributable to business written in the United States.

In addition to these trusts, the group shall maintain in trust a surplus of which one hundred million dollars ($100,000,000) shall be held jointly for the benefit of the United States domiciled ceding insurers of any member of the group for all years of account. Each incorporated member of the group shall not be engaged in any business other than underwriting as a member of the group and shall be subject to the same level of regulation and solvency control by the group's domiciliary insurance regulator as are the unincorporated members. Within 90 days after its financial statements are due to be filed with the group's domiciliary insurance regulator, the group shall provide to the Commissioner an annual certification by the group's domiciliary insurance regulator of the solvency of each underwriter member or, if a certification is unavailable, financial statements prepared by independent public accountants of each underwriter member of the group.

d. Repealed by Session Laws 2001-223, s. 3.1. For applicability, see note.

(5) Credit shall be allowed when the reinsurance is ceded to an assuming insurer not meeting the requirements of subdivisions (1), (2), (3), or (4) of this subsection, but only with respect to the insurance of risks located in jurisdictions where the reinsurance is required by applicable law or regulation of that jurisdiction.

(6) If the assuming insurer is not licensed or accredited to transact insurance or reinsurance in this State, the credit permitted by subdivisions (3)

and (4) of this subsection shall not be allowed unless the assuming insurer agrees in the reinsurance agreements:

a. That if the assuming insurer fails to perform its obligations under the terms of the reinsurance agreement, the assuming insurer, at the ceding insurer's request, shall submit to the jurisdiction of any court of competent jurisdiction in any state of the United States, shall comply with all requirements necessary to give the court jurisdiction, and shall abide by the final decision of the court or of any appellate court if there is an appeal; and

b. To designate the Commissioner or a designated attorney as its true and lawful attorney upon whom may be served any lawful process in any action, suit, or proceeding begun by or on behalf of the ceding company.

This subdivision does not affect the obligation of the parties to a reinsurance agreement to arbitrate their disputes, if the obligation is created in the agreement.

(7) If the assuming insurer does not meet the requirements of subdivision (1), (2), or (3) of this subsection, the credit permitted by subdivision (4) of this subsection shall not be allowed unless the assuming insurer agrees in the trust agreements to the following conditions:

a. Notwithstanding any other provisions in the trust instrument, if the trust fund is inadequate because it contains an amount less than the amount required by sub-subdivision of this subsection, or if the grantor of the trust has been declared insolvent or placed into receivership, rehabilitation, liquidation, or similar proceedings under the laws of its state or country of domicile, the trustee shall comply with an order of the public official with regulatory oversight over the trust or with an order of a court of competent jurisdiction directing the trustee to transfer to the public official with regulatory oversight all of the assets of the trust fund.

b. The assets shall be distributed by, and claims shall be filed with and valued by, the public official with regulatory oversight in accordance with the laws of the state in which the trust is domiciled that are applicable to the liquidation of domestic insurance companies.

c. If the public official with regulatory oversight determines that the assets of the trust fund or any part thereof are not necessary to satisfy the claims of the United States ceding insurers of the grantor of the trust, those assets shall be returned by the public official with regulatory oversight to the trustee for distribution in accordance with the trust agreement.

    d.   The grantor shall waive any right otherwise available to it under United States law that is inconsistent with this provision.

(c)   This section applies to all reinsurance cessions made on or after January 1, 1992, under reinsurance agreements that have an inception, anniversary, or renewal date on or after January 1, 1992. (1991, c. 681, s. 22; 1993, c. 452, s. 42; 1993 (Reg. Sess., 1994), c. 678, s. 8; 1995, c. 193, s. 13; c. 360, s. 2(g); 2001-223, s. 3.1; 2009-451, s. 21.15(a).)

§ 58-7-25: Repealed by Session Laws 1991, c. 681, s. 23.

§ 58-7-26. Asset or reduction from liability for reinsurance ceded by a domestic insurer to an assuming insurer not meeting the requirements of G.S. 58-7-21.

(a)   An asset or a reduction from liability for reinsurance ceded by a domestic insurer to an assuming insurer not meeting the requirements of G.S. 58-7-21 shall be allowed in an amount not exceeding the liabilities carried by the ceding insurer. The reduction shall be in the amount of funds held by or on behalf of the ceding insurer, including funds held in trust for the ceding insurer, under a reinsurance contract with the assuming insurer as security for the payment of obligations thereunder, if the security is held in the United States subject to withdrawal solely by, and under the exclusive control of, the ceding insurer; or, in the case of a trust, held in a qualified United States financial institution as defined in subsection (c) of this section. This security may be in the form of:

(1)   Cash;

(2)   Securities that are listed by the Securities Valuation Office of the NAIC and qualifying as admitted assets;

(3)   Clean, irrevocable, unconditional letters of credit, issued or confirmed by a qualified United States financial institution, as defined in subsection (b) of this section, effective no later than December 31 of the year for which the filing is

being made, and in the possession of, or in trust for, the ceding company on or before the filing date of its annual statement. Letters of credit meeting applicable standards of issuer acceptability as of the dates of their issuance (or confirmation) shall, notwithstanding the issuing (or confirming) institution's subsequent failure to meet applicable standards of issuer acceptability, continue to be acceptable as security until their expiration, extension, renewal, modification or amendment, whichever occurs first; or

(4) Any other form of security acceptable to the Commissioner.

(b) For purposes of subdivision (a)(3) of this section, a "qualified United States financial institution" means an institution that:

(1) Is organized, or in the case of a United States office of a foreign banking organization licensed, under the laws of the United States or any of its states;

(2) Is regulated, supervised, and examined by United States federal or state authorities having regulatory authority over banks and trust companies; and

(3) Has been determined by either the Commissioner or the Securities Valuation Office of the NAIC to meet such standards of financial condition and standing as are considered necessary and appropriate to regulate the quality of financial institutions whose letters of credit will be acceptable to the Commissioner.

(c) A "qualified United States financial institution" means, for purposes of those provisions of this section specifying those institutions that are eligible to act as a fiduciary of a trust, an institution that:

(1) Is organized, or in the case of a United States branch or agency office of a foreign banking organization licensed, under the laws of the United States or any of its states and has been granted authority to operate with fiduciary powers; and

(2) Is regulated, supervised, and examined by federal or state authorities having regulatory authority over banks and trust companies.

(d) This section applies to all reinsurance cessions made on or after January 1, 1992, under reinsurance agreements that have an inception, anniversary, or renewal date on or after January 1, 1992. (1991, c. 681, s. 22; 2001-223, s. 3.2; 2006-105, s. 1.3.)

§ 58-7-30. Insolvent ceding insurer.

(a) Notwithstanding any other provision of this Article, no credit shall be allowed, as an admitted asset or as a reduction from liability, to any ceding insurer for reinsurance, unless the reinsurance is payable by the assuming insurer, on the basis of reported claims allowed by the court overseeing the liquidation against the ceding insurer under the contract or contracts reinsured without diminution because of the insolvency of the ceding insurer, directly to the ceding insurer or to its domiciliary receiver except (1) where the contract or other written agreement specifically provides for another payee of the reinsurance in the event of the insolvency of the ceding insurer or (2) where the assuming insurer, with the consent of the direct insured or insureds, has assumed the policy obligations of the ceding insurer as direct obligations of the assuming insurer to the payees under the policies and in substitution of the obligations of the ceding insurer to the payees.

(b) No credit shall be allowed, as an admitted asset or as a reduction from liability, to any ceding insurer for reinsurance, unless the reinsurance is documented by a policy, certificate, treaty, or other form of agreement that is properly executed by an authorized officer of the assuming insurer. If the reinsurance is ceded through an underwriting manager or agent, the manager or agent shall provide to the domestic ceding insurer evidence of the manager or agent's authority to assume reinsurance for and on behalf of the assuming insurer. The evidence shall consist of either an acceptable letter of authority executed by an authorized officer of the assuming insurer or a copy of the actual agency agreement between the underwriting manager or agent and the assuming insurer; and the evidence shall be specific as to the classes of business within the authority and as to the term of the authority. If there is any conflict between this subsection and Article 9 of this Chapter, the provisions of Article 9 govern.

(c) The reinsurance agreement may provide that the domiciliary liquidator of an insolvent ceding insurer shall give written notice to the assuming insurer of the pendency of a claim against the ceding insurer on the contract reinsured within a reasonable time after the claim is filed in the liquidation proceeding. During the pendency of the claim, any assuming insurer may investigate the claim and interpose at its own expense in the proceeding where the claim is to be adjudicated, any defenses which it deems available to the ceding insurer or its liquidator. The expense may be filed as a claim against the insolvent ceding insurer to the extent of a proportionate share of the benefit which may accrue to the ceding insurer solely as a result of the defense undertaken by the assuming insurer. Where two or more assuming insurers are involved in the same claim and a majority in interest elect to interpose a defense to the claim, the expense shall be apportioned in accordance with the terms of the reinsurance agreement as though the expense had been incurred by the ceding insurer. (1985, c. 572, s. 1; 1995, c. 193, s. 14; c. 517, s. 4; 2001-223, s. 3.3.)

§ 58-7-31. Life and health reinsurance agreements.

(a)   Notwithstanding any other provision of this Article, this section applies to every domestic life and accident and health insurer, to every other licensed life and accident and health insurer that is not subject to a substantially similar statute or administrative rule in its domiciliary state, and to every licensed property and casualty insurer with respect to its accident and health business. This section does not apply to assumption reinsurance, yearly renewable term reinsurance, nor to certain nonproportional reinsurance, such as stop loss or catastrophe reinsurance.

(b)   No insurer shall, for reinsurance ceded, reduce any liability or establish any asset in any financial statement filed with the Commissioner if, by the terms of the reinsurance agreement, in substance or effect, any of the following conditions exist:

(1)   Renewal expense allowances provided or to be provided to the ceding insurer by the reinsurer in any accounting period, are not sufficient to cover anticipated allocable renewal expenses of the ceding insurer on the portion of the business reinsured, unless a liability is established for the present value of the shortfall, using assumptions equal to the applicable statutory reserve basis on the business reinsured. Those expenses include commissions, premium taxes, and direct expenses including, but not limited to, billing, valuation, claims, and maintenance expected by the company at the time the business is reinsured.

(2)   The ceding insurer can be deprived of surplus or assets at the reinsurer's option or automatically upon the occurrence of some event, such as the insolvency of the ceding insurer; except that termination of the reinsurance agreement by the reinsurer for nonpayment of reinsurance premiums or other

amounts due, such as modified coinsurance reserve adjustments, interest, and adjustments on funds withheld, and tax reimbursements, are not a deprivation of surplus or assets.

(3) The ceding insurer is required to reimburse the reinsurer for negative experience under the reinsurance agreement; except that neither offsetting experience refunds against current and prior years' losses under the reinsurance agreement nor payment by the ceding insurer of an amount equal to the current and prior years' losses under the reinsurance agreement upon voluntary termination of in-force reinsurance by the ceding insurer are a reimbursement to the reinsurer for negative experience. Voluntary termination does not include situations where termination occurs because of unreasonable provisions that allow the reinsurer to reduce its risk under the reinsurance agreement.

(4) The ceding insurer must, at specific points in time scheduled in the reinsurance agreement, terminate or automatically recapture all or part of the reinsurance ceded.

(5) The reinsurance agreement involves the possible payment by the ceding insurer to the reinsurer of amounts other than from income realized from the reinsured policies. No ceding company shall pay reinsurance premiums or other fees or charges to a reinsurer that are greater than the direct premiums collected by the ceding company.

(6) The treaty does not transfer all of the significant risk inherent in the business being reinsured. The following table identifies for a representative sampling of products or type of business, the risks that are considered to be significant. For products not specifically included, the risks determined to be significant shall be consistent with this table.

Risk Categories:

a.= Morbidity.

b.= Mortality.

c.= Lapse. (This is the risk that a policy will voluntarily terminate before the recoupment of a statutory surplus strain experienced at issue of the policy.)

d.= Credit Quality (C1). (This is the risk that invested assets supporting the reinsured business will decrease in value. The main hazards are that assets will default or that there will be a decrease in earning power. It excludes market value declines due to changes in interest rate.)

e.= Reinvestment (C3). (This is the risk that interest rates will fall and funds reinvested [coupon payments or monies received upon asset maturity or call] will therefore earn less than expected. If asset durations are less than liability durations, the mismatch will increase.)

f.= Disintermediation (C3). (This is the risk that interest rates will rise and policy loans and surrenders increase or maturing contracts do not renew at anticipated rates of renewal. If asset durations are greater than the liability durations, the mismatch will increase. Policyholders will move their funds into new products offering higher rates. The company may have to sell assets at a loss to provide for these withdrawals.)

+= Significant   0 = Insignificant

RISK CATEGORY	a	b	c	d	e	f
Health Insurance - other than LTC/LTD*	+	0	+	0	0	0
Health Insurance - LTC/LTD*	+	0	+	+	+	0
Immediate Annuities	0	+	0	+	+	0
Single Premium Deferred Annuities	0	0	+	+	+	+
Flexible Premium Deferred Annuities	0	0	+	+	+	+
Guaranteed Interest Contracts	0	0	0	+	+	+

+	+	+	Other Annuity Deposit Business	0	0	+
+	+	+	Single Premium Whole Life	0	+	+
+	+	+	Traditional Non-Par Permanent	0	+	+
0	0	0	Traditional Non-Par Term	0	+	+
+	+	+	Traditional Par Permanent	0	+	+
0	0	0	Traditional Par Term	0	+	+
+	+	+	Adjustable Premium Permanent	0	+	+
+	+	+	Indeterminate Premium Permanent	0	+	+
+	+	+	Universal Life Flexible Premium	0	+	+
+	+	+	Universal Life Fixed Premium	0	+	+
+	+	+	Universal Life Fixed Premium	0	+	+

(dump-in premiums allowed)

*LTC = Long-Term Care Insurance

*LTD = Long-Term Disability Insurance

(7) a. The credit quality, reinvestment, or disintermediation risk is significant for the business reinsured and the ceding company does not (other than for the classes of business excepted in subdivision (7)b. of this section) either transfer the underlying assets to the reinsurer or legally segregate such assets in a trust or escrow account or otherwise establish a mechanism satisfactory to the Commissioner that legally segregates, by contract or contractual provisions, the underlying assets.

b. Notwithstanding the requirements of subdivision (7)a. of this section, the assets supporting the reserves for the following classes of business and any classes of business that do not have a significant credit quality, reinvestment, or disintermediation risk may be held by the ceding company without segregation of those assets:

- Health Insurance - LTC/LTD

- Traditional Non-Par Permanent

- Traditional Par Permanent

- Adjustable Premium Permanent

- Indeterminate Premium Permanent

- Universal Life Fixed Premium

(no dump-in premiums allowed)

The associated formula for determining the reserve interest rate adjustment must use a formula that reflects the ceding company's investment earnings and incorporates all realized and unrealized gains and losses reflected in the statutory statement. The following is an acceptable formula:

$$\text{Rate} = \frac{2(I + CG)}{X + Y - I - CG}$$

Where: I is the net investment income.

CG is capital gains less capital losses.

X is the current year cash and invested assets plus investment income due and accrued less borrowed money.

Y is the same as X but for the prior year.

(8) Settlements are made less frequently than quarterly or payments due from the reinsurer are not made in cash within 90 days after the settlement date.

(9) The ceding insurer is required to make representations or warranties not reasonably related to the business being reinsured.

(10) The ceding insurer is required to make representations or warranties about future performance of the business being reinsured.

(11) The reinsurance agreement is entered into for the principal purpose of producing significant surplus aid for the ceding insurer, typically on a temporary basis, while not transferring all of the significant risks inherent in the business reinsured and, in substance or effect, the expected potential liability to the ceding insurer remains basically unchanged.

(c) Notwithstanding subsection (b) of this section, an insurer may, with the prior approval of the Commissioner, take such reserve credit or establish such asset as the Commissioner deems to be consistent with the insurance laws or rules of this State, including actuarial interpretations or standards adopted by the Commissioner.

(d) (1) Reinsurance agreements entered into after October 1, 1993, that involve the reinsurance of business issued prior to the effective date of the reinsurance agreements, along with any subsequent amendments thereto, shall be filed by the ceding company with the Commissioner within 30 days after its date of execution. Each filing shall include data detailing the financial impact of the transaction. The ceding insurer's actuary who signs the financial statement actuarial opinion with respect to valuation of reserves shall consider this statute and any applicable actuarial standards of practice when determining the proper credit in financial statements filed with the Commissioner. The actuary should maintain adequate documentation and be prepared upon request to describe the actuarial work performed for inclusion in the financial statements and to demonstrate that such work conforms to this statute.

(2) Any increase in surplus net of federal income tax resulting from arrangements described in subdivision (d)(1) of this section shall be identified

separately on the insurer's statutory financial statement as a surplus item (aggregate write-ins for gains and losses in surplus in the Capital and Surplus Account, page 4 of the Annual Statement) and recognition of the surplus increase as income shall be reflected on a net of tax basis in the "Reinsurance Ceded" line, page 4 of the Annual Statement as earnings emerge from the business reinsured.

(e) No reinsurance agreement or amendment to any reinsurance agreement may be used to reduce any liability or to establish any asset in any financial statement filed with the Commissioner, unless the reinsurance agreement, amendment, or a binding letter of intent has been duly executed by both parties no later than the "as of date" of the financial statement.

(f) In the case of a letter of intent, a reinsurance agreement or an amendment to a reinsurance agreement must be executed within a reasonable period of time, not exceeding 90 days after the execution date of the letter of intent, in order for credit to be granted for the reinsurance ceded.

(g) The reinsurance agreement shall contain provisions that provide that:

(1) The reinsurance agreement shall constitute the entire reinsurance agreement between the parties with respect to the business being reinsured thereunder and that there are no understandings between the parties other than as expressed in the reinsurance agreement; and

(2) Any change or modification to the reinsurance agreement shall be null and void unless made by amendment to the reinsurance agreement and signed by both parties.

(h) Insurers subject to this section shall reduce to zero by December 31, 1994, any reserve credits or assets established with respect to reinsurance agreements entered into prior to October 1, 1993, that, under the provisions of this section, would not be entitled to recognition of such reserve credits or assets; provided, however, that such reinsurance agreements shall have been in compliance with laws or regulations in existence immediately preceding October 1, 1993. (1993, c. 452, s. 4; 1993 (Reg. Sess., 1994), c. 678, s. 9; 1995, c. 193, ss. 15, 16; 2001-223, ss. 3.4, 3.5.)

§ 58-7-32: Repealed by Session Laws 1993, c. 452, s. 65.

§ 58-7-33. Minimum policyholders' surplus to assume property or casualty reinsurance.

(a)   Notwithstanding any other provision of law, no domestic property or casualty insurer with less than ten million dollars ($10,000,000) in policyholders' surplus may, without the Commissioner's prior written approval, assume reinsurance on any risk that it is otherwise permitted to assume except where the reinsurance is:

(1)   Required by applicable law or regulation; or

(2)   Assumed under pooling arrangement among members of the same holding company system.

(b)   This section applies to reinsurance contracts entered into or renewed on or after July 13, 1991.

(c)   This section does not invalidate any reinsurance contract that was entered into before July 13, 1991, as between the parties to the contract. (1991, c. 681, s. 26.)

§ 58-7-35. Manner of creating such corporations.

The procedure for organizing such corporations is as follows: The proposed incorporators, not less than 10 in number, a majority of whom must be residents of the State, shall subscribe articles of association setting forth their intention to form a corporation; its proposed name, which must not so closely resemble the name of an existing corporation doing business under the laws of this State as to be likely to mislead the public, and must be approved by the Commissioner; the class of insurance it proposes to transact and on what business plan or principle; the place of its location within the State, and if on the stock plan, the amount of its capital stock. The words "insurance company," "insurance association," or "insurance society" or "life" or "casualty" or "indemnity," or an acceptable alternative approved by the Commissioner, must be a part of the title of any such corporation. The certificate of incorporation must be subscribed and sworn to by the incorporators before an officer authorized to take acknowledgment of deeds, who shall forthwith certify the certificate of incorporation, as so made out and signed, to the Commissioner at his office in the City of Raleigh. The Commissioner shall examine the certificate, and if he approves of it and finds that the requirements of the law have been complied with, shall certify such facts, by certificate on such articles, to the Secretary of State. Upon the filing in the office of the Secretary of State of the certificate of incorporation and attached certificates, and the payment of a charter fee in the amount required for private corporations, and the same fees to the Secretary of State, the Secretary of State shall cause the certificate and accompanying certificates to be recorded in his office, and shall issue a certificate in the following form:

Be it known that, whereas (here the names of the subscribers to the articles of association shall be inserted) have associated themselves with the intention of forming a corporation under the name of (here the name of the corporation shall be inserted), for the purpose (here the purpose declared in the articles of association shall be inserted), with a capital (or with a permanent fund) of (here the amount of capital or permanent fund fixed in the articles of association shall be inserted), and have complied with the provisions of the statute of this State in such case made and provided, as appears from the following certified articles of association: (here copy articles of association and accompanying certificates). Now, therefore, I (here the name of the Secretary shall be inserted), Secretary of State, hereby certify that (here the names of the subscribers to the articles of association shall be inserted), their associates and successors, are legally organized and established as, and are hereby made, an existing corporation under the name of (here the name of the corporation shall be inserted), with such articles of association, and have all the powers, rights, and privileges and are subject to the duties, liabilities, and restrictions which by law appertain thereto.

Witness my official signature hereunto subscribed, and the seal of the State of North Carolina hereunto affixed, this the _____ day of_____, in the year ____ (in these blanks the day, month, and year of execution of this certificate shall be inserted; and in the case of purely mutual companies, so much as relates to capital stock shall be omitted).

The Secretary of State shall sign the certificate and cause the seal of the State to be affixed to it, and such certificate of incorporation and certificate of the Secretary of State has the effect of a special charter and is conclusive evidence of the organization and establishment of the corporation. The Secretary of State shall also cause a record of his certificate to be made, and a certified copy of this record may be given in evidence with the same effect as the original certificate.

Subject to G.S. 58-8-5, any proposed change in the articles of incorporation shall be filed with the Commissioner, who shall examine the change. If the Commissioner approves the change, the Commissioner shall place a certificate of approval on the change, and forward it to the Secretary of State. (1899, c. 54, s. 25; 1903, c. 438, ss. 2, 3; Rev., s. 4727; C.S., s. 6328; 1957, c. 98; 1987 (Reg. Sess., 1988), c. 975, s. 15; 1989, c. 485, s. 50; 1991, c. 720, ss. 4, 53; 1993, c. 504, s. 4.)

§ 58-7-37. Background of incorporators and proposed management personnel.

(a) Before a license is issued to a new domestic insurance company, each key person must furnish the Commissioner a complete set of the applicant's fingerprints. The applicant's fingerprints shall be certified by an authorized law enforcement officer. The fingerprints of every applicant shall be forwarded to the State Bureau of Investigation for a search of the applicant's criminal history record file, if any. If warranted, the State Bureau of Investigation shall forward a set of the fingerprints to the Federal Bureau of Investigation for a national criminal history record check. An applicant shall pay the cost of the State and any national criminal history record check of the applicant.

(b) As used in this section, "key person" means a proposed officer, director, or any other individual who will be in a position to influence the operating decisions of a domestic insurance company.

(c) The Commissioner may refuse to approve the formation or initial license of a new domestic insurance company under this Article if, after notice to the applicant and an opportunity for a hearing, the Commissioner finds as to the incorporators or other key person any one or more of the following conditions:

(1) Any untrue material statement regarding the background or experience of any incorporator or other key person;

(2) Violation of, or noncompliance with, any insurance laws, or of any rule or order of the Commissioner or of a commissioner of another state by any incorporator or other key person;

(3) Obtaining or attempting to obtain the license through misrepresentation or fraud;

(4) An incorporator or other key person has been convicted of a felony;

(5) An incorporator or other key person has been found to have committed any unfair trade practice or fraud;

(6) An incorporator or other key person has used fraudulent, coercive, or dishonest practices, or has acted in a manner that is incompetent, untrustworthy, or financially irresponsible; or

(7) An incorporator or other key person has held such a position in another insurance company that has had its license suspended or revoked by any state.

(d) If the Commissioner disapproves of the formation or initial license, the Commissioner shall notify the applicant and advise the applicant in writing of the reasons for the disapproval. Within 30 days after receipt of notification, the applicant may make written demand upon the Commissioner for a hearing to determine the reasonableness of the Commissioner's action. The hearing shall be scheduled within 30 days after the date of receipt of the written demand.

(e) For the purposes of investigation under this section, the Commissioner shall have all the power conferred by G.S. 58-2-50 and other applicable provisions of this Chapter.

(f) The Commissioner may adopt rules to set standards for obtaining background information on each incorporator or other key person of a proposed new domestic insurance company. (2001-223, s. 4.1; 2013-199, s. 2.)

§ 58-7-40. First meeting; organization; license.

The first meeting for the purpose of organization under such charter shall be called by a notice signed by one or more of the subscribers to the certificate of incorporation, stating the time, place, and purpose of the meeting; and at least seven days before the appointed time a copy of this notice shall be given to each subscriber, left at his usual place of business or residence, or duly mailed to his post-office address, unless the signers waive notice in writing. Whoever gives the notice must make affidavit thereof, which affidavit shall include a copy of the notice and be entered upon the records of the corporation. At the first meeting, or any adjournment thereof, an organization shall be effected by the choice of a temporary clerk, who shall be sworn; by the adoption of bylaws; and by the election of directors and such other officers as the bylaws require; but at this meeting no person may be elected director who has not signed the certificate of incorporation. The temporary clerk shall record the proceedings until the election and qualification of the secretary. The directors so chosen shall elect a president, secretary, and other officers which under the bylaws they are so authorized to choose. The president, secretary, and a majority of the directors shall forthwith make, sign, and swear to a certificate setting forth a copy of the certificate of incorporation, with the names of the subscribers thereto, the date of the first meeting and of any adjournments thereof, and shall submit such certificate and the records of the corporation to the Commissioner of Insurance, who shall examine the same, and who may require such other evidence as he deems necessary. If upon his examination the Commissioner of Insurance approves of the bylaws and finds that the requirements of the law have been complied with, he shall issue a license to the company to do business in the State, as is provided for in this Chapter. (1899, c. 54, s. 25; 1903, c. 438, ss. 2, 3; Rev., s. 4728; C.S., s. 6329.)

§ 58-7-45. Bylaws; classification and election of directors; amendments.

(a) A domestic company may adopt bylaws for the conduct of its business that are not repugnant to law or its articles of incorporation and therein provide for the division of its board of directors into two, three, or four classes, and the election thereof at its annual meetings so that the members of one class only shall retire and their successors be chosen each year. Vacancies in any such class may be filled by election by the board for the unexpired term.

(b) Any change in the bylaws of a domestic company shall be promptly filed with the Commissioner. (1899, c. 54, s. 22; Rev., s. 4724; C.S., s. 6330; 1993, c. 504, s. 5.)

§ 58-7-46. Notification to Commissioner for president or chief executive officer changes.

All domestic insurers organized under the laws of this Chapter shall provide the Commissioner written notice of any change that occurs in the position of president or chief executive officer of the insurer no later than 30 days after the change. Notice shall include the name of the insurer, the name of the person previously holding the position of president or chief executive officer, the name of the person currently holding the position, and the date the position change took place. (2005-215, s. 6.)

§ 58-7-50. Maintenance and removal of records and assets.

(a)   Every domestic insurer shall maintain its home or principal office in this State and keep therein complete records of its assets, transactions, and affairs, specifically including:

(1)   Financial records;

(2)   Corporate records;

(3)   Reinsurance documents;

(4)   All accounting transactions;

(5)   Claim files; and

(6)   Payment of claims, in accordance with such methods and systems as are customary or suitable as to the kind or kinds of insurance transacted.

(b)   Every domestic insurer shall have and maintain its assets in this State, except as to:

(1)   Real property and personal property appurtenant thereto lawfully owned by the insurer and located outside this State; and

(2)   Such property of the insurer as may be customary, necessary, and convenient to enable and facilitate the operation of its branch offices, regional home offices, and operations offices, located outside this State as referred to in G.S. 58-7-55.

(c) The removal from this State of all or a part of the records or assets of a domestic insurer except pursuant to a plan of merger or consolidation approved by the Commissioner or for such reasonable purposes and periods of time as may be approved by the Commissioner in writing in advance of such removal, or concealment of such records or assets or part thereof from the Commissioner is prohibited. Any person who, without the prior approval of the Commissioner, removes or attempts to remove such records or assets or part thereof from the office or offices in which they are required to be kept and maintained under subsection (a) of this section or who conceals or attempts to conceal such records from the Commissioner, in violation of this subsection, shall be guilty of a Class I felony. Upon any removal or attempted removal of such records or assets or upon retention of such records or assets or part thereof outside this State, beyond the period therefor specified in the consent of the Commissioner under which consent the records were so removed thereat, or upon concealment of or attempt to conceal records or assets in violation of this section, the Commissioner may institute delinquency proceedings against the insurer pursuant to the provisions of Article 30 of this Chapter.

(d) This section is subject to the exceptions provided in G.S. 58-7-55. The Commissioner may allow a domestic insurer to maintain certain records or assets outside this State.

(e) Every domestic insurer that has its home or principal office in a location outside this State on October 1, 1993, shall petition the Commissioner for approval to continue to operate in that manner. The Commissioner, in determining whether to approve or disapprove the petition, shall consider the exceptions of G.S. 58-7-55, as well as any other factors that might affect the Commissioner's ability to regulate the insurer, or that might affect the insurer's ability to service or protect its policyholders. (1985 (Reg. Sess., 1986), c. 1013, s. 7; 1989, c. 452, s. 3; 1993, c. 452, s. 5; c. 539, s. 1270; 1994, Ex. Sess., c. 24, s. 14(c); 1998-212, s. 26B(a).)

§ 58-7-55. Exceptions to requirements of G.S. 58-7-50.

The provisions of G.S. 58-7-50 shall not be deemed to prohibit or prevent an insurer from:

(1) Establishing and maintaining branch offices or regional home offices in other states where necessary or convenient to the transaction of its business

and keeping therein the detailed records and assets customary and reasonably necessary for the servicing of its insurance in force and affairs in the territory served by such an office, as long as such records and assets are made readily available at such office for examination by the Commissioner at his request.

(2)   Having, depositing, or transmitting funds and assets of the insurer in or to jurisdictions outside this State as required by other jurisdictions as a condition of transacting insurance in such jurisdictions reasonably and customarily required in the regular course of its business.

(3)   Establishing and maintaining its principal operations offices, its usual operations records, and such of its assets as may be necessary or convenient for the purpose, in another state in which the insurer is authorized to transact insurance in order that general administration of its affairs may be combined with that of an affiliated insurer or insurers, but subject to the following conditions:

a.   That the Commissioner consents in writing to such removal of offices, records, and assets from this State upon evidence satisfactory to him that the same will facilitate and make more economical the operations of the insurer, and will not unreasonably diminish the service or protection thereafter to be given the insurer's policyholders in this State and elsewhere;

b.   That the insurer will continue to maintain in this State its principal corporate office or place of business, and maintain therein available to the inspection of the Commissioner complete records of its corporate proceedings and a copy of each financial statement of the insurer current within the preceding five years, including a copy of each interim financial statement prepared for the information of the insurer's officers or directors;

c.   That, upon the written request of the Commissioner, the insurer will with reasonable promptness produce at its principal corporate offices in this State for examination or for subpoena, its records or copies thereof relative to a particular transaction or transactions of the insurer as designated by the Commissioner in his request; and

d.   That if at any time the Commissioner finds that the conditions justifying the maintenance of such offices, records, and assets outside of this State no longer exist, or that the insurer has willfully and knowingly violated any of the conditions stated in sub-subdivisions b. and c., the Commissioner may order the return of such offices, records, and assets to this State within such reasonable time, not less than six months, as may be specified in the order; and that for failure to comply with such order, as thereafter modified or extended, if any, the Commissioner shall suspend or revoke the insurer's license.

(4)   Placing its investment assets in one or more custodial accounts inside or outside of this State with banks, trust companies, or other similar institutions pursuant to custodial agreements approved by the Commissioner.

(5)   Permitting policyholder and certificate holder records and claims and other information to be kept and maintained by agents, general agents, third-party administrators, creditors, employers, associations, and others in the ordinary course of business in a manner customary or suitable to the kind or kinds of insurance transacted; provided, however, that the insurer shall, upon reasonable notice, make available to the Commissioner or his designee any records or other information permitted by this subsection to be maintained outside this State. (1985 (Reg. Sess., 1986), c. 1013, s. 7; 1999-132, s. 9.1.)

§ 58-7-60. Approval as a domestic insurer.

Any insurer that is organized under the laws of any other state and is licensed to transact the business of insurance in this State may become a domestic insurer by (i) complying with laws and regulations regarding the organization and licensing of a domestic insurer of the same type; (ii) designating its principal place of business at a place in this State; and (iii) obtaining the approval of the Commissioner. Such domestic insurer shall be entitled to like certificates of authority to transact business in this State and shall be subject to the authority and jurisdiction of this State. Articles of Incorporation of such domestic insurer may be amended to provide that the corporation is a continuation of the corporate existence of the original foreign corporation through adoption of this State as its corporate domicile and that the original date of incorporation in its original domicilliary state is the date of incorporation of such domestic insurer. (1987, c. 752, s. 10.)

§ 58-7-65. Conversion to foreign insurer.

Any domestic insurer may, upon the approval of the Commissioner, transfer its domicile to any other state in which it is licensed to transact the business of insurance. Upon such a transfer such insurer shall cease to be a domestic insurer and shall be licensed in this State, if qualified, as a foreign insurer. The Commissioner shall approve any such proposed transfer unless he determines that such transfer is not in the interest of the policyholders of this State. (1987, c. 752, s. 10.)

§ 58-7-70. Effects of redomestication.

The license, agent appointments and licenses, rates, and other items that the Commissioner authorizes or grants, in his discretion, that are in existence at the time any insurer licensed by the Commissioner transfers its corporate domicile to this or any other state by merger, consolidation, or any other lawful method, shall continue in full force and effect upon the transfer if the insurer remains duly licensed by the Commissioner. All outstanding policies of any transferring insurer shall remain in full force and effect and need not be endorsed as to any new name of the insurer or its new location unless so ordered by the Commissioner. Every transferring insurer shall file new policy forms with the Commissioner on or before the effective date of the transfer, but may use existing policy forms with appropriate endorsements if allowed by, and under such conditions as approved by, the Commissioner: Provided, however, every such transferring insurer shall (i) notify the Commissioner of the details of the proposed transfer and (ii) promptly file any resulting amendments to corporate documents filed or required to be filed with the Commissioner. (1987, c. 752, s. 10; 1999-132, s. 9.1; 2000-140, s. 11; 2001-223, s. 4.2.)

§ 58-7-73. Dissolutions of insurers.

Upon reaching a determination of intent to dissolve and before filing articles of dissolution with the Office of the Secretary of State, a domestic insurer organized under this Chapter shall file a plan of dissolution for approval by the Commissioner. At such time the Commissioner may restrict the license of the insurer. In order to proceed with a dissolution, the plan must be approved by the Commissioner. (2002-187, s. 2.4.)

§ 58-7-75. Amount of capital and/or surplus required; impairment of capital or surplus.

The amount of capital and/or surplus requisite to the formation and organization of companies under the provisions of Articles 1 through 64 of this Chapter shall be as follows:

(1) Stock Life Insurance Companies. - A stock corporation may be organized in the manner prescribed in this Chapter and licensed to do the business of life insurance, only when it has paid-in capital of at least six hundred thousand dollars ($600,000) and a paid-in initial surplus of at least nine hundred thousand dollars ($900,000), and it may in addition do the kind of business specified in G.S. 58-7-15(2), without having additional capital or surplus. Every such company shall at all times thereafter maintain a minimum capital of not less than six hundred thousand dollars ($600,000) and a minimum surplus of at least one hundred fifty thousand dollars ($150,000). Provided that, any such corporation may do either or both of the kinds of insurance authorized for stock accident and health insurance companies, as set out in G.S. 58-7-15(3)a. and b., where its charter so permits, and only as long as it maintains a minimum capital and surplus equal to the sum of the minimum capital and surplus requirements of this subdivision and the minimum capital and surplus requirements of subdivision (2) of this section.

(1a) Non-Stock Life Insurance Companies. - A nonstock corporation, not inclusive of a corporation organized pursuant to subdivision (6) of this section, may be organized in the manner prescribed in this Chapter and licensed to do the business of life insurance, only when it has a paid in initial surplus of at least one million five hundred thousand dollars ($1,500,000) and it may in addition do the kind of business specified in G.S. 58-7-15(2), without having additional surplus. Every such corporation shall at all times thereafter maintain a minimum surplus of at least seven hundred fifty thousand dollars ($750,000). Provided that, any such corporation may conduct the kind of insurance authorized for stock accident and health insurance companies, as set out in G.S. 58-7-15(3)a. and b., where its charter so permits, and only as long as it maintains a minimum surplus equal to the sum of the minimum surplus requirements of this subdivision and the minimum surplus requirements of subdivision (2a) of this section.

(2) Stock Accident and Health Insurance Companies.

a. A stock corporation may be organized in the manner prescribed in this Chapter and licensed to do only the kind of insurance specified in G.S. 58-7-15(3)a, when it has paid-in capital of not less than four hundred thousand dollars ($400,000), and a paid-in initial surplus of at least six hundred thousand dollars ($600,000). Every such company shall at all times thereafter maintain a minimum capital of not less than four hundred thousand dollars ($400,000) and a minimum surplus of at least one hundred thousand dollars ($100,000).

b. Any company organized under the provisions of paragraph a of this subdivision may, by the provisions of its original charter or any amendment thereto, acquire the power to do the kind of business specified in G.S. 58-7-15(3)b, if it has a paid-in capital of at least six hundred thousand dollars ($600,000) and a paid-in initial surplus of at least nine hundred thousand dollars ($900,000). Every such company shall at all times maintain a minimum capital of not less than six hundred thousand dollars ($600,000) and a minimum surplus of at least one hundred fifty thousand dollars ($150,000).

(2a) Non-Stock Accident and Health Insurance Companies.

a. A non-stock corporation, not inclusive of a corporation organized pursuant to subdivision (6) of this section, may be organized in the manner prescribed in this Chapter and licensed to do only the kind of insurance specified in G.S. 58-7-15(3)a. when it has a paid in initial surplus of at least one million dollars ($1,000,000). Every such corporation shall at all times thereafter maintain a minimum surplus of at least five hundred thousand dollars ($500,000).

b. Any non-stock corporation organized under the provisions of sub-subdivision a. of this subdivision may, by the provisions of its original charter or any amendment thereto, acquire the power to do the kind of business specified in G.S. 58-7-15(3)b., if it has a paid-in initial surplus of at least one million five hundred thousand dollars ($1,500,000). Every such corporation shall at all times maintain a minimum surplus of at least seven hundred fifty thousand dollars ($750,000).

(3) Stock Fire and Marine Companies. - A stock corporation may be organized in the manner prescribed in this Chapter and licensed to do one or more of the kinds of insurance specified in G.S. 58-7-15 (4), (5), (6), (7), (8), (11), (12), (19), (20), (21) and (22) only when it has a paid-in capital of not less than eight hundred thousand dollars ($800,000) and a paid-in initial surplus of not less than one million two hundred thousand dollars ($1,200,000). Every

such company shall at all times thereafter maintain a minimum capital of not less than eight hundred thousand dollars ($800,000) and a minimum surplus of at least two hundred thousand dollars ($200,000). Provided that, any such corporation may do all the kinds of insurance authorized for casualty, fidelity and surety companies, as set out in subdivision (4) of this section where its charter so permits, and when and so long as it meets and thereafter maintains a minimum capital and surplus equal to the sum of the minimum capital and surplus requirements of this subdivision and the minimum capital and surplus requirements of subdivision (4) of this section.

(4) Stock Casualty and Fidelity and Surety Companies. - A stock corporation may be organized in the manner prescribed in this Chapter and licensed to do one or more of the kinds of insurance specified in G.S. 58-7-15 (3), (6), (7), (8), (9), (10), (11), (12), (13), (14), (15), (16), (17), (18), (19), (21), (22), and (23) only when it has a paid-in capital of not less than one million dollars ($1,000,000) and a paid-in initial surplus of not less than one million five hundred thousand dollars ($1,500,000). Every such company shall at all times thereafter maintain a minimum capital of not less than one million dollars ($1,000,000) and a minimum surplus of at least two hundred fifty thousand dollars ($250,000).

(5) Mutual Fire and Marine Companies.

a. Limited assessment companies. - A limited assessment mutual company may be organized in the manner prescribed in this Chapter and licensed to do one or more kinds of insurance specified in G.S. 58-7-15 (4), (5), (6), (7), (8), (11), (12), (19), (20), (21) and (22) only when it has no less than five hundred thousand dollars ($500,000) of insurance in not fewer than 500 separate risks subscribed with a paid-in initial surplus of at least three hundred thousand dollars ($300,000), which surplus shall at all times be maintained. The assessment liability of a policyholder of a company organized in accordance with the provisions of this sub-subdivision shall not be limited to less than five annual premiums; provided, the limited assessment company may reduce the assessment liability of its policyholders from such five annual premiums to one additional annual premium when the free surplus of the company amounts to not less than three hundred thousand dollars ($300,000), which surplus shall at all times be maintained.

b. Assessable mutual companies. - An assessable mutual company may be organized in the manner prescribed in this Chapter and licensed to do one or more of the kinds of insurance specified in G.S. 58-7-15 (4), (5) and (6), with an unlimited assessment liability of its policyholders only when it has not less than five hundred thousand dollars ($500,000) of insurance in not fewer than 500 separate risks subscribed with a paid-in initial surplus equal to twice the amount of the maximum net retained liability under the largest policy of insurance issued by the company; but not less than sixty thousand dollars ($60,000); which surplus shall at all times be maintained. Provided the company, when its charter so permits, in addition may be licensed to do one or more of the kinds of insurance specified in G.S. 58-7-15 (7), (8), (11), (12), (19), (20), (21) and (22), with an unlimited assessment liability of its policyholders, when its free surplus amounts to not less than sixty thousand dollars ($60,000), which surplus shall at all times be maintained.

c. Nonassessable mutual companies. - A nonassessable mutual company may be organized in the manner prescribed in this Chapter and licensed to do one or more of the kinds of insurance specified in G.S. 58-7-15 (4), (5), (6), (7), (8), (11), (12), (19), (20), (21) and (22) and may be authorized to issue policies under the terms of which a policyholder is not liable for any assessments in addition to the premium set out in the policy only when it has not less than five hundred thousand dollars ($500,000) of insurance in not fewer than 500 separate risks subscribed with a paid-in initial surplus of not less than eight hundred thousand dollars ($800,000), which surplus shall at all times be maintained.

d. Town or county mutual insurance companies. - A town or county mutual insurance company with unlimited assessment liability may be organized in the manner prescribed in this Chapter and licensed to do the kinds of insurance specified in G.S. 58-7-15(4) only when it has not less than fifty thousand dollars ($50,000) of insurance in force in not fewer than 50 separate risks subscribed with a paid-in initial surplus of not less than fifteen thousand dollars ($15,000), which surplus shall at all times be maintained. A town or county mutual insurance company may, in addition to writing the business specified in G.S. 58-7-15(4) cover in the same policy the hazards usually insured against under an extended coverage endorsement when the company has not less than five hundred thousand dollars ($500,000) of insurance in force in not fewer than 500 separate risks and maintains a surplus at all times of not less than one hundred twenty thousand dollars ($120,000): Provided, that the company may not operate in more than six adjacent counties in this State. Any company authorized under this section before July 1, 1991, shall be permitted to continue to do the same kinds of business that it was authorized to do prior to July 1, 1991, without being required to increase its surplus; however, the insurer shall increase its surplus to the required amounts on or before July 1, 1992. The requirements of this sub-subdivision as to surplus shall apply to such companies as a prerequisite to writing additional lines of business, and to such companies as a prerequisite to commencing business if unlicensed prior to July 1, 1991.

(6) Mutual Life, Accident and Health Insurance Companies. - A nonassessable mutual insurance company may be organized in the manner prescribed in this Chapter, and licensed to do only one or more of the kinds of insurance specified in G.S. 58-7-15 (1), (2) and (3) when it has complied with the requirements of this Chapter and with those set forth in sub-subdivisions a through d of this subdivision, inclusive, whichever shall be applicable.

a. If organized to do only the kinds of insurance specified in G.S. 58-7-15 (1) and (2) the company shall have not less than 500 bona fide applications for life insurance in an aggregate amount not less than five hundred thousand dollars ($500,000), and shall have received from each such applicant in cash the full amount of one annual premium on the policy for which the applicant applied, in an aggregate amount at least equal to ten thousand dollars ($10,000), and shall in addition have a paid-in initial surplus of two hundred thousand dollars ($200,000), and shall have and maintain at all times a minimum surplus of one hundred thousand dollars ($100,000).

b. If organized to do only the kind of insurance specified in paragraph a of G.S. 58-7-15(3) the company shall have not less than 250 bona fide applications for that insurance, and shall have received from each applicant in cash the full amount of one annual premium on the policy for which the applicant applied, in an aggregate amount of at least ten thousand dollars ($10,000), and shall have a paid-in initial surplus of two hundred thousand dollars ($200,000) and shall have and maintain at all times a minimum surplus of one hundred thousand dollars ($100,000).

c. If organized to do the kinds of insurance specified in G.S. 58-7-15 (1) and (3)a, the company shall have complied with the provisions of sub-subdivisions a and b of this subdivision.

d. If organized to do the kind of insurance specified in G.S. 58-7-15(3)b, in addition to the kind or kinds of insurance designated in any one of the preceding sub-subdivisions of this subdivision, the company shall have a paid-in initial surplus of at least five hundred thousand dollars ($500,000) and shall maintain a minimum surplus of at least three hundred thousand dollars ($300,000).

(7) Organization of Mutual Casualty, Fidelity and Surety Companies.

a. Nonassessable, mutual companies. - A mutual insurance company with no assessment liability provided for its policyholders may be organized in the manner prescribed in this Chapter and licensed to do one or more of the kinds of insurance specified in G.S. 58-7-15 (3), (6), (7), (8), (9), (10), (11), (12), (13), (14), (15), (16), (17), (18), (19), (21) and (22) when it has a minimum paid-in initial surplus of one million dollars ($1,000,000) and not less than five hundred thousand dollars ($500,000) in insurance subscribed in not less than 500 separate risks. The surplus of the company shall at all times be maintained at or above that amount.

b. Assessable mutual companies. - A mutual insurance company with assessment liability provided for its policyholders may be organized in the manner prescribed in this Chapter and licensed to do one or more of the kinds of insurance specified in G.S. 58-7-15 (3), (6), (7), (8), (9), (10), (11), (12), (13), (14), (15), (16), (17), (18), (19), (21) and (22) when it has a minimum paid-in initial surplus of four hundred thousand dollars ($400,000) and not less than five hundred thousand dollars ($500,000) of insurance subscribed in not less than 500 separate risks. The company shall at all times maintain a surplus in an amount not less than four hundred thousand dollars ($400,000). The assessment liability of a policyholder of the company shall not be limited to less than one annual premium.

(8) Organization of Mutual Multiple Line Companies.

a. Assessable mutual companies. - A company may do all the kinds of insurance authorized to be done by a company organized under the provisions of sub-subdivision (5)a, and sub-subdivision (7)b of this subdivision, where its charter so permits when and if it meets the combined minimum requirements of those sub-subdivisions. The assessment liability of policyholders of such a company shall not be limited to less than one annual premium within any one policy year.

b. Nonassessable mutual companies. - A company may do all the kinds of insurance authorized to be done by a company organized under the provisions of sub-subdivision (5)c, and sub-subdivision (7)a of this subdivision, where its charter so permits when and if it meets the combined minimum requirements of those paragraphs. The policyholders of such a company shall not be subject to any assessment liability.

(9) Repealed by Session Laws 1991, c. 644, s. 32.

(10) Impairment of Capital and/or Surplus. - Whenever the Commissioner finds from a financial statement made by any company, or from a report of examination of any company, that its admitted assets are less than the aggregate amount of its liabilities and its outstanding capital stock, required minimum surplus, or both, the Commissioner shall determine, in accordance with G.S. 58-2-165 and other applicable provisions of this Chapter, the amount of the impairment of capital, surplus, or both and issue an order in writing requiring the company to eliminate the impairment within such period of not more than 90 days as the Commissioner shall designate. The Commissioner may, by order served upon the company, prohibit the company from issuing any new policies while the impairment exists. If at the expiration of the designated period the company has not satisfied the Commissioner that the impairment has been eliminated, an order for the rehabilitation or liquidation of the company may be entered as provided in Article 30 of this Chapter.

(11) The Commissioner may require an insurer to have and maintain a larger amount of capital or surplus than prescribed in this section, based upon the volume and kinds of insurance transacted by the insurer and on the principles of risk-based capital as determined by the NAIC or the Commissioner. (1899, c. 54, s. 26; 1903, c. 438, s. 4; Rev., s. 4729; 1907, c. 1000, s. 5; 1913, c. 140, s. 2; C.S., s. 6332; 1929, c. 284, s. 1; 1945, c. 386; 1947, c. 721; 1963, c. 943; 1965, c. 947; 1967, c. 300; 1971, c. 536; 1973, c. 686; 1979, c. 421, s. 1; 1983, c. 472; 1985, c. 666, s. 75; 1985 (Reg. Sess., 1986), c. 1013, s. 10; 1989, c. 485, s. 53; 1991, c. 644, s. 32; c. 681, s. 27; 1995, c. 193, s. 17; 2001-223, s. 5.1; 2007-127, s. 4; 2008-124, s. 2.6.)

§ 58-7-80. Capital stock fully paid in cash.

The capital stock shall be paid in cash within 12 months from the date of the charter or certificate of organization, and no certificate of full shares and no policies may be issued until the whole capital is paid in. A majority of the directors shall certify on oath that the money has been paid by the stockholders for their respective shares and is held as the capital of the company invested or to be invested as required by G.S. 58-7-75. (1899, c. 54, s. 27; Rev., s. 4730; C.S., s. 6333; 1945, c. 386.)

§§ 58-7-85 through 58-7-90: Repealed by Session Laws 1991, c. 681, s. 30.

§ 58-7-95. Establishment of separate accounts by life insurance companies.

(a) When used in this section, "variable contract" shall mean any individual or group contract issued by an insurance company providing for life insurance or annuity benefits or contractual payments or values which vary so as to reflect investment results of any segregated portfolio of investments or of a designated separate account or accounts in which amounts received or retained in connection with any of such contracts have been placed.

(b) Any domestic life insurance company may, pursuant to resolution of its board of directors, establish one or more separate accounts and may allocate to such account or accounts amounts (including without limitation proceeds applied under optional modes of settlement or under dividend options) to provide for life insurance, guaranteed investment contracts, or annuities (and benefits incidental thereto) payable in fixed or variable amounts or both.

(c) In addition to the amounts allocated under subsection (b), such company may allocate from its general accounts to such separate account or accounts additional amounts, which may include an initial allocation to establish such account; provided, that such company shall be entitled to withdraw at any time, in whole or in part, its participation in any separate account to which funds have been allocated as provided in this subsection (c), and to receive, upon withdrawal, its proportionate share of the value of the assets of the separate account at the time of withdrawal.

(d) Except as hereinafter provided, the amounts allocated to any separate account and accumulations thereon may be invested and reinvested without regard to any requirements or limitations prescribed by the laws of this State governing the investments of life insurance companies; provided, that to the extent that the company's reserve liability with regard to (i) benefits guaranteed as to amount and duration, and (ii) funds guaranteed as to principal amount or stated rate of interest is maintained in any separate account, a portion of the assets of such separate account at least equal to such reserve liability shall be, except as the Commissioner may otherwise approve, invested in accordance with the laws of this State governing the investments of life insurance companies. The investments in such separate account or accounts shall not be taken into account in applying the investment limitations applicable to other investments of the company.

(e)   Repealed by Session Laws 2001-223, s. 6.3, effective June 15, 2001.

(f)   Repealed by Session Laws 2001-223, s. 6.3, effective June 15, 2001.

(g)   The life insurance company shall maintain in each separate account assets with a value at least equal to the reserves and other contract liabilities with respect to the account, except as may otherwise be approved by the Commissioner.

(h)   The income, if any, and gains and losses, realized or unrealized, from assets allocated to each account shall be credited to or charged against the account without regard to other income, gains or losses of the company.

(i)   Unless otherwise approved by the Commissioner, assets allocated to a separate account shall be valued at their market value on the date of valuation, or if there is no readily available market, then as provided under the terms of the contract or the rules or other written agreement applicable to such separate account; provided, that unless otherwise approved by the Commissioner that portion of the assets of such separate account equal to the company's reserve liability with regard to the guaranteed benefits and funds referred to in subsection (d) hereof, if any, shall be valued in accordance with the rules otherwise applicable to the company's assets. The reserve liability for variable contracts shall be determined in accordance with actuarial procedures that recognize the variable nature of the benefits provided and any mortality guarantees.

(j)   If and to the extent so provided under the applicable contracts, that portion of the assets of any such separate account equal to the reserves and other contract liabilities with respect to such account shall not be chargeable with liabilities arising out of any other business the company may conduct.

(k)   The life insurance company shall have the power and the company's charter shall be deemed amended to authorize such company to do all things necessary under any applicable state or federal law in order that variable contracts may be lawfully sold or offered for sale. To the extent such company deems it necessary to comply with any applicable federal or state laws, such company, with respect to any separate account, including without limitation any separate account which is a management investment company or a unit investment trust, may provide, for persons having an interest therein, appropriate voting and other rights and special procedures for the conduct of the business of such account, including without limitation special rights and procedures relating to investment policy, investment advisory services, selection of independent public accountants, and the selection of a committee, the members of which need not be otherwise affiliated with such company, to manage the business of such account. This provision shall not affect existing laws pertaining to the voting rights of the life insurance company's policyholders.

(l)   Amounts allocated to a separate account in the exercise of the power granted by this section shall be owned by the company, and the company shall not be, or hold itself out to be, a trustee with respect to such amounts.

(m)   The company shall not, in connection with the allocation of investments or expenses, or in any other respect, discriminate unfairly between separate accounts or between separate and other accounts, but this provision shall not require the company to follow uniform investment policies for its accounts.

(n)   No sale, exchange or other transfer of assets may be made by a company between any of its separate accounts or between any other investment account and one or more of its separate accounts unless, in case of a transfer into a separate account, such transfer is made solely to establish the account or to support the operation of the contracts with respect to the separate account to which the transfer is made, and unless such transfer, whether into or from a separate account, is made (i) by a transfer of cash, or (ii) by a transfer of securities having a readily determinable market value, provided that such transfer of securities is approved by the Commissioner. The Commissioner may approve other transfers among such accounts if, in his opinion, such transfers would not be inequitable.

(o)   Any contract providing benefits payable in variable amounts delivered or issued for delivery in this State shall contain a statement of the essential features of the procedure to be followed by the company in determining the dollar amount of such variable benefits. Any such contract under which the benefits vary to reflect investment experience, including a group contract and any certificate in evidence of variable benefits issued thereunder, shall state that such dollar amount will so vary and shall contain on its first page a statement to the effect that the benefits thereunder are on a variable basis.

(p)   Any variable annuity contract providing benefits payable in variable amounts issued under this section may include as an incidental benefit provision for payment on death during the deferred period of an amount not in excess of the greater of the sum of the premiums or stipulated payments paid under the contract or the value of the contract at time of death or any other incidental amount approved by the Commissioner; such contracts will be deemed not to be contracts of life insurance and therefore not subject to the provisions of the insurance law governing life insurance contracts. Provision for any other benefit on death during the deferred period will be subject to such insurance provisions.

(q)   No domestic life insurance company and no other life insurance company shall deliver or issue for delivery within this State any contracts under this section unless it is licensed or organized to do a life insurance or annuity business in this State, and the Commissioner is satisfied that its financial condition and its methods of operation in connection with the issuance of such contracts will not render its operation hazardous to the public or its policyholders in this State. In determining the qualification of a company requesting authority to deliver such contracts within this State, the Commissioner shall consider, among other things:

(1)   The history and financial condition of the company;

(2)   The character, responsibility and general fitness of the officers and directors of the company; and

(3)   The law and regulations under which the company is authorized in the state of domicile to issue variable annuity contracts. The state of entry of an alien company shall be deemed its place of domicile for this purpose.

If the company is a subsidiary of an admitted life insurance company, or affiliated with such company through common management or ownership, it may be deemed by the Commissioner to have met the provisions of this subsection if either it or the parent or affiliated company meets the requirements hereof.

(r)   The Commissioner shall have sole and exclusive authority to regulate the issuance by life insurance companies and the sale of such contracts and to issue such reasonable rules and regulations as may be necessary to carry out the purposes and provisions of this section, and such contracts and the life insurance companies which issue them shall not be subject to the Securities Law of North Carolina nor to the jurisdiction of the Secretary of State thereunder.

(s)   Except for G.S. 58-58-61 and G.S. 58-58-120 in the case of a variable annuity contract, G.S. 58-58-55, 58-58-120, and 58-58-140(1) in the case of a variable life insurance policy, and except as otherwise provided in this section, all pertinent provisions of this Chapter apply to separate accounts and contracts issued in connection with separate accounts. Any individual variable life insurance contract, delivered or issued for delivery within this State, shall contain reinstatement and nonforfeiture provisions appropriate to that contract. Any group variable life insurance contract, delivered or issued for delivery within this State, shall contain grace provisions appropriate to that contract. Any individual variable annuity contract, delivered or issued for delivery within this State, shall contain reinstatement provisions appropriate to that contract. (1965, c. 166; 1969, c. 616, s. 2; 1971, c. 831, s. 2; 1973, c. 490; 1979, c. 409, s. 10; 1991, c. 720, s. 4; 1991 (Reg. Sess., 1992), c. 837, s. 7; 2001-223, ss. 6.1, 6.2, 6.3, 6.4; 2003-144, s. 3.)

§ 58-7-100: Repealed by Session Laws 1991, c. 681, s. 30.

§ 58-7-105. Authority to increase or reduce capital stock.

The Commissioner shall, upon application, examine the proceedings of domestic companies to increase or reduce their capital stock, and when found conformable to law shall issue certificates of authority to such companies to transact business upon such increased or reduced capital: Provided, that in no event shall the said capital stock be reduced to an amount less than that required upon organization of such company in G.S. 58-7-75. He shall not allow stockholders' obligations of any description as part of the assets or capital of any stock insurance company unless the same are secured by competent collateral. (1899, c. 54, s. 15; Rev., s. 4732; C.S., s. 6335; 1945, c. 386; 1991, c. 720, s. 4.)

§ 58-7-110. Assessment of shares; revocation of license.

When the net assets of a company organized under this Article do not amount to more than the amount required in G.S. 58-7-75 for its original capital, it may make good its capital to the original amount by assessment of its stock. Shares on which such an assessment is not paid within 60 days after demand shall be forfeitable and may be canceled by vote of the directors and new shares issued to make up the deficiency. If such company does not, within three months after notice from the Commissioner to that effect, make good its capital or reduce the same, as allowed by this Article, its authority to transact new business of insurance shall be revoked by the Commissioner. (1899, c. 54, s. 28; 1903, c. 438, s. 4; Rev., s. 4733; C.S., s. 6336; 1945, c. 386; 1991, c. 720, s. 4.)

§ 58-7-115. Increase of capital stock.

Any company organized under the provisions of Articles 1 through 64 of this Chapter may issue pro rata to its stockholders certificates of any portion of its surplus which shall be considered an increase of its capital to the amount of such certificates. As used in this section, "surplus" means earned surplus; provided, however, issuance of certificates out of paid-in and contributed surplus will be permitted on a case-by-case basis, with the prior approval of the Commissioner. The issuance of those certificates shall not lower the total surplus of the insurer to an amount less than that required to be maintained by G.S. 58-7-75. The company may, at a meeting called for the purpose, vote to increase the amount and number of shares of its capital stock, and to issue certificates therefor when paid for in full. In whichever method the increase is made, the company shall, within 30 days after the issue of such certificates, submit to the Commissioner a certificate setting forth the amount of the increase and the facts of the transaction, signed and sworn to by its president and secretary and a majority of its directors. If the Commissioner finds that the facts conform to the law, he shall endorse his approval thereof; and upon filing such certificate so endorsed with the Secretary of State, and the payment of a fee of five dollars ($5.00) for filing the same, the company may transact business upon the capital as increased, and the Commissioner shall issue his certificate to that effect. (1899, c. 54, s. 29; Rev., s. 4734; C.S., s. 6337; 1945, c. 386; 1991, c. 720, s. 4; 1993, c. 452, s. 6.)

§ 58-7-120. Reduction of capital stock.

When the capital stock of a company organized under this Article is impaired, the company may, upon a vote of the majority of the stock represented at a meeting legally called for that purpose, reduce its capital stock and the number of shares thereof to an amount not less than the minimum sum required by law, but no part of its assets and property shall be distributed to its stockholders. Within 10 days after such meeting the company must submit to the Commissioner a certificate setting forth the proceedings thereof and the amount of the reduction and the assets and liabilities of the company, signed and sworn to by its president, secretary, and a majority of its directors. The Commissioner shall examine the facts in the case, and if they conform to law, and in his judgment the proposed reduction may be made without prejudice to the public, he shall endorse his approval upon the certificate. Upon filing the certificate so endorsed with the Secretary of State and paying a filing fee of five dollars ($5.00), the company may transact business upon the basis of the reduced capital as though it were original capital, and its charter shall be deemed to be amended to conform thereto, and the Commissioner shall issue his certificate to that effect. The company may, by a majority vote of its directors, after the reduction, require the return of the original certificates of stock held by each stockholder in exchange for new certificates it may issue in lieu thereof for such number of shares as each stockholder is entitled to in the proportion that the reduced capital bears to the original capital. (1899, c. 54, s. 30; Rev., s. 4735; C.S., s. 6338; 1991, c. 720, s. 4.)

§ 58-7-125. Dividends not payable when capital stock impaired; liability of stockholders for unlawful dividends.

No dividend shall be paid by any company incorporated in this State when its capital stock is impaired, or when such payment would have the effect of impairing its capital stock; and any dividend so paid subjects the stockholders receiving it to a joint and several liability to the creditors of said company to the extent of the dividend so paid. (1899, c. 54, s. 31; 1903, c. 536, s. 3; Rev., s. 4736; C.S., s. 6339; 1945, c. 386.)

§ 58-7-130. Dividends and distributions to stockholders.

(a) Each domestic insurance company in North Carolina shall be restricted by the Commissioner from the payment of any dividends or other distributions to its stockholders whenever the Commissioner determines from examination of the company's financial condition that the payment of future dividends or other distributions would cause a hazardous financial condition, impair the financial soundness of the company or be detrimental to its policyholders, and those restrictions shall continue in force until the Commissioner specifically permits the payment of dividends or other distributions to stockholders by the company through a written authorization.

(b) A domestic stock insurance company shall not declare or pay dividends or other distributions to its stockholders from any source other than unassigned surplus without the Commissioner's prior written approval. For purposes of this section, "unassigned surplus" means an amount equal to the unassigned funds of a company as reflected in the company's most recent financial statement filed with the Commissioner under G.S. 58-2-165, including all or part of the surplus arising from unrealized capital gains or revaluation of assets.

(c) A transfer out of paid-in and contributed surplus to common or preferred capital stock will be permitted on a case-by-case basis, with the Commissioner's prior approval, depending on the necessity for a company to make the transfer.

(d) Nothing in this section and no action taken by the Commissioner in any way restricts the liability of stockholders under G.S. 58-7-125.

(e) Dividends and other distributions paid to stockholders are subject to the requirements and limitations of G.S. 58-19-25(d) and G.S. 58-19-30(c). (1945, c. 386; 1991, c. 720, s. 9; 2001-223, s. 5.2; 2002-187, s. 2.5; 2006-105, s. 3.1.)

§ 58-7-135: Repealed by Session Laws 1993, c. 452, s. 65.

§ 58-7-140. Certain officers debarred from commissions.

No officer or other person whose duty it is to determine the character of the risk, and upon whose decision the application shall be accepted or rejected by an insurance company, shall receive as any part of his compensation a commission upon the premiums, but his compensation shall be a fixed salary and such share in the net profits as the directors may determine. Nor shall such officer or person be an employee of any officer or agent of the company. (1899, c. 54, s. 32; 1903, c. 438, s. 4; Rev., s. 4738; C.S., s. 6347; 1945, c. 386.)

§ 58-7-145. Restrictions on purchase and sale of equity securities of domestic companies.

(a) Statement of Ownership of Equity Securities. - Every person who is directly or indirectly the beneficial owner of more than ten percent (10%) of any class of any equity security of a domestic stock insurance company or who is a director or an officer of such company shall file in the office of the Commissioner on or before the first day of June, 1966, or within 10 days after he becomes such beneficial owner, director or officer, a statement, in such form as the Commissioner may prescribe, of the amount of all equity securities of such company of which he is the beneficial owner, and within 10 days after the close of each calendar month thereafter if there has been a change in such ownership during such month, shall file in the office of the Commissioner a statement, in such form as the Commissioner may prescribe, indicating his ownership at the close of the calendar month and such changes in his ownership as have occurred during such calendar month.

(b) Profit Made from Sale of Equity Security Held Less than Six Months. - For the purpose of preventing the unfair use of information which may have been obtained by such beneficial owner, director, or officer by reason of his relationship to such company, any profit realized by him from any purchase and sale, or any sale and purchase, of any equity security of such company within a period of less than six months, unless such security was acquired in good faith in connection with a debt previously contracted, shall inure to and be recoverable by the company, irrespective of any intention on the part of such beneficial owner, director or officer in entering into such transaction of holding the security purchased or of not repurchasing the security sold for a period exceeding six months. Suit to recover such profit may be instituted at law or in equity in any court of competent jurisdiction by the company, or by the owner of any equity security of the company in the name and in behalf of the company, if the company shall fail or refuse to bring such suit within 60 days after request or shall fail diligently to prosecute the same thereafter; but no such suit shall be brought more than two years after the date such profit was realized. This section shall not be construed to cover any transaction where such beneficial owner was not such both at the time of the purchase and sale, or the sale and purchase, of the equity security involved, or any transaction or transactions which the Commissioner by rules and regulations may exempt as not comprehended within the purpose of this section.

(c) Delivery of Security Sold. - It shall be unlawful for any such beneficial owner, director or officer, directly or indirectly, to sell any equity security of such company if the person selling the security or his principal (i) does not own the security sold, or (ii) if owning the security, does not deliver it against such sale within 20 days thereafter, or does not within five days after such sale deposit it in the mails or other usual channels of transportation; but no person shall be deemed to have violated this section if he proves that notwithstanding the exercise of good faith he was unable to make such delivery or deposit within such time, or that to do so would cause undue inconvenience or expense.

(d) Sales by Dealers. - The provisions of subsection (b) shall not apply to any purchase and sale, or sale and purchase, and the provisions of subsection (c) shall not apply to any sale, of an equity security of a domestic stock insurance company not then or theretofore held by him in an investment account, by a dealer in the ordinary course of his business and incident to the establishment or maintenance by him of a primary or secondary market (otherwise than on an exchange as defined in the Securities Exchange Act of 1934) for such security. The Commissioner may, by such rules and regulations as he deems necessary or appropriate in the public interest, define and prescribe terms and conditions with respect to securities held in an investment account and transactions made in the ordinary course of business and incident to the establishment or maintenance of a primary or secondary market.

(e) Arbitrage Transactions. - The provisions of subsections (a), (b) and (c) of this section shall not apply to foreign or domestic arbitrage transactions unless made in contravention of such rules and regulations as the Commissioner may adopt in order to carry out the purposes of this section.

(f) "Equity Security" Defined. - The term "equity security" when used in this section means any stock or similar security; or any security convertible, with or without consideration, into such a security, or carrying any warrant or right to subscribe to or purchase such a security; or any such warrant or right; or any other security which the Commissioner shall deem to be of similar nature and consider necessary or appropriate, by such rules and regulations as he may prescribe in the public interest or for the protection of investors, to treat as an equity security.

(g) Exemptions from Requirements of Section. - The provisions of subsections (a), (b) and (c) hereof shall not apply to equity securities of a domestic stock insurance company if

(1) Such securities shall be registered, or shall be required to be registered, pursuant to section 12 of the Securities Exchange Act of 1934, as amended, or if

(2) Such domestic stock insurance company shall not have any class of its equity securities held of record by 100 or more persons on the last business day of the year next preceding the year in which equity securities of the company would be subject to the provisions of subsections (a), (b) and (c) hereof except for the provisions of this subdivision (2).

(h) Rules and Regulations of Commissioner. - The Commissioner shall have the power to make such rules and regulations as may be necessary for the execution of the functions vested in him by subsections (a) through (g) hereof, and may for such purpose classify domestic stock insurance companies, securities, and other persons or matters within his jurisdiction. No provision of subsections (a), (b) and (c) hereof imposing any liability shall apply to any act done or omitted in good faith in conformity with any rule or regulation of the Commissioner, notwithstanding that such rule or regulation may, after such act or omission, be amended or rescinded or determined by judicial or other authority to be invalid for any reason.

(i) Severability. - If any part or provision of this section or the application thereof to any person or circumstance be adjudged invalid by any court of competent jurisdiction, such judgment shall be confined in its operation to the part, provision or application directly involved in the controversy in which such judgment shall have been rendered and shall not affect or impair the validity of the remainder of this section or the application thereof to other persons or circumstances. (1965, c. 127, s. 2.)

§ 58-7-150. Consolidation.

(a) A domestic insurer may consolidate with another insurer, subject to the following conditions:

(1) The plan of consolidation must be submitted to and be approved by the Commissioner before the consolidation.

(2) The Commissioner shall not approve the plan unless the Commissioner finds that it is fair, equitable to policyholders, consistent with law, and will not

conflict with the public interest. If the Commissioner disapproves the plan, the Commissioner shall state the reasons for the disapproval and call for a hearing.

(3) No director, officer, member or subscriber of any such insurer, except as is expressly provided by the plan of consolidation, shall receive any fee, commission, other compensation or valuable consideration whatever, for in any manner aiding, promoting or assisting in the consolidation.

(4) Any consolidation as to an incorporated domestic insurer shall in other respects be governed by the general laws of this State relating to business corporations. The consolidation of a domestic mutual insurer may be effected by vote of two thirds of the members voting thereon pursuant to such notice and procedure as the Commissioner may prescribe.

(b) Reinsurance of all or substantially all of the insurance obligations or risks of existing or in-force policies of a domestic insurer by another insurer under an assumption reinsurance agreement, as defined in G.S. 58-10-25(a)(2), shall be deemed a consolidation for the purposes of this section. This section does not apply to consolidations to the extent regulated by Article 19 or other Articles of this Chapter.

(c) Repealed by Session Laws 2005-424, s. 1.3, effective January 1, 2006, and applicable to applications filed, licenses issued, and licenses continued on or after that date. (1947, c. 923; 1955, c. 905; 1985, c. 572, s. 4; 1989 (Reg. Sess., 1990), c. 1069, s. 10; 1993, c. 452, s. 7; 1993 (Reg. Sess., 1994), c. 678, s. 10; 1995, c. 193, s. 18; c. 507, s. 11A(c); 2001-223, ss. 7.1, 7.2; 2005-424, s. 1.3.)

§ 58-7-155: Repealed by Session Laws 2005-424, s. 1.3, effective January 1, 2006, and applicable to applications filed, licenses issued, and licenses continued on or after that date.

§ 58-7-160. Investments unlawfully acquired.

Whenever it appears by examination as authorized by law that a domestic insurer has acquired any assets in violation of the law in force on the date of the acquisition, the Commissioner shall disallow the amount of the assets, if wholly ineligible, or the amount of the value thereof in excess of any limitation prescribed by this Chapter and shall deduct that amount as a nonadmitted asset of the insurer. (1991, c. 681, s. 29.)

§ 58-7-162. Allowable or admitted assets.

In any determination of the financial condition of an insurer, there shall be allowed as assets only those assets owned by an insurer and that consist of:

(1) Cash in the possession of the insurer, or in transit under its control, and including the true balance of any deposit in a solvent United States bank, savings and loan association, credit union, or trust company, and the balance of any such deposit in an insolvent United States bank, savings and loan association, credit union, or trust company, to the extent insured by a federal agency.

(2) Investments, securities, properties, and loans acquired or held in accordance with this Chapter.

(3) Premium notes, policy loans, and other policy assets and liens on policies and certificates of life insurance and annuity contracts and accrued interest thereon, in an amount not exceeding the legal reserve and other policy liabilities carried on each individual policy.

(4) The net amount of uncollected and deferred premiums and annuity considerations in the case of a life insurer.

(5) Repealed by Session Laws 2003-212, s. 5, effective October 1, 2003.

(6) All premiums in the course of collection not more than 90 days past due, excluding commissions payable thereon, due from any person that solely or in combination with the person's affiliates owes the insurer an amount that equals or exceeds five percent (5%) of the insurer's surplus as regards policyholders, but only if:

a. The premiums collected by the person or affiliates and not remitted to the insurer are held in a trust account with a bank or other depository approved by the Commissioner. The funds shall be held as trust funds and may not be commingled with any other funds of the person or affiliates. Disbursements from the trust account may be made only to the insurer, the insured, or, for the purpose of returning premiums, a person that is entitled to returned premiums on behalf of the insured. A written copy of the trust agreement shall be filed with and approved by the Commissioner before becoming effective. The Commissioner shall disapprove any trust agreement filed under this sub-subdivision that does not assure the safety of the premiums collected. The investment income derived from the trust may be allocated as the parties consider to be proper. The person or affiliates shall deposit premiums collected into the trust account within 15 business days after collection; or

b. The person or affiliates shall provide to the insurer, and the insurer shall maintain in its possession, an unexpired, clean, irrevocable letter of credit, payable to the insurer, issued for a term of no less than one year and in conformity with the requirements set forth in this sub-subdivision, the amount of which equals or exceeds the liability of the person or affiliates to the insurer, at all times during the period that the letter of credit is in effect, for premiums collected by the person or affiliates. The letter of credit shall be issued under arrangements satisfactory to the Commissioner and the letter shall be issued by a banking institution that is a member of the Federal Reserve System and that has a financial standing satisfactory to the Commissioner; or

c. The person or affiliates shall provide to the insurer, and the insurer shall maintain in its possession, evidence that the person or affiliates have purchased and have currently in effect a financial guaranty bond, payable to the insurer, issued for a term of not less than one year and that is in conformity with the requirements set forth in this sub-subdivision, the amount of which equals or exceeds the liability of the person or affiliates to the insurer, at all times during which the financial guaranty bond is in effect, for the premiums collected by the person or persons. The financial guaranty bond shall be issued under an arrangement satisfactory to the Commissioner and the financial guaranty bond shall be issued by an insurer that is authorized to transact that business in this State, that has a financial standing satisfactory to the Commissioner, and that is neither controlled nor controlling in relation to either the insurer or the person or affiliates for whom the bond is purchased.

Premiums receivable under this subdivision will not be allowed as an admitted asset if a financial evaluation by the Commissioner indicates that the person or affiliates are unlikely to be able to pay the premiums as they become due. The financial evaluation shall be based on a review of the books and records of the controlling or controlled person.

(7) Repealed by Session Laws 2003-212, s. 5, effective October 1, 2003.

(8) Notes and like written obligations not past due, taken for premiums other than life insurance premiums, on policies permitted to be issued on that basis, to the extent of the unearned premium reserves carried thereon.

(9) The full amount of reinsurance which is recoverable by a ceding insurer from a solvent reinsurer and is authorized under G.S. 58-7-21.

(10) Amounts receivable by an assuming insurer representing funds withheld by a solvent ceding insurer under a reinsurance treaty.

(11) Deposits or equities recoverable from underwriting associations, syndicates, and reinsurance funds, or from any suspended banking institution, to the extent considered by the Commissioner to be available for the payment of losses and claims and at values to be determined by the Commissioner.

(12) Electronic and mechanical machines, including operating and system software constituting a management information system.

(13) Other assets, not inconsistent with the provisions of this section, considered by the Commissioner to be available for the payment of losses and claims, at values to be determined by the Commissioner. (1991, c. 681, s. 29; 1993, c. 452, s. 8; 1995 (Reg. Sess., 1996), c. 659, s. 1; 2003-212, ss. 4-6; 2011-221, s. 4.)

§ 58-7-163. Assets not allowed.

In addition to assets impliedly excluded by the provisions of G.S. 58-7-162, the following expressly shall not be allowed as assets in any determination of the financial condition of an insurer:

(1) Repealed by Session Laws 2003-212, s. 7, effective October 1, 2003.

(2) Advances (other than policy loans) to officers, directors, and controlling stockholders, whether secured or not, and advances to employees, agents, and other persons on personal security only.

(3)   Stock of the insurer or any material equity therein or loans secured thereby, or any material proportionate interest in the stock acquired or held through the ownership by the insurer of an interest in another firm, corporation, or business unit.

(4)   Repealed by Session Laws 2003-212, s. 7, effective October 1, 2003.

(5)   The amount, if any, by which the aggregate book value of investments as carried in the ledger assets of the insurer exceeds the aggregate value of the investments as determined under this Chapter.

(6)   Bonds, notes, or other evidences of indebtedness that are secured by mortgages or deeds of trust that are in default, to the extent of the cost or carrying value that is in excess of the value as determined pursuant to other provisions of this Chapter.

(7)   Repealed by Session Laws 2003-212, s. 7, effective October 1, 2003.

(8)   Certificates of contribution, surplus notes, or other similar evidences of indebtedness, to the extent that admission of these investments results in the double counting of these investments in the reporting entity's balance sheet.

(9)   Any asset that is encumbered in any manner unless the asset is authorized under G.S. 58-7-187 or G.S. 58-7-162(13). (1991, c. 681, s. 29; 1993, c. 452, s. 9; 1993 (Reg. Sess., 1994), c. 678, s. 11; 2003-212, s. 7.)

§ 58-7-165. Eligible investments.

(a)   Insurers shall invest in or lend their funds on the security of, and shall hold as invested assets, only eligible investments as prescribed in this Chapter.

(b)   Any particular investment held by an insurer on December 31, 1991, that was a legal investment when it was made, and that the insurer was legally entitled to possess immediately before January 1, 1992, is an eligible investment.

(c)   Eligibility of an investment shall be determined as of the date of its making or acquisition, except as stated otherwise in this Chapter.

(d) Any investment limitation based upon the amount of the insurer's assets or particular funds shall relate to those assets or funds shown by the insurer's annual statement as of the December 31 preceding the date of acquisition of the investment by the insurer, or, if applicable, as shown by the most current quarterly financial statement filed by the insurer. (1991, c. 681, s. 29.)

§ 58-7-167. General qualifications.

(a) No security or investment, other than real or personal property acquired under G.S. 58-7-187, is eligible for acquisition unless it is interest-bearing or interest-accruing, is entitled to receive dividends if and when declared and paid, or is otherwise income-producing, is not then in default in any respect, and the insurer is entitled to receive for its exclusive account and benefit the interest or income accruing thereon.

(b) No security or investment shall be eligible for purchase at a price above its market value unless it is approved by the Commissioner and is valued in accordance with valuation procedures of the NAIC that have been adopted by the Commissioner.

(c) This Chapter does not prohibit the acquisition by an insurer of other or additional securities or property if received as a dividend, as a lawful distribution of assets, or under a lawful and bona fide agreement of bulk reinsurance, merger, or consolidation. Any investment so acquired that is not otherwise eligible under this Chapter shall be disposed of under G.S. 58-7-188 if the investment is in property or securities. (1991, c. 681, s. 29.)

§ 58-7-168. Authorization of investment.

An insurer shall not make any investment or loan, other than a policy loan or annuity contract loan of a life insurer, unless the investment or loan is authorized or approved by the insurer's board of directors or by a committee authorized by the board and charged with the supervision or making of the investment or loan. The minutes of any such committee shall be recorded and regular reports of the committee shall be submitted to the board of directors. (1991, c. 681, s. 29.)

§ 58-7-170. Diversification.

(a) Every insurer must maintain an amount equal to its entire policyholder-related liabilities and the minimum capital and surplus required to be maintained by the insurer under this Chapter invested in coin or currency of the United States and in investments authorized under this Chapter, other than the investments authorized under G.S. 58-7-183 or G.S. 58-7-187, except G.S. 58-7-187(b)(1).

(b) Investments eligible under subsection (a), except investments acquired under G.S. 58-7-183, are subject to the following limitations, other limitations of this section, and any other limitations that are expressly provided for in any provision under which the investment is authorized:

(1) The cost of investments made by insurers in stock authorized by G.S. 58-7-173 shall not exceed twenty-five percent (25%) of the insurer's admitted assets, provided that no more than twenty percent (20%) of the insurer's admitted assets shall be invested in common stock; and the cost of an investment in stock of any one corporation shall not exceed three percent (3%) of the insurer's admitted assets. Notwithstanding any other provision in this Chapter, the financial statement carrying value of all stock investments shall be used for the purpose of determining the asset value against which the percentage limitations are to be applied. Investments in the voting securities of a depository institution, or any company that controls a depository institution, shall not exceed five percent (5%) of the insurer's admitted assets. As used in this subdivision, "depository institution" has the same meaning as in section 3 of the Federal Deposit Insurance Act, 12 U.S.C. § 1813; and includes any foreign bank that maintains a branch, an agency, or a commercial lending company in the United States.

(2) The cost of Canadian investments authorized by G.S. 58-7-173 shall not exceed forty percent (40%) of the insurer's admitted assets in the aggregate, provided that no more than twenty-five percent (25%) of the insurer's admitted assets shall be invested in Canadian investments authorized by G.S. 58-7-173(11).

(c) The cost of investments made by an insurer in mortgage loans authorized by G.S. 58-7-179 with any one person, or in mortgage-backed securities authorized by G.S. 58-7-173(1), (2), (8), or (17), and backed by a single collateral pool, shall not exceed three percent (3%) of the insurer's admitted assets. An insurer shall not invest in additional mortgage loans or mortgage-backed securities without the Commissioner's consent if the admitted value of all those investments held by the insurer exceeds an aggregate of sixty percent (60%) of the admitted assets of the insurer. Within the aggregate sixty percent (60%) limitation, the admitted value of all mortgage-backed securities permitted by G.S. 58-7-173(17) shall not exceed thirty-five percent (35%) of the admitted assets of the insurer. The admitted value of other mortgage loans permitted by G.S. 58-7-179 shall not exceed forty percent (40%) of the admitted assets of the insurer. Mortgage-backed securities authorized by G.S. 58-7-173(1), (2), or (8) shall only be subject to the single collateral pool limitation and the sixty percent (60%) aggregate limitation. No later than January 31, 1999, an insurer that has mortgage investments that exceed the limitations specified in this subsection shall submit to the Commissioner a plan to bring the amount of mortgage investments into compliance with the specified limitations by January 1, 2004.

(d)   Without the Commissioner's prior written approval, the cost of investments permitted under G.S. 58-7-173 and G.S. 58-7-178, and that are classified as medium to lower quality obligations, other than obligations of subsidiaries or affiliated corporations as that term is defined in G.S. 58-19-5, shall be limited to:

(1)   No more than twenty percent (20%) of an insurer's admitted assets;

(2)   No more than ten percent (10%) of an insurer's admitted assets in obligations designated a 4, 5, or 6 in accordance with the Purposes and Procedures Manual of the NAIC Securities Valuation Office;

(3)   No more than three percent (3%) of an insurer's admitted assets in obligations designated a 5 or 6 in accordance with the Purposes and Procedures Manual of the NAIC Securities Valuation Office; and

(4)   No more than one percent (1%) of an insurer's admitted assets in obligations designated a 6 in accordance with the Purposes and Procedures Manual of the NAIC Securities Valuation Office.

(5),(6) Repealed by Session Laws 1993, c. 452, s. 11.

(e)   As used in subsections (d), (f), (g), and (h) of this section, "medium to lower quality obligations" means obligations designated a 3, 4, 5, or 6 in accordance with the Purposes and Procedures Manual of the NAIC Securities Valuation Office.

(f) Each insurer shall possess and maintain adequate documentation to establish that its investments in medium to lower quality obligations do not exceed the limitations under subsection (d) of this section.

(g),(h) Repealed by Session Laws 2005-215, s. 7, effective July 20, 2005.

(i) Failure to obtain the Commissioner's prior written approval shall result in any investments in excess of those permitted by subsection (d) of this section not being allowed as an asset of the insurer.

(j) The Commissioner may limit the extent of an insurer's deposits with any financial institution if the Commissioner determines that the financial solvency of the insurer is threatened by a deposit in excess of insured limits.

(k) The provisions of this section supersede any inconsistent provision of section 106 of the Secondary Mortgage Market Enhancement Act of 1984, 15 U.S.C. § 77r-1, to the extent permitted by that Act. (1991, c. 681, s. 29; 1993, c. 452, ss. 10-13; c. 504, s. 43; 1993 (Reg. Sess., 1994), c. 678, s. 12; 1998-212, s. 26B(i); 2001-215, s. 3; 2001-223, ss. 8.1, 8.2; 2005-215, s. 7.)

§ 58-7-172. Cash and deposits.

An insurer may have funds in coin or currency of the United States on hand or on deposit in any solvent national or state bank, savings and loan association, credit union, or trust company. (1991, c. 681, s. 29; 2011-221, s. 5.)

§ 58-7-173. Permitted insurer investments.

An insurer may invest in:

(1) Bonds, notes, warrants, and other evidences of indebtedness that are direct obligations of the U.S. Government or for which the full faith and credit of the U.S. Government is pledged for the payment of principal and interest.

(2) Loans insured or guaranteed as to principal and interest by the U.S. Government or by any agency or instrumentality of the U.S. Government to the extent of the insurance or guaranty.

(3) Student loans insured or guaranteed as to principal by the U.S. Government or by any agency or instrumentality of the U.S. Government to the extent of the insurance or guaranty.

(4) Bonds, notes, warrants, and other securities not in default that are the direct obligations of any state or United States territory or the government of Canada or any Canadian province, or for which the full faith and credit of such state, government, or province has been pledged for the payment of principal and interest.

(5) Bonds, notes, warrants, and other securities not in default of any county, district, incorporated city, or school district in any state of the United States, or the District of Columbia, or in any Canadian province, that are the direct obligations of the county, district, city, or school district and for payment of the principal and interest of which the county, district, city, or school district has lawful authority to levy taxes or make assessments.

(6) Bonds, notes, certificates of indebtedness, warranties, or other evidences of indebtedness that are payable from revenues or earnings specifically pledged therefor of any public toll bridge, structure, or improvement owned by any state, incorporated city, or legally constituted public corporation or commission, all within the United States or Canada, for the payment of the principal and interest of which a lawful sinking fund has been established and is being maintained and if no default by the issuer in payment of principal or interest has occurred on any of its bonds, notes, warrants, or other securities within five years prior to the date of investment therein.

(7) Bonds, notes, certificates of indebtedness, warrants, or other evidences of indebtedness that are valid obligations issued, assumed, or guaranteed by the United States, any state, any county, city, district, political subdivision, civil division, or public instrumentality of any such government or unit thereof, or in any province of Canada; if by statute or other legal requirements the obligations are payable as to both principal and interest from revenues or earnings from the whole or any part of any utility supplying water, gas, a sewage disposal facility, electricity, or any other public service, including but not limited to a toll road or toll bridge.

(8) Bonds, debentures, or other securities of the following agencies, whether or not those obligations are guaranteed by the U.S. Government:

a. Fannie Mae, and stock thereof when acquired in connection with the sale of mortgage loans to the Association.

b. Any federal land bank, when the securities are issued under the Farm Loan Act;

c. Any federal home loan bank, when the securities are issued under the Home Loan Bank Act;

d. The Home Owners' Loan Corporation, created by the Home Owners' Loan Act of 1933;

e. Any federal intermediate credit bank, created by the Agricultural Credits Act;

f. The Central Bank for Cooperatives and regional banks for cooperatives organized under the Farm Credit Act of 1933, or by any of such banks; and any notes, bonds, debentures, or other similar obligations, consolidated or otherwise, issued by farm credit institutions under the Farm Credit Act of 1971;

g. Any other similar agency of the U.S. Government that is of similar financial quality.

(9) Bonds, debentures, or other securities of public housing authorities, issued under the Housing Act, of 1949, the Municipal Housing Commission Act, or the Rural Housing Commission Act, or issued by any public housing authority or agency in the United States, if the bonds, debentures, or other securities are secured by a pledge of annual contributions to be paid by the United States or any United States agency.

(10) Obligations issued, assumed, or guaranteed by the International Bank for Reconstruction and Development, the International Finance Corporation, the Inter-American Development Bank, the Asian Development Bank, or the African Development Bank; and the cost of investments made under this subdivision in any one institution shall not exceed three percent (3%) of the insurer admitted assets.

(11) Bonds, notes, or other interest-bearing or interest-accruing obligations of any solvent institution organized under the laws of the United States, of any state, Canada or any Canadian province; provided the instruments are designated and valued in accordance with the Purposes and Procedures Manual of the NAIC Securities Valuation Office. The cost of investments made under this subdivision in any one issuer shall not exceed three percent (3%) of an insurer's admitted assets.

(12) Secured obligations of duly constituted churches and of church-holding companies; and the cost of investments made under this subdivision shall not exceed three percent (3%) of the insurer's admitted assets.

(13) Equipment trust obligations or certificates adequately secured and evidencing an interest in transportation equipment, wholly or in part within the United States, and the right to receive determined portions of rental, purchase, or other fixed obligatory payments for the use or purchase of that transportation equipment; and the cost of investments made under this subdivision shall not exceed twenty percent (20%) of the insurer's admitted assets.

(14) Share or savings accounts of credit unions, savings and loan associations or building and loan associations.

(15) Loans with a maturity not in excess of 12 years from the date thereof that are secured by the pledge of securities eligible for investment under this Chapter or by the pledge or assignment of life insurance policies issued by other insurers authorized to transact insurance in this State. On the date made, no such loan shall exceed in amount seventy-five percent (75%) of the market value of the collateral pledged, except that loans upon the pledge of U.S. Government bonds and loans upon the pledge or assignment of life insurance policies shall not exceed ninety-five percent (95%) of the market value of the bonds or the cash surrender value of the policies pledged. The market value of the collateral pledge shall at all times during the continuance of the loans meet or exceed the miminum percentages herein. Loans made under this section shall not be renewable beyond a period of 12 years from the date of the loan.

(16) Stocks, common or preferred, of any corporation created or existing under the laws of the United States, any U.S. territory, Canada or any Canadian province, or of any state. An insurer may invest in stocks, common or preferred, of any corporation created or existing under the laws of any foreign country other than Canada subject to the provisions of G.S. 58-7-178.

(17)   Mortgage-backed securities that are designated a 1 or 2 in accordance with the Purposes and Procedures Manual of the NAIC Securities Valuation Office including, without limitation, collateral mortgage obligations backed by a pool of mortgages of the kind, class, and investment quality as those eligible for investment under G.S. 58-7-179. (1991, c. 681, s. 29; 1993, c. 105, s. 1; c. 452, s. 14; c. 504, s. 44; 2001-223, ss. 8.3, 8.4, 8.5, 8.6, 8.7, 8.8; 2001-487, s. 14(g); 2005-215, ss. 8, 9; 2011-221, s. 6.)

§ 58-7-175. Policy loans.

A life insurer may lend to its policyholder, upon pledge of the policy as collateral security, any sum not exceeding the cash loan value of the policy; or may lend against pledge or assignment of any of its supplementary contracts or other contracts or obligations, as long as the loan is adequately secured by the pledge or assignment. Loans so made are eligible investments of the insurer. (1991, c. 681, s. 29.)

§ 58-7-177: Repealed by Session Laws 2001-223, s. 8.9.

§ 58-7-178. Foreign or territorial investments.

(a)   An insurer authorized to transact insurance in a foreign country or any U.S. territory may have funds invested in securities that may be required for that authority and for the transaction of that business, provided the funds and securities are substantially of the same kinds, classes, and investment grades as those otherwise eligible for investment under this Chapter. The aggregate amount of investments under this subsection shall not exceed the amount that the insurer is required by law to invest in the foreign country or United States territory, or one and one-half times the amount of reserves and other obligations under the contracts, whichever is greater.

(b)   An insurer, whether or not it is authorized to do business or has outstanding insurance contracts on lives or risks in any foreign country, may invest in bonds, notes, or stocks of any foreign country or alien corporation that are substantially of the same kinds, classes, and investment grades as those otherwise eligible for investment under this Chapter. The aggregate cost of investments under this subsection shall not exceed ten percent (10%) of the insurer's admitted assets, provided that the cost of investments in any one foreign country under this subsection shall not exceed three percent (3%) of the insurer's admitted assets.

(c)   Canadian securities eligible for investment under other provisions of this Chapter are not subject to this section. (1991, c. 681, s. 29; 2001-223, s. 8.11; 2001-487, s. 103(b); 2002-187, s. 2.6; 2005-215, s. 10.)

§ 58-7-179. Mortgage loans.

(a)   An insurer may invest any of its funds in bonds, notes, or other evidences of indebtedness that are secured by first mortgages or deeds of trust upon improved real property located in the United States, any U.S. territory, or Canada, or that are secured by first mortgages or deeds of trust upon leasehold estates having an unexpired term of not less than 30 years, inclusive of the terms that may be provided by enforceable options of renewal, as long as the loan matures at least 20 years before the expiration of such lease, in improved real property located in the United States, any U.S. territory, or Canada. In all cases the security for the loan must be a first lien upon the real property, and there must not be any condition or right of reentry or forfeiture not insured against under which, in the case of real property other than leaseholds, the lien can be cut off or subordinated or otherwise disturbed, or under which, in the case of leaseholds, the insurer cannot continue the lease in force for the duration of the loan. Nothing herein prohibits any investment because of the existence of any prior lien for ground rents, taxes, assessments, or other similar charges not yet delinquent. This section does not prohibit investment in mortgages or similar obligations when made under G.S. 58-7-180.

(b)   "Improved real property" means all farmlands used for tillage, crops, or pasture; timberlands; and all real property on which permanent improvements, and improvements under construction or in process of construction, suitable for residential, institutional, commercial, or industrial use are situated.

(c)   No such mortgage loan or loans made or acquired by an insurer on any one property shall, at the time of investment by the insurer, exceed the larger of the following amounts, as applicable:

(1) Ninety-five percent (95%) of the value of the real property or leasehold securing the real property in the case of a mortgage on a dwelling primarily intended for occupancy by not more than four families if they insure down to seventy-five percent (75%) with a licensed mortgage insurance company, or seventy-five percent (75%) of the value in the case of other real estate mortgages;

(2) The amount of any insurance or guaranty of the loan by the United States or by an agency or instrumentality thereof; or

(3) The percentage-of-value limit on the amount of the loan applicable under subdivision (1) of this subsection, plus the amount by which the excess of the loan over the percentage-of-value limit is insured or guaranteed by the United States or by any agency or instrumentality thereof.

(d) In the case of a purchase money mortgage given to secure the purchase price of real estate sold by the insurer, the amount lent or invested shall not exceed the unpaid part of the purchase price.

(e) Nothing in this section prohibits an insurer from renewing or extending a loan for the original or a lesser amount where a shrinkage in value of the real estate securing the loan would cause its value to be less than the amount otherwise required in relation to the amount of the loan. (1991, c. 681, s. 29; 2003-212, s. 11.)

§ 58-7-180. Chattel mortgages.

(a) In connection with a mortgage loan on the security of real estate designed and used primarily for residential purposes only, where the mortgage loan was acquired under G.S. 58-7-179, an insurer may lend or invest an amount not exceeding twenty percent (20%) of the amount lent on or invested in such real estate mortgage on the security of a chattel mortgage to be amortized by regular periodic payments with a term of not more than five years, and representing a first and prior lien, except for taxes not then delinquent, on personal property constituting durable equipment owned by the mortgagor and kept and used in the mortgaged premises.

(b) For the purposes of this section, the term "durable equipment" includes only mechanical refrigerators, air-conditioning equipment, mechanical laundering machines, heating and cooking stoves and ranges, and, in addition, in the case of apartment houses and hotels, room furniture and furnishings.

(c)   Before the acquisition of a chattel mortgage under this section, items of property to be included therein shall be separately appraised by a qualified appraiser and the fair market value determined. No such chattel mortgage loan shall exceed in amount the same ratio of loan to the value of the property as is applicable to the companion loan on the real property.

(d)   This section does not prohibit an insurer from taking liens on personal property as additional security for any investment otherwise eligible under this Chapter. (1991, c. 681, s. 29.)

§ 58-7-182. Special investments by title insurers.

In addition to other investments eligible under this Chapter, a title insurer may invest and have invested an amount not exceeding the greater of three hundred thousand dollars ($300,000) or fifty percent (50%) of that part of its policyholders' surplus that exceeds the minimum surplus required by G.S. 58-7-75 in its abstract plant and equipment, in loans secured by mortgages on abstract plants and equipment, and, with the Commissioner's consent, in stocks of abstract companies. (1991, c. 681, s. 29.)

§ 58-7-183. Special consent investments.

(a)   After satisfying the requirements of this Chapter, any funds of an insurer in excess of its reserves and policyholders' surplus required to be maintained may be invested:

(1)   Without limitation in any investments otherwise authorized by this Chapter; or

(2)   In such other investments not specifically authorized by this Chapter as long as any single interest investment does not exceed two percent (2%) of admitted assets and the aggregate of the investments does not exceed the lesser of five percent (5%) of the insurer's total admitted assets or sixty percent

(60%) of the amount by which the insurer's policyholders' surplus exceeds the minimum required to be maintained.

The limitations in subdivision (2) of this subsection may be exceeded if approved in writing by the Commissioner.

(b)   In no case shall the investments authorized under this section being held by an insurer be greater than the amount by which the insurer's policyholders' surplus exceeds the minimum required to be maintained.

(c)   Notwithstanding the provisions of this section, an insurer may not invest in investments prohibited by this Chapter. (1991, c. 681, s. 29; 1993, c. 452, s. 14.1, c. 504, s. 6.)

§ 58-7-185. Prohibited investments and investment underwriting.

(a)   In addition to investments excluded under other provisions of this Chapter, except with prior approval by the Commissioner, an insurer shall not directly or indirectly invest in or lend its funds upon the security of:

(1)   Issued shares of its own capital stock, except in connection with a plan for purchase of the shares by the insurer's officers, employees, or agents. No such stock shall, however, constitute an asset of the insurer in any determination of its financial condition.

(2)   Except with the Commissioner's consent, securities issued by any corporation or enterprise, the controlling interest of which is or will after acquisition by the insurer be held directly or indirectly by the insurer or any combination of the insurer and the insurer's directors, officers, parent corporation, subsidiaries, or controlling stockholders. Investments in subsidiaries under G.S. 58-19-10 are not subject to this provision.

(3)   Repealed by Session Laws 2001-223, s. 8.13.

(b)   No insurer shall underwrite or participate in the underwriting of an offering of securities or property by any other person. (1991, c. 681, s. 29; 2001-223, ss. 8.12, 8.13.)

§ 58-7-187. Real estate, in general.

(a) An insurer shall not directly or indirectly acquire or hold real estate except as authorized in this section.

(b) An insurer may acquire and hold:

(1) Land and buildings thereon used or acquired for use as its principal home office and branch offices, or used in conjunction with such offices, for the convenient transaction of its own business.

(2) Real property acquired in satisfaction in whole or in part of loans, mortgages, liens, judgments, decrees, or debts previously owing to the insurer, in the course of its business.

(3) Real property acquired in part payment of the consideration on the sale of other real property owned by it, if the transaction effects a net reduction in the insurer's investment in real estate.

(4) Real property acquired by gift or devise or through merger, consolidation, or bulk reinsurance of another insurer under this Chapter.

(5) Additional real property and equipment incident to real property, if necessary or convenient for the enhancement of the marketability or sale value of real property previously acquired or held by it under subdivisions (2) through (4) of this subsection.

(c) An insurer may acquire and hold real property for investment, subject to the following conditions:

(1) The amount shall not exceed in the aggregate the lesser of five percent (5%) of the insurer's admitted assets or fifteen percent (15%) of the insurer's capital and surplus.

(2) The amount in any one property shall not exceed one percent (1%) of the insurer's admitted assets.

(3) The amount in unimproved land shall not exceed one-half of one percent (0.5%) of the insurer's admitted assets.

(4) There shall be no time limit for the disposal of investment real estate.

(d) The amount in real property acquired and held by an insurer shall not exceed fifteen percent (15%) of the insurer's admitted assets; but the Commissioner may permit an insurer to invest in real property in such increased amount as the Commissioner considers to be proper. (1991, c. 681, s. 29.)

§ 58-7-188. Time limit for disposal of ineligible property and securities; effect of failure to dispose.

(a) Any property or securities lawfully acquired by an insurer that it could not otherwise have invested in or lent its funds upon at the time of the acquisition shall be disposed of within three years from the date of acquisition, unless within that period the security has attained to the standard of eligibility; except that any security or property acquired under any agreement of bulk reinsurance, merger, or consolidation may be retained for a longer period if so provided in the plan for the reinsurance, merger, or consolidation as approved by the Commissioner under this Chapter. Upon application by the insurer and proof that forced sale of any such property or security would materially injure the insurer's interests, the Commissioner may extend the disposal period for an additional reasonable time.

(b) Any property or securities lawfully acquired and held by an insurer after expiration of the period for their disposal or any extension of the period granted by the Commissioner shall not be allowed as an asset of the insurer. (1991, c. 681, s. 29.)

§ 58-7-190: Repealed by Session Laws 1993, c. 452, s. 65.

§ 58-7-192. Valuation of securities and investments.

(a) through (c) Repealed by Session Laws 2003-212, s. 8, effective October 1, 2003.

(d) No valuations shall be greater than any applicable valuation or method contained in the latest edition of the NAIC publications entitled "Purposes and Procedures Manual of the NAIC Securities Valuation Office" or the "Accounting Practices and Procedures Manual", unless the Commissioner determines that another valuation method is appropriate when it results in a more conservative valuation.

(e) Repealed by Session Laws 2003-212, s. 8, effective October 1, 2003. (1991, c. 681, s. 29; 1993, c. 452, ss. 15, 16; 2001-223, s. 8.14; 2003-212, s. 8.)

§ 58-7-193. Valuation of property.

(a), (b) Repealed by Session Laws 2003-212, s. 9, effective October 1, 2003.

(c) Personal property acquired pursuant to chattel mortgages made in accordance with G.S. 58-7-180 shall not be valued at an amount greater than the unpaid balance of principal on the defaulted loan at the date of acquisition, or the fair market value of the property, whichever amount is less.

(d) If the Commissioner and an insurer do not agree on the value of real or personal property of an insurer, in carrying out the Commissioner's responsibilities under this section, the Commissioner may retain the services of a qualified real or personal property appraiser. The insurer shall reimburse the Commissioner for the costs of the services of any appraiser incurred with respect to the Commissioner's responsibilities under this section. (1991, c. 681, s. 29; 2003-212, s. 9.)

§ 58-7-195: Repealed by Session Laws 2003-212, s. 10, effective October 1, 2003.

§ 58-7-197. Replacing certain assets; reporting certain liabilities.

(a) The Commissioner, upon determining that an insurer's asset has not been valued according to this Chapter or that it does not qualify as an asset, shall require the insurer to properly revalue an improperly valued asset or replace a nonadmitted asset with an asset suitable to the Commissioner within 90 days after the determination.

(b) The Commissioner, upon determining that an insurer has failed to report certain liabilities that should have been reported, shall require that the insurer report those liabilities to the Commissioner within 90 days after notice to the insurer.

(c) When the Commissioner determines that an admitted asset held by any insurer is of doubtful value or is without ascertainable value on a public exchange, unless the insurer establishes a value by placing the asset upon the market and obtaining a bona fide offer for the asset, the Commissioner may have the asset appraised, and the appraisal shall be the true value of the asset. No asset may be carried in an insurer's financial statement under G.S. 58-2-165 at an appraised value established by the insurer unless the Commissioner's prior written approval is obtained.

(d) When any admitted asset defaults as to principal or in the payment of interest or dividends after it has been purchased by an insurer, the asset shall subsequently be carried at its market value or, after notice and opportunity for hearing, at a value determined by the Commissioner.

(e) Whenever it appears to the Commissioner that an insurer has acquired any asset in violation of this Chapter, the Commissioner shall disallow, in whole or in part, the amount of the asset that is prohibited by this Chapter. In any determination of the financial position of the insurer, that amount shall be deducted as a nonadmitted asset of the insurer. (1991, c. 681, s. 29.)

§ 58-7-198. Assets of foreign or alien insurers.

The Commissioner may refuse a new or renewal license to any foreign or alien insurer upon finding that its assets do not comply in substance with the investment requirements and limitations imposed by this Chapter upon like domestic insurers whenever authorized to do the same kinds of insurance business. (1991, c. 681, s. 29.)

§ 58-7-200. Investment transactions.

(a) The transactions specified in subsections (b) through (e) of this section are expressly allowed or prohibited as provided in this section and to the extent they are not in conflict with other provisions of this Chapter.

(b) An insurer may engage in derivative transactions under the provisions and limitations of G.S. 58-7-205.

(c) No insurer shall directly or indirectly invest in, or lend its funds to, any of its directors, officers, controlling stockholders, or any other person in which an officer, director, or controlling stockholder is substantially interested, nor shall any director, officer, or controlling stockholder directly or indirectly accept the funds.

(d) No director, officer, or controlling stockholder of any insurer shall receive any money or valuable thing, either directly or indirectly or through any substantial interest in any other person, for negotiating, procuring, recommending, or aiding in any purchase or sale of property or loan from the insurer; or be monetarily interested either as principal, corporation, agent, or beneficiary, in any such purchase, sale, or loan; and no financial obligation of any such director, officer, or stockholder shall be guaranteed by the insurer. "Substantial interest in any other person" means an interest equivalent to ownership or control by a director, officer, or controlling stockholder or the aggregate ownership or control by all directors, officers, and controlling stockholders of the same insurer of those percentages or more of the stock of the person, as defined under "control" in G.S. 58-19-5(2).

(e) Nothing in this section prohibits:

(1) A director or officer of any insurer from receiving the usual salary, compensation, or emoluments for services rendered in the ordinary course of that person's duties as a director or officer, if the salary, compensation, or emolument is authorized by vote of the board of directors of the insurer;

(2) Any insurer in connection with the relocation of the place of employment of an officer, including any relocation in connection with the initial employment of the officer, from (i) making, or the officer from accepting therefrom, a mortgage loan to the officer on real property owned by the officer that is to serve as the officer's residence or (ii) acquiring, or the officer from selling thereto, at not more than its fair market value, the officer's prior residence;

(3) The payment to a director or officer of any such insurer who is a licensed attorney-at-law of fees in connection with loans made by the insurer if and when the fees are paid by the borrower and do not constitute a charge against the insurer;

(4) An insurer from making a loan upon a policy held therein by the borrower not in excess of the policy's net value; or

(5) Subject to G.S. 58-19-30 and G.S. 58-7-163, an insurer from advancing funds to directors, officers, or controlling stockholders, for expenses reasonably expected to be incurred in the ordinary course of the insurer's business, as authorized or approved by the insurer's board of directors or by individuals authorized by the board and charged with the supervision or making of the advances. (1991, c. 681, s. 29; 2001-223, ss. 8.15, 8.16; 2007-127, s. 8.)

§ 58-7-205. Derivative transactions.

(a) As used in this section, the following terms have the following meanings:

(1) "Business entity" includes a sole proprietorship, corporation, limited liability company, association, partnership, joint stock company, joint venture, mutual fund, trust, joint tenancy or other similar form of business organization, whether for-profit or not-for-profit.

(2) "Counterparty exposure" amount means:

a. The amount of credit risk attributable to a derivative instrument entered into with a business entity other than through a qualified exchange, qualified foreign exchange, or cleared through a qualified clearinghouse ("over-the-counter derivative instrument"). The amount of credit risk equals:

1. The market value of the over-the-counter derivative instrument if the liquidation of the derivative instrument would result in a final cash payment to the insurer; or

2. Zero if the liquidation of the derivative instrument would not result in a final cash payment to the insurer.

b. If over-the-counter derivative instruments are entered into under a written master agreement which provides for netting of payments owed by the respective parties and the domicile of the counterparty is either within the United States or, if not within the United States, within a foreign jurisdiction listed in the Purposes and Procedures of the Securities Valuation Office of the NAIC as eligible for netting, the net amount of credit risk shall be the greater of zero or the net sum of:

1. The market value of the over-the-counter derivative instruments entered into under the agreement, the liquidation of which would result in a final cash payment to the insurer; and

2. The market value of the over-the-counter derivative instruments entered into under the agreement, the liquidation of which would result in a final cash payment by the insurer to the business entity.

c. For open transactions, market value shall be determined at the end of the most recent quarter of the insurer's fiscal year and shall be reduced by the market value of acceptable collateral held by the insurer or placed in escrow by one or both parties.

(3) "Derivative instrument" means an agreement, option, instrument, or a series or combination thereof:

a. To make or take delivery of, or assume or relinquish, a specified amount of one or more underlying interests, or to make a cash settlement in lieu thereof; or

b. That has a price, performance, value, or cash flow based primarily upon the actual or expected price level, performance, value, or cash flow of one or more underlying interests.

Derivative instruments include options, warrants used in a hedging transaction and not attached to another financial instrument, caps, floors, collars, swaps, forwards, futures, and any other agreements, options, or instruments substantially similar thereto or any series or combination thereof. Derivative instruments shall additionally include any agreements, options, or instruments permitted under rules adopted under subsection (c) of this section. Derivative instruments shall not include an investment authorized by G.S. 58-7-173, 58-7-175, 58-7-178, 58-7-179, 58-7-180, and 58-7-187.

(4) "Derivative transaction" means any transaction involving the use of one or more derivative instruments.

(5) "Qualified clearinghouse" means a clearinghouse for, and subject to the rules of, a qualified exchange or a qualified foreign exchange. The clearinghouse provides clearing services, including acting as a counterparty to each of the parties to a transaction such that the parties no longer have credit risk as to each other.

(6) "Qualified exchange" means:

a. A securities exchange registered as a national securities exchange, or a securities market regulated under the Securities Exchange Act of 1934 (15 U.S.C. §§ 78, et seq.), as amended;

b. A board of trade or commodities exchange designated as a contract market by the Commodity Futures Trading Commission, or any successor thereof;

c. Private Offerings, Resales and Trading through Automated Linkages (PORTAL);

d. A designated offshore securities market as defined in Securities Exchange Commission Regulation S, 17 C.F.R. Part 230, as amended; or

e. A qualified foreign exchange.

(7) "Qualified foreign exchange" means a foreign exchange, board of trade, or contract market located outside the United States, its territories or possessions:

a. That has received regulatory comparability relief under Commodity Futures Trading Commission Rule 30.10 (as set forth in Appendix C to Part 30 of the CFTC's Regulations, 17 C.F.R. Part 30);

b. That is, or its members are, subject to the jurisdiction of a foreign futures authority that has received regulatory comparability relief under Commodity Futures Trading Commission Rule 30.10 (as set forth in Appendix C to Part 30 of the CFTC's Regulations, 17 C.F.R. Part 30) as to futures transactions in the jurisdiction where the exchange, board of trade, or contract market is located; or

c. Upon which foreign stock index futures contracts are listed that are the subject of no-action relief issued by the CFTC's Office of General Counsel, but an exchange, board of trade, or contract market that qualifies as a "qualified foreign exchange" only under this paragraph shall only be a "qualified foreign exchange" as to foreign stock index futures contracts that are the subject of the no-action relief under this paragraph.

(8) "Replication transaction" means a derivative transaction that is intended to replicate the investment in one or more assets that an insurer is authorized to acquire or sell under this section or G.S. 58-7-165. A derivative transaction that is entered into as a hedging transaction shall not be considered a replication transaction.

(b) An insurer may, directly or indirectly through an investment subsidiary, engage in derivative transactions under this section under the following conditions:

(1) An insurer may use derivative instruments under this section to engage in hedging transactions and certain income generation transactions as may be further defined by rules adopted by the Commissioner.

(2) An insurer shall be able to demonstrate to the Commissioner the intended hedging characteristics and the ongoing effectiveness of the derivative transaction or combination of the transactions through cash flow testing or other appropriate analyses.

(c) The Commissioner may adopt reasonable rules for investments and transactions under this section including, but not limited to, rules which impose financial solvency standards, valuation standards, and reporting requirements.

(d) An insurer may enter into hedging transactions under this section if, as a result of and after giving effect to the transaction:

(1) The aggregate statement value of options, caps, floors, and warrants not attached to another financial instrument purchased and used in hedging transactions then engaged in by the insurer does not exceed seven and one-half percent (7.5%) of its admitted assets;

(2) The aggregate statement value of options, caps, and floors written in hedging transactions then engaged in by the insurer does not exceed three percent (3%) of its admitted assets; and

(3) The aggregate potential exposure of collars, swaps, forwards, and futures used in hedging transactions then engaged in by the insurer does not exceed six and one-half percent (6.5%) of its admitted assets.

(e) An insurer may enter into the following types of income generation transactions if, as a result of and after giving effect to the transactions, the aggregate statement value of the fixed income assets that are subject to call or that generate the cash flows for payments under the caps or floors, plus the face value of fixed income securities underlying a derivative instrument subject to call, plus the amount of the purchase obligations under the puts, does not exceed ten percent (10%) of its admitted assets:

(1) Sales of covered call options on noncallable fixed-income securities, callable fixed-income securities if the option expires by its terms before the end of the noncallable period, or derivative instruments based on fixed income securities;

(2) Sales of covered call options on equity securities, if the insurer holds in its portfolio, or can immediately acquire through the exercise of options, warrants, or conversion rights already owned, the equity securities subject to call during the complete term of the call option sold;

(3) Sales of covered puts on investments that the insurer is permitted to acquire under this Chapter, if the insurer has escrowed or entered into a custodian agreement segregating cash or cash equivalents with a market value equal to the amount of its purchase obligations under the put during the complete term of the put option sold; or

(4) Sales of covered caps or floors, if the insurer holds in its portfolio the investments generating the cash flow to make the required payments under the caps or floors during the complete term that the cap or floor is outstanding.

(f) An insurer shall include all counterparty exposure amounts in determining compliance with the limitations of G.S. 58-7-170.

(g) Under rules that may be adopted by the Commissioner, additional transactions involving the use of derivative instruments in excess of the limits of subsection (d) of this section or for other risk management purposes may be approved by the Commissioner.

(h) An insurer shall establish guidelines and internal procedures as follows:

(1) Before engaging in a derivative transaction, an insurer shall establish written guidelines that shall be used for effecting and maintaining the transactions. The guidelines shall:

a. Address investment or, if applicable, underwriting objectives, and risk constraints such as credit risk limits;

b. Address permissible transactions and the relationship of those transactions to its operations, such as a precise identification of the risks being hedged by a derivative transaction; and

c. Require compliance with internal control procedures.

(2) An insurer shall have a system for determining whether a derivative instrument used for hedging has been effective.

(3) An insurer shall have a credit risk management system for over-the-counter derivative transactions that measures credit risk exposure using the counterparty exposure amount.

(4) An insurer's board of directors shall, in accordance with G.S. 58-7-168:

a. Approve the guidelines required by subdivision (1) of this subsection and the systems required by subdivisions (2) and (3) of this subsection; and

b. Determine whether the insurer has adequate professional personnel, technical expertise and systems to implement investment practices involving derivatives.

(i) An insurer shall maintain documentation and records relating to each derivative transaction, such as:

(1) The purpose or purposes of the transaction;

(2) The assets or liabilities to which the transaction relates;

(3) The specific derivative instrument used in the transaction;

(4) For over-the-counter derivative instrument transactions, the name of the counterparty and counterparty exposure amount; and

(5) For exchange-traded derivative instruments, the name of the exchange and the name of the firm that handled the trade.

(j) Each derivative instrument shall be:

(1) Traded on a qualified exchange;

(2) Entered into with, or guaranteed by, a business entity;

(3) Issued or written by or entered into with the issuer of the underlying interest on which the derivative instrument is based; or

(4) Entered into with a qualified foreign exchange. (2001-223, s. 8.17.)

Article 8.

Mutual Insurance Companies.

§ 58-8-1. Mutual insurance companies organized; requisites for doing business.

No policy may be issued by a mutual company until the president and the secretary of the company have certified under oath that every subscription for insurance in the list presented to the Commissioner for approval is genuine, and made with an agreement with every subscriber for insurance that he will take the policies subscribed for by him within 30 days after the granting of a license to the company by the Commissioner to issue policies. Any person making a false oath in respect to the certificate is guilty of a Class I felony. (1899, c. 54, ss. 25, 32, 34; 1901, c. 391, s. 3; 1903, c. 438, s. 4; Rev., s. 4738; 1911, c. 93; C.S., s. 6346; 1945, c. 386; 1989 (Reg. Sess., 1990), c. 1054, s. 4; 1993 (Reg. Sess., 1994), c. 767, s. 24.)

§ 58-8-5. Manner of amending charter.

(a) A domestic mutual insurance company may hereafter amend its charter in the following manner only:

(1) A meeting of the board of directors shall be called in accordance with the bylaws, specifying the amendment to be voted upon at such meeting;

(2) If at such meeting two thirds of the directors present vote in favor of the proposed amendment, then the president and secretary shall under oath make a certificate to this effect, which certificate shall set forth the call for such meeting, the service of such call upon all directors, and the minutes of the meeting relating to the adoption of the proposed amendment;

(3) If the meeting at which the proposed amendment is to be considered is a special meeting, rather than a regular annual meeting of policyholders, such special meeting can be called only after the Commissioner has given his approval in writing;

(4) If at such policyholders' meeting two thirds of those voting in person or by proxy shall vote in favor of any proposed amendment, the president and secretary shall make a certificate under oath setting forth such fact together with the full text of the amendment thus approved. Said certificate shall, within 30 days after such meeting, be submitted to the Commissioner for his approval as conforming to the requirements of law, and it shall be the duty of the Commissioner to act upon all proposed amendments within 10 days after the filing of such certificate with him.

(b) All charter amendments heretofore issued upon application of the board of directors of any domestic mutual insurance company are hereby validated, if otherwise legally adopted. (1943, c. 170; 1947, c. 721; 1991, c. 720, s. 4; 2001-223, s. 9.1.)

§ 58-8-10. Policyholders are members of mutual companies.

Every person insured by a mutual insurance company is a member while that person's policy is in force, entitled to one vote for each policy that person holds, and must be notified of the time and place of holding the company's meetings by a written notice or by an imprint upon the back of each policy, receipt, or certificate of renewal, as follows:

The insured is hereby notified that by virtue of this policy the insured is a member of the _____ insurance company, and that the annual meetings of the company are held at its home office on the _____ day of_____, in each year, at _____ o'clock.

The blanks shall be duly filled in print and are a sufficient notice. A corporation that becomes a member of a mutual insurance company may authorize any person to represent the corporation; and this representative has all the rights of an individual member. A person holding property in trust may insure it in a mutual insurance company, and as trustee assume the liability and be entitled to the rights of a member; but is not personally liable upon the contract of insurance. Members may vote by proxies, dated and executed within one year after receipt, and returned and recorded on the books of the company three days or more before the meeting at which they are to be used. (1899, c. 54, s. 33; Rev., s. 4739; C.S., s. 6348; 1945, c. 386; 1947, c. 721; 1998-211, s. 37.1(a).)

§ 58-8-15. Directors in mutual companies.

Every mutual insurance company shall elect by ballot a board of not less than seven directors, who shall manage and conduct its business and hold office for one year or for such term as the bylaws provide and until their successors are qualified. The directors need not be residents of this State or members of the company. In companies with a guaranty capital, no more than one-half of the directors shall be elected by the holders of guaranty capital, except where guaranty capital holders are policyholders. Policyholders which are holders of guaranty capital shall be entitled to one vote for each policy that person holds and one vote for each unit of guaranty capital that person holds. (1899, c. 54, s. 33; Rev., s. 4739; C.S., s. 6349; 1945, c. 386; 1971, c. 751; 2003-212, s. 14.)

§ 58-8-20. Mutual companies with a guaranty capital.

(a)   A mutual insurance company formed as provided in Articles 1 through 64 of this Chapter, in lieu of the contributed surplus required for the organization of mutual companies under the provisions of G.S. 58-7-75, or a mutual insurance company now existing, may, with the prior approval of the

Commissioner, tender a guaranty capital offering of not less than fifty thousand dollars ($50,000), divided into units of one hundred dollars ($100.00) each, which shall be invested in the same manner as is provided in this Chapter for the investment of the capital stock of insurance companies.

(a1) Guaranty capital may be issued by an existing domestic mutual insurance company only under the following terms and conditions:

(1) To aid and assist a financially troubled domestic mutual insurance company which otherwise faces rehabilitation or liquidation by this Department; or

(2) For any other reason as presented in a petition to the Commissioner and which is found by the Commissioner to be reasonable, justifiable, and in the best interest of all the policyholders of the company.

Guaranty capital issued under subdivision (2) of this subsection shall require written notification of the action proposed by the board of directors of the company to be mailed to the policyholders of the company not less than 30 days before the meeting when the action may be taken. The written notification shall be advertised in two newspapers of general circulation, approved by the Commissioner, not less than three times a week for a period of not less than four weeks before the meeting. The written notification to policyholders shall include a proxy statement to allow policyholders to vote on the proposed action without personal attendance at the meeting, and the Commissioner shall approve both the written notification and the proxy statement. The proposed action shall be effected by a vote of two-thirds of the policyholders voting thereon in person or by proxy.

(b) The board of directors of a company may distribute interest to the holders of guaranty capital in accordance with the guaranty capital filing approved by the Department.

(c) Guaranty capital shall be applied to the payment of losses only when the company has exhausted its cash in hand and the invested assets, exclusive of uncollected premiums, and when thus impaired, the directors may make good the whole or any part of it by assessments upon the contingent funds of the company at the date of such impairment.

(d) Guaranty capital holders are entitled to one vote per unit of guaranty capital. Guaranty capital holders who are not policyholders are not entitled to participate in the policyholder votes prescribed under subdivision (a1)(2) and subsection (e) of this section.

(e) Guaranty capital may be reduced or retired by vote of the policyholders of the company and the assent of the Commissioner, if the net assets of the company above its reserve and all other claims and obligations, exclusive of guaranty capital, for two years immediately preceding and including the date of its last annual statement, is not less than twenty-five percent (25%) of the guaranty capital. Written notice of the proposed action on the part of the company must be mailed to each policyholder of the company not less than 30 days before the meeting when the action may be taken, and must also be advertised in two papers of general circulation, approved by the Commissioner, not less than three times a week for a period of not less than four weeks before the meeting. The written notification to policyholders shall include a proxy statement to allow policyholders to vote on the proposed action without personal attendance at the meeting, and the Commissioner shall approve both the written notification and the proxy statement. An affirmative vote of at least two-thirds of the policyholders voting in person or by proxy is required to adopt the proposed action.

(f) No insurance company with guaranty capital shall distribute to its holders of guaranty capital its assets, except as provided in the guaranty capital filing as approved by the Commissioner.

(g) In the event of a merger, demutualization, or other event where the entity ceases to exist, guaranty capital shall only be returned or repaid to the holders of guaranty capital to the extent that the guaranty capital has been contributed together with accrued interest as specified in the filing approved by the Commissioner. (1899, c. 54, s. 34; Rev., s. 4740; 1911, c. 196, s. 3; C.S., s. 6350; 1945, c. 386; 1971, c. 752; 1981, c. 723; 1989, c. 320; 1991, c. 720, s. 10; 1993, c. 452, s. 17; 2003-212, s. 15; 2005-215, s. 26.)

§ 58-8-25. Dividends to policyholders.

(a) Any participating or dividend-paying company, stock or mutual or foreign or domestic, that writes other than life insurance or workers' compensation insurance and employers' liability insurance in connection therewith, may declare and pay a dividend to policyholders from its unassigned surplus, as reflected in the company's most recent annual or quarterly statement filed with the Commissioner under G.S. 58-2-165, which shall include only its surplus in excess of any required minimum surplus. No such dividend shall be paid unless it is fair and equitable and for the best interest of the company and its policyholders. In declaring any dividend to its policyholders, any such company may make reasonable classifications of policies expiring during a fixed period, upon the basis of each general kind of insurance covered by those policies and by territorial divisions of the location of risks by states, except that in fixing the amount of dividends to be paid on each general kind of insurance, the dividends shall be uniform in rate and applicable to the majority of risks within that general kind of insurance, and exceptions may be made as to any class or classes of risk and a different rate or amount of dividends paid on the class or classes if the conditions applicable to the class or classes differ substantially from the condition applicable to the kind of insurance as a whole. Every such company shall have an equal rate of dividend for the same term on all policies insuring risks in the same classification. The payment of dividends to policyholders shall not be contingent upon the maintenance or renewal of the policy. All dividends shall be paid to the policyholder unless a written assignment of those dividends is executed. Neither the payment of dividends nor the rate of the dividends may be guaranteed by any company, or its agent, before the declaration of the dividend by the board of directors of the company. The holders of policies of insurance issued by a company in compliance with the orders of any public official, bureau or committee, in conformity with any statutory requirement or voluntary arrangement, for the issuance of insurance to risks not otherwise acceptable to the company, may be established as a separate class of risks.

(b) Any participating or dividend-paying company, stock or mutual or foreign or domestic, that writes workers' compensation insurance and employers' liability insurance in connection therewith may declare and pay a dividend to policyholders from its unassigned surplus, as reflected in the company's most recent statement filed with the Commissioner under G.S. 58-2-165, which shall include only its surplus in excess of any required minimum surplus. No such dividend shall be paid unless it is fair and equitable and for the best interest of the company and its policyholders. In declaring any dividend to its policyholders, any such company may make reasonable classifications of policies expiring during a fixed period. The payment of dividends to policyholders shall not be contingent upon the maintenance or renewal of the policy. All dividends shall be paid to the policyholder unless a written assignment of those dividends is executed. Neither the payment of dividends nor the rate of the dividends may be guaranteed by any company, or its agent, before the declaration of the dividend by the board of directors of the company. The holders of policies of insurance issued by a company in compliance with the orders of any public official, bureau, or committee, in conformity with any statutory requirement or voluntary arrangement, for the issuance of insurance to risks not otherwise acceptable to the company, may be established as a separate class of risks. (1899, c. 54, s. 35; Rev., s. 4741; C.S., s. 6351; 1935, c. 89; 1945, c. 386; 1947, c. 721; 1955, c. 645; 1983, c. 374, ss. 2, 3; 2001-223, s. 9.2.)

§ 58-8-30. Contingent liability of policyholders.

Every insurance company shall in its bylaws and policies prescribe the contingent liability, if any, of its members for the payment of losses, reserves and expenses not provided for by its assets, which contingent liability shall be in accordance with the provisions of G.S. 58-7-75. Each member is liable for the payment of his proportionate share of any assessments made by the company in accordance with the law, his contract and the bylaws of the company on account of losses incurred while he was a member, if he is notified of such assessment within one year after the expiration of his policy. When any reduction is made in the contingent liability of members, it shall apply proportionately to all policies in force. (1945, c. 386.)

§ 58-8-35. Contingent liability printed on policy.

Every insurance company licensed to do business in this State shall print on each policy in clear and explicit language the full contingent liability of its members. (1945, c. 386; 1991, c. 644, s. 1; 1991 (Reg. Sess., 1992), c. 837, s. 2.)

§ 58-8-36. Administrative fees.

Statewide multiline limited assessable mutual insurance companies are not subject to the provisions of G.S. 58-33-85(b). (2011-196, s. 12.)

§ 58-8-40. Nonassessable policies; foreign or alien companies.

No foreign or alien insurance company shall be licensed to issue in this State nonassessable policies unless it has a free surplus equal in amount to that required of a domestic insurance company, writing the same kind or kinds of insurance, and in addition thereto has fully complied with the requirements of the government under which it was organized; and no foreign or alien insurance company may be licensed to do business in this State to issue assessable policies if it issues nonassessable policies in any other state or country unless all policies shall state that any assessment shall be for the exclusive benefit of holders of policies which provide for such contingent liability and the holders of policies subject to assessment shall not be liable to assessment in an amount greater in proportion to the total deficiency than the ratio that the deficiency attributable to the assessable business bears to the total deficiency. (1945, c. 386.)

§ 58-8-45. Waiver of forfeiture in policies assigned or pledged; notice of assignment; payment of assessment or premium by assignee or mortgagee.

When any policy of insurance is issued by any mutual insurance company or association other than life, organized under the laws of this State and such policy is assigned or pledged as collateral security for the payment of a debt, such company or association, by its president and secretary or other managing officers, may insert in such policy so assigned or pledged, or attach thereto as a rider thereon, a provision or provisions to be approved by the Commissioner, whereby any or all conditions of the policy which work a suspension or forfeiture and especially the provisions of the statute which limits such corporation to insure only property of its members, may be waived in such case for the benefit of the assignee or mortgagee. In case any such company or association shall consent to such assignment of any policy or policies, or the proceeds thereof, it may nevertheless at any time thereafter, by its president and secretary or such other officer as may be authorized by the board of directors, cancel such policy by giving the assignee or mortgagee not less than 10 days' notice in writing: Provided, however, a longer period may be agreed upon by the company or association and such assignee or mortgagee. And the president and secretary of such company or association, with the approval of the Commissioner, may agree with the assignee or mortgagee upon an assessment or premium to be paid to the insurer in case the insured shall not pay the same, which shall not be less than such a rate or sum of money as may be produced by the average assessments or premiums made or charged by like company or association during a period of five years next preceding the year of such agreement and assignment. When an assignment is made as herein provided the policy or policies so assigned or pledged, subject to the conditions herein, shall remain in full force and effect for the benefit of the assignee or mortgagee, notwithstanding the title or ownership of the assured to the property insured, or to any interest therein, shall be in any manner changed, transferred or encumbered. (Ex. Sess., 1920, c. 79; C.S. s. 6351(a); 1945, c. 386; 1991, c. 720, s. 4.)

§ 58-8-50. Guaranty against assessments prohibited.

If any director, officer, or agent of a mutual insurance company, either officially or privately, gives a guarantee to a policyholder of the company against an assessment to which that policyholder would otherwise be liable, the director, officer, or agent shall be punished by a fine not exceeding one thousand dollars ($1,000) for each offense. (1899, c. 54, s. 100; Rev., s. 3496; C.S., s. 6352; 1945, c. 386; 2003-212, s. 16.)

§ 58-8-55. Manner of making assessments; rights and liabilities of policyholders.

When a mutual insurance company is not possessed of cash funds above its reserve sufficient for the payment of insured losses and expenses, it must make an assessment for the amount needed to pay such losses and expenses upon its members liable to assessment therefor in proportion to their several liabilities. The company shall cause to be recorded in a book kept for that purpose the order for the assessment, together with a statement which must set forth the condition of the company at the date of the order, the amount of its cash assets and deposits, notes, or other contingent funds liable to the assessment, the amount the assessment calls for, and the particular losses or liabilities it is made to provide for. This record must be made and signed by the directors who voted for the order before any part of the assessment is collected, and any person liable to the assessment may inspect and take a copy of the same. When, by reason of depreciation or loss of its funds or otherwise, the cash assets of such company, after providing for its other debts, are less than the required premium reserve upon its policies, it must make good the deficiency by assessment in the manner above provided. If the directors are of the opinion that the company is liable to become insolvent they may, instead of such assessment, make two assessments, the first determining what each policyholder must equitably pay or receive in case of withdrawal from the company and having his policy canceled; the second, what further sum each must pay in order to reinsure the unexpired term of his policy at the same rate as the whole was insured at first. Each policyholder must pay or receive according to the first assessment, and his policy shall be cancelled unless he pays the sum further determined by the second assessment, in which case his policy continues in force; but in neither case may a policyholder receive or have credited to him more than he would have received on having his policy canceled by a vote of the directors under the bylaws. (1899, c. 54, ss. 36, 37; Rev., s. 4742; C.S., s. 6353; 1945, c. 386.)

§ 58-8-60. Independent charters for members of the Farmers Mutual Fire Insurance Association of North Carolina.

(a) Each branch of the Farmers Mutual Fire Insurance Association of North Carolina ("Association"), created by Chapter 343 of the 1893 Private Laws of North Carolina, as amended, shall adopt articles of incorporation by a majority vote of its board of directors.

(b) The articles of incorporation shall provide for the name of the corporation, to be approved by the Commissioner; the kinds of insurance it proposes to transact and on what business plan or principle; and the place of its location in the State. The certificate of incorporation must be subscribed and sworn to by a majority of the board of directors before an officer authorized to take acknowledgement of deeds, who shall certify the certificate to the Commissioner. The Commissioner shall review the certificate and articles of incorporation and file them with the Secretary of State in accordance with G.S. 58-7-35.

(c) The independently chartered former branches of the Association shall transact the same kinds of insurance and operate under the same business plan as they did as members of the Association. The assets of each independently chartered former branch shall remain the assets of the corporation to which the branch is converted pursuant to this section.

(d) The independently chartered former branches of the Association may change their methods of operation upon compliance with G.S. 58-8-5 and applicable provisions of this Chapter.

(e) The corporations created under this section are subject to applicable provisions of this Chapter.

(f) The corporations created under this section shall enjoy the same rights, privileges, and exemptions as enjoyed by the former Association.

(g) No officer nor member of the board of directors of an independently chartered former branch shall incur any liability for actions taken in good faith pursuant to this section. (1993, c. 495, s. 1; 2005-424, s. 1.4.)

Article 9.

Reinsurance Intermediaries.

§ 58-9-1: Repealed by Session Laws 1993, c. 452, s. 65.

§ 58-9-2. Reinsurance intermediaries.

(a) As used in this Article:

(1) "Actuary" means a person who meets the standards of a qualified actuary, as specified in the NAIC Annual Statement Instructions, as amended or clarified by rule or order of the Commissioner, for the type of insurer for which an intermediary is establishing loss reserves.

(2) "Broker" means any person, other than an officer or employee of a ceding insurer, who solicits, negotiates, or places reinsurance cessions or retrocessions on behalf of a ceding insurer without the authority or power to bind reinsurance on behalf of the ceding insurer.

(3) "Commissioner" includes the Commissioner's authorized deputies and employees.

(4) "Controlling person" means any person who directly or indirectly has the power to direct or cause to be directed the management, control, or activities of an intermediary.

(5) "Intermediary" means any person who acts as a broker, as defined in G.S. 58-33-10(3), in soliciting, negotiating, or procuring the making of any reinsurance contract or binder on behalf of a ceding insurer; or acts as a broker, as defined in G.S. 58-33-10(3), in accepting any reinsurance contract on behalf of an assuming insurer. "Intermediary" includes a broker or a manager, as those terms are defined in this section.

(6) "Manager" means any person who has authority to bind or manages all or part of the assumed reinsurance business of a reinsurer (including the management of a separate division, department, or underwriting office) and acts as an agent for the reinsurer. The following persons are not managers, with respect to a reinsurer:

a. An employee of a reinsurer;

b. A United States manager of the United States branch of an alien reinsurer;

c. An underwriting manager who, pursuant to contract, manages all the reinsurance operations of a reinsurer, is under common control with the reinsurer under Article 19 of this Chapter, and whose compensation is not based on the volume of premiums written;

d. The manager of a group, association, pool, or organization of insurers that engages in joint underwriting or joint reinsurance and that is subject to examination by the insurance regulator of the state in which the manager's principal business office is located.

(7) "Producer" means an insurance agent or insurance broker licensed under Article 33 of this Chapter or an intermediary licensed under this Article.

(8) "Qualified United States financial institution" means a bank that:

a. Is organized, or in the case of a United States office of a foreign banking organization is licensed, under the laws of the United States or any state;

b. Is regulated, supervised, and examined by federal or state authorities having regulatory authority over banks and trust companies; and

c. Has been determined by the Securities Valuation Office of the NAIC to meet its standards of financial condition and standing in order to issue letters of credit.

(9) "Reinsurer" means any insurer that is licensed by the Commissioner and that is authorized to assume reinsurance.

(b) No person shall act as a broker in this State if the broker maintains an office either directly, as a member or employee of a noncorporate entity, or as an officer, director, or employee of a corporation:

(1) In this State, unless the broker is a producer in this State; or

(2) In another state, unless the broker is a producer in this State or another state having a law or rule substantially similar to this Article or unless the broker is licensed under this Article as a nonresident intermediary.

(c) No person shall act as a manager:

(1) For a reinsurer domiciled in this State, unless the manager is a producer in this State;

(2) In this State, if the manager maintains an office directly, as a member or employee of a noncorporate entity, or as an officer, director, or employee of a corporation in this State, unless the manager is a producer in this State;

(3) In another state for a foreign insurer, unless the manager is a producer in this State or another state having a law or rule substantially similar to this Article, or the manager is licensed in this State as a nonresident intermediary.

(d) Every manager subject to subsection (c) of this section shall demonstrate to the Commissioner that he has evidence of financial responsibility in the form of fidelity bonds or liability insurance to cover the manager's contractual obligations. If any manager cannot demonstrate this evidence, the Commissioner shall require the manager to:

(1) Maintain a separate fidelity bond in favor of each reinsurer represented in an amount that will cover those obligations and which bond is issued by an authorized insurer; or

(2) Maintain an errors and omissions liability insurance policy in an amount that will cover those obligations and which policy is issued by a licensed insurer. (1993, c. 452, s. 19; 1995, c. 193, s. 20; 2001-203, s. 27; 2002-187, s. 2.7.)

§ 58-9-5: Repealed by Session Laws 1993, c. 452, s. 65.

§ 58-9-6. Licensing.

(a) The Commissioner shall issue an intermediary license or an exemption from the license, subject to G.S. 58-9-2(b)(2) or G.S. 58-9-2(c)(3), to any person who has complied with the requirements of this Article. A license issued to a non corporate entity authorizes all of the members of the entity and any designated employees to act as intermediaries under the license, and those persons shall be named in the application and any supplements. A license issued to a corporation authorizes all of the officers and any designated employees and directors of the corporation to act as intermediaries on behalf of the corporation, and those persons shall be named in the application and any supplements.

(b) If an applicant for an intermediary license is a nonresident, the applicant, before receiving a license, shall designate the Commissioner as his agent for service of legal process and shall furnish the Commissioner with the name and address of a resident of this State upon whom notices or orders of the Commissioner or process affecting the nonresident intermediary may be served. The licensee shall notify the Commissioner in writing of every change in his designated agent for service of process within five business days after the change, and the change shall not become effective until acknowledged by the Commissioner.

(c) The Commissioner shall refuse to issue an intermediary license if:

(1) The applicant, anyone named on the application, or any member, principal, officer, or director of the applicant is not trustworthy;

(2) Any controlling person of the applicant is not trustworthy to act as an intermediary; or

(3) Any of the persons in subdivisions (1) and (2) of this subsection has given cause for revocation or suspension of the license or has failed to comply with any prerequisite for the issuance of the license.

Upon written request, the Commissioner shall furnish a summary of the basis for refusal to issue a license.

(d) Attorneys-at-law licensed by this State are exempt from this section when they are acting in their professional capacities. (1993, c. 452, s. 20; 2001-223, s. 10.1.)

§ 58-9-10: Repealed by Session Laws 1993, c. 452, s. 65.

§ 58-9-11. Broker and insurer transactions.

(a) Transactions between a broker and the insurer it represents as a broker shall only be entered into pursuant to a written authorization, specifying the responsibilities of each party. The authorization shall include provisions to the effect that:

(1) The insurer may terminate the broker's authority at any time.

(2) The broker will render accounts to the insurer that accurately detail all material transactions, including information necessary to support all commissions, charges, and other fees received by or owing to the broker and will remit all funds due to the insurer within 30 days after receipt by the broker.

(3) All funds collected for the insurer's account will be held by the broker in a fiduciary capacity in a qualified United States financial institution.

(4) The broker will comply with this Article.

(5) The broker will comply with the written standards established by the insurer for the cession or retrocession of all risks.

(6) The broker will disclose to the insurer any relationship with any reinsurer to which business will be ceded or retroceded.

(7) The broker will annually provide the insurer with an audited statement of the broker's financial condition, which statement will be prepared by an independent certified public accountant.

(8) The insurer will have access and the right to copy and audit all accounts and records maintained by the broker related to its business, in a form usable by the insurer.

(9) For at least 10 years after the expiration of each contract of reinsurance transacted by the broker, the broker will keep a complete record for each transaction showing:

a. The type of contract, limits, underwriting restrictions, classes or risks, and territory;

b. Period of coverage, including effective and expiration dates, cancellation provisions, and notice required of cancellation;

c. Reporting and settlement requirements of balances;

d. Rate or rates used to compute the reinsurance premium;

e. Names and addresses of assuming reinsurers;

f. Rates of all reinsurance commissions, including the commissions on any retrocession handled by the broker;

g. Related correspondence and memoranda;

h. Proof of placement;

i. Details regarding retrocessions handled by the broker, including the identity of retrocessionaires and percentage of each contract assumed or ceded;

j. Financial records, including premium and loss accounts; and

k. When the broker procures a reinsurance contract on behalf of a licensed ceding insurer:

1. Directly from any assuming reinsurer, written evidence that the assuming reinsurer has agreed to assume the risk; or

2. If placed through a representative of the assuming reinsurer, other than an employee, written evidence that the reinsurer has delegated binding authority to the representative.

(b) An insurer shall not engage the services of any person to act as a broker on its behalf unless the person is licensed under G.S. 58-9-6 or exempted under this Article. An insurer shall not employ an individual who is employed by a broker with which it transacts business, unless the broker is under common control with the insurer under Article 19 of this Chapter. (1993, c. 452, s. 21; 2001-223, s. 10.2.)

§ 58-9-15: Repealed by Session Laws 1993, c. 452, s. 65.

§ 58-9-16. Manager and reinsurer transactions.

(a) Transactions between a manager and the reinsurer it represents as a manager shall only be entered into pursuant to a written contract, specifying the responsibilities of each party, which shall be approved by the reinsurer's board of directors. At least 30 days before the reinsurer assumes or cedes business through the manager, a certified copy of the approved contract shall be filed with the Commissioner for approval. The contract shall include provisions to the effect that:

(1) The reinsurer may terminate the contract for cause upon written notice to the manager. The reinsurer may immediately suspend the authority of the manager to assume or cede business during the pendency of any dispute regarding the cause for termination.

(2) The manager will render accounts to the reinsurer accurately detailing all material transactions, including information necessary to support all commissions, charges, and other fees received by or owing to the manager and

will remit all funds due under the contract to the reinsurer at least once every month.

(3) All funds collected for the reinsurer's account will be held by the manager in a fiduciary capacity in a qualified United States financial institution. The manager may retain no more than three months' estimated claims payments and allocated loss adjustment expenses. The manager shall maintain a separate bank account for each reinsurer that it represents.

(4) For at least 10 years after the expiration of each contract of reinsurance transacted by the manager, the manager will keep a complete record for each transaction showing:

a. The type of contract, limits, underwriting restrictions, classes or risks, and territory;

b. Period of coverage, including effective and expiration dates, cancellation provisions and notice required of cancellation, and disposition of outstanding reserves on covered risk;

c. Reporting and settlement requirements of balances;

d. Rate used to compute the reinsurance premium;

e. Names and addresses of reinsurers;

f. Rates of all reinsurance commissions, including the commissions on any retrocessions handled by the manager;

g. Related correspondence and memoranda;

h. Proof of placement;

i. Details regarding retrocessions handled by the manager, as permitted by G.S. 58-9-21, including the identity of retrocessionaires and percentage of each contract assumed or ceded;

j. Financial records, including, but not limited to, premium and loss accounts; and

k. When the manager places a reinsurance contract on behalf of a ceding insurer:

1. Directly from any assuming reinsurer, written evidence that the assuming reinsurer has agreed to assume the risk; or

2. If placed through a representative of the assuming reinsurer, other than an employee, written evidence that the reinsurer has delegated binding authority to the representative.

(5) The reinsurer will have access and the right to copy all accounts and records maintained by the manager related to its business in a form usable by the reinsurer.

(6) The contract cannot be assigned in whole or in part by the manager.

(7) The manager will comply with the written underwriting and rating standards established by the insurer for the acceptance, rejection, or cession of all risks.

(8) The rates, terms, and purposes of commissions, charges, and other fees that the manager may levy against the reinsurer shall be set forth.

(9) If the contract permits the manager to settle claims on behalf of the reinsurer:

a. All claims will be reported to the reinsurer in a timely manner;

b. A copy of the claim file will be sent to the reinsurer at its request or as soon as it becomes known that the claim:

1. Has the potential to exceed an amount set by the reinsurer and approved by the Commissioner;

2. Involves a coverage dispute;

3. May exceed the manager's claims settlement authority;

4. Is open for more than six months; or

5. Is closed by payment of an amount set by the reinsurer and approved by the Commissioner.

c. All claim files will be the joint property of the reinsurer and manager. However, upon an order of liquidation of the reinsurer, the files shall become the sole property of the reinsurer or its estate; the manager shall have reasonable access to and the right to copy the files on a timely basis; and

d. Any settlement authority granted to the manager may be terminated for cause upon the reinsurer's written notice to the manager or upon the termination of the contract. The reinsurer may suspend the settlement authority during the pendency of the dispute regarding the cause of termination.

(10) If the contract provides for a sharing of interim profits by the manager, the interim profits will not be paid until one year after the end of each underwriting period for property business and five years after the end of each underwriting period for casualty business and not until the adequacy of reserves on remaining claims has been verified pursuant to G.S. 58-9-21.

(11) The manager will annually provide the reinsurer with an audited statement of its financial condition prepared by an independent certified public accountant.

(12) The reinsurer shall at least semiannually conduct an on-site review of the underwriting and claims processing operations of the manager.

(13) The manager will disclose to the reinsurer any relationship it has with any insurer before ceding or assuming any business with the insurer pursuant to this contract.

(14) Within the scope of its actual or apparent authority, the acts of the manager shall be deemed to be the acts of the reinsurer on whose behalf it is acting.

(b) A manager shall not:

(1) Cede retrocessions on behalf of the reinsurer, except that the manager may cede facultative retrocessions pursuant to obligatory facultative agreements if the contract with the reinsurer contains reinsurance underwriting guidelines for the retrocessions. The guidelines shall include a list of reinsurers with which the automatic agreements are in effect, and for each reinsurer, the

coverages and amounts or percentages that may be reinsured, and commission schedules.

(2) Commit the reinsurer to participate in reinsurance syndicates.

(3) Appoint any producer without assuring that the producer is duly licensed to transact the type of reinsurance for which he is appointed.

(4) Without prior approval of the reinsurer, pay or commit the reinsurer to pay a claim settlement with a retrocessionaire, without prior approval of the reinsurer. If prior approval is given, a report must be promptly forwarded to the reinsurer.

(5) Collect any payment from a retrocessionaire or commit the reinsurer to any claim settlement with a retrocessionaire, without prior approval of the reinsurer. If prior approval is given, a report must be promptly forwarded to the reinsurer.

(6) Jointly employ an individual who is employed by the reinsurer unless the manager is under common control with the reinsurer under Article 19 of this Chapter.

(7) Appoint a submanager. (1993, c. 452, s. 22.)

§ 58-9-20: Repealed by Session Laws 1993, c. 452, s. 65.

§ 58-9-21. Miscellaneous provisions.

(a) A reinsurer shall not engage the services of any person to act as a manager on its behalf unless the person is licensed under G.S. 58-9-6 or exempted under this Article.

(b) If a manager establishes loss reserves, the reinsurer shall annually obtain the opinion of an actuary attesting to the adequacy of loss reserves established for losses incurred and outstanding on business produced by the manager. This opinion shall be in addition to any other required loss reserve certification.

(c) Binding authority for all retrocessional contracts or participation in reinsurance syndicates shall be given to an officer of the reinsurer who is not affiliated with the manager.

(d) Within 30 days after termination of a contract with a manager, the reinsurer shall provide written notification of the termination to the Commissioner.

(e) A reinsurer shall not appoint to its board of directors any officer, director, employee, controlling person, or subproducer of its manager. This Article does not apply to relationships governed by Article 19 of this Chapter or G.S. 58-3-165.

(f) An intermediary is subject to examination by the Commissioner. The Commissioner shall have access to all books, bank accounts, and records of an intermediary in a form usable to the Commissioner. A manager may be examined as if it were the reinsurer. (1993, c. 452, s. 23; 2001-223, s. 10.3.)

§ 58-9-22. Compliance with orders.

An intermediary shall comply with any order of a court of competent jurisdiction or a duly constituted arbitration panel requiring the production of nonprivileged documents by the intermediary or the testimony of an employee or other individual otherwise under the control of the intermediary with respect to any reinsurance transaction for which it acted as an intermediary. (2009-172, s. 1.)

§ 58-9-25: Repealed by Session Laws 1993, c. 452, s. 65.

§ 58-9-26. Sanctions.

(a) If the Commissioner determines that any person has not materially complied with this Article or with any rule adopted or order issued under this Article, after notice and opportunity to be heard, the Commissioner may order:

(1) For each separate violation, a civil penalty under the procedures in G.S. 58-2-70(d); or

(2) Revocation or suspension of the person's license.

If the Commissioner finds that because of a material noncompliance that an insurer or reinsurer has suffered any loss or damage, the Commissioner may maintain a civil action brought by or on behalf of the insurer or reinsurer and its policyholders and creditors for recovery of compensatory damages for the benefit of the insurer or reinsurer and its policyholders and creditors or for other appropriate relief.

(b) If an order of rehabilitation or liquidation of the insurer has been entered under Article 30 of this Chapter, and the receiver appointed under that order determines that any person has not materially complied with this Article, or any rule adopted or order issued under this Article, and the insurer suffered any loss or damage from the material noncompliance, the receiver may maintain a civil action for recovery of damages or other appropriate sanctions for the benefit of the insurer. (1993, c. 452, s. 24.)

§ 58-9-30: Repealed by Session Laws 1993, c. 452, s. 65.

Article 10.

Miscellaneous Insurer Financial Provisions.

Part 1. Conversion of Stock and Mutual Insurers.

§ 58-10-1. Stock to mutual insurer conversion.

Any domestic stock life insurance corporation may become a mutual life insurance corporation, and to that end may carry out a plan for the acquisition of shares of its capital stock: Provided, however, that such plan (i) shall have been adopted by a vote of a majority of the directors of such corporation; (ii) shall have been approved by a vote of the holders of two thirds of the stock outstanding at the time of issuing the call for a meeting for that purpose; (iii) shall have been submitted to the Commissioner and shall have been approved by him in writing, and (iv) shall have been approved by a majority vote of the policyholders (including, for the purpose of this Part, the employer or the president, secretary or other executive officer of any corporation or association to which a master group policy has been issued, but excluding the holders of certificates or policies issued under or in connection with a master group policy) voting at said meeting, called for that purpose, at which meeting only such policyholders whose insurance shall then be in force and shall have been in force for at least one year prior to such a meeting shall be entitled to vote; notice of such a meeting shall be given by mailing such notice, postage prepaid, from the home office of such corporation at least 30 days prior to such meeting to such policyholders at their last known post-office addresses: Provided, that personal delivery of such written notice to any policyholder may be in lieu of mailing the same; and such meeting shall be otherwise provided for and conducted in such a manner as shall be provided in such plan: Provided, however, that policyholders may vote in person, by proxy, or by mail; that all such votes shall be cast by ballot, and a representative of the Commissioner shall supervise and direct the methods and procedure of said meeting and appoint an adequate number of inspectors to conduct the voting at said meeting who shall have power to determine all questions concerning the verification of the ballots, the ascertainment of the validity thereof, the qualifications of the voters, and the canvass of the vote, and who shall certify to the said representative and to the corporation the results thereof, and with respect thereto shall act under such rules and regulations as shall be prescribed by the Commissioner; that all necessary expenses incurred by the Commissioner or his representative shall be paid by the corporation as certified to by said Commissioner. Every payment for the acquisition of any shares of the capital stock of such corporation, the purchase price of which is not fixed by such plan, shall be subject to the approval of the Commissioner: Provided, that neither such plan, nor any payment thereunder, nor any payment not fixed by such plan, shall be approved by the Commissioner, if the making of such payment shall reduce the assets of the corporation to an amount less than the entire liabilities of the corporation, including therein the net values of its outstanding contracts according to the standard adopted by the Commissioner, and also all other funds, contingent reserves and surplus which the corporation is required by order or direction of the Commissioner to maintain, save so much of the surplus as shall have been appropriated or paid under such plan. (1937, c. 231, s. 1; 1991, c. 720, s. 4; 1995, c. 318, s. 1; 2001-223, s. 9.3.)

§ 58-10-5. Stock acquired to be turned over to voting trust until all stock acquired; dividends repaid to corporation for beneficiaries.

If a domestic stock life insurance corporation shall determine to become a mutual life insurance corporation it may, in carrying out any plan to that end under the provisions of G.S. 58-10-1, acquire any shares of its own stock by gift, devise, or purchase. And until all such shares are acquired, any shares so acquired shall be acquired in trust for the policyholders of the corporation as hereinafter provided, and shall be assigned and transferred on the books of the corporation to not less than three nor more than five trustees, and be held by them in trust and be voted by such trustees at all corporate meetings at which stockholders have the right to vote until all of the capital stock of such corporation is acquired, when the entire capital stock shall be retired and canceled; and thereupon, unless sooner incorporated as such, the corporation shall be and become a mutual life insurance corporation without capital stock. Said trustees shall be appointed and vacancies shall be filled as provided in the plan adopted under G.S. 58-10-1. Said trustees shall file with the corporation and with the Commissioner a verified acceptance of their appointments and declaration that they will faithfully discharge their duties as such trustees. After the payment of such dividends to stockholders or former stockholders as may have been provided in the plan adopted under G.S. 58-10-1, all dividends and other sums received by said trustees on said shares of stock so acquired, after paying the necessary expenses of executing said trust, shall be immediately repaid to said corporation for the benefit of all who are or may become policyholders of said corporation and entitled to participate in the profits thereof, and shall be added to and become a part of the surplus earned by said corporation, and be apportionable accordingly as a part of said surplus among said policyholders. (1937, c. 231, s. 2; 1991, c. 720, s. 4; 2011-284, s. 55.)

§ 58-10-10. Mutual to stock insurer conversion.

(a)   A domestic mutual insurer may convert to a domestic stock insurer under a plan that is approved in advance by the Commissioner.

(b)   The Commissioner shall not approve the plan unless:

(1)   It is fair and equitable to the insurer's policyholders.

(2) It is adopted by the insurer's board of directors in accordance with the insurer's bylaws and approved by a vote of not less than two-thirds of the insurer's members voting on it in person, by proxy, or by mail at a meeting called for the purpose of voting on the plan, pursuant to reasonable notice and procedure as approved by the Commissioner. If the company is a life insurer, the right to vote may be limited, as its bylaws provide, to members whose policies are other than term or group policies and have been in effect for more than one year.

(3) Each policyholder's equity in the insurer is determinable under a fair and reasonable formula approved by the Commissioner. The equity shall be based upon the insurer's entire statutory surplus after deducting certificates of contribution, guaranty capital certificates, and similar evidences of indebtedness included in an insurer's statutory surplus.

(4) The policyholders entitled to vote on the plan and participate in the purchase of stock and distribution of assets include all policyholders on the date the plan was adopted by the insurer's board of directors.

(5) The plan provides that each policyholder specified in subdivision (4) of this subsection receives a preemptive right to acquire a proportionate part of all of the proposed capital stock of the insurer or of all of the stock of a corporation affiliated with the insurer within a designated reasonable period as the part is determinable under the plan of conversion; and to apply toward the purchase of the stock the amount of the policyholder's equity in the insurer under subdivision (3) of this subsection. The plan must provide for an equitable distribution of fractional interests.

(6) The plan provides for payment to each policyholder of the policyholder's entire equity in the insurer; with that payment to be applied toward the purchase of stock to which the policyholder is entitled preemptively or to be made in cash, or both. The cash payment may not exceed fifty percent (50%) of each policyholder's equity. The stock purchased, together with the cash payment, if any, shall constitute full payment and discharge of the policyholder's equity as an owner of the mutual insurer.

(7) Shares are to be offered to policyholders at a price not greater than that of shares to be subsequently offered to others.

(8) The Commissioner finds that the insurer's management has not, through reduction of volume of new business written, through policy cancellations, or

through any other means, sought to (i) reduce, limit, or affect the number or identity of the insurer's members entitled to participate in the plan or (ii) secure for the individuals constituting management any unfair advantage through the plan.

(9) The plan, when completed, provides that the insurer's capital and surplus are not less than the minimum required of a domestic stock insurer transacting the same kinds of insurance, are reasonable in relation to the insurer's outstanding liabilities, and are adequate to meet its financial needs.

(c) With respect to an insurer with a guaranty capital, the conversion plan shall be approved by a vote of not less than two-thirds of the insurer's guaranty capital shareholders and policyholders as provided for in subdivision (b)(2) of this section. The plan may provide for the issuance of stock in exchange for outstanding guaranty capital shares at their redemption value subject to the conditions in subsection (b) of this section.

(d) The Commissioner may schedule a public hearing on the proposed conversion plan.

(e) The Commissioner may retain, at the mutual insurer's expense, any attorneys, actuaries, economists, accountants, or other experts not otherwise a part of the Commissioner's staff as may be reasonably necessary to assist the Commissioner in reviewing the proposed conversion plan.

(f) The corporate existence of the mutual company continues in the stock company created under this section. All assets, rights, franchises, and interests of the former mutual insurer, in and to real or personal property, are deemed to be transferred to and vested in the stock insurer, without any other deed or transfer; and the stock insurer simultaneously assumes all of the obligations and liabilities of the former mutual insurer.

(g) No director, officer, or employee of the insurer shall receive:

(1) Any fee, commission, compensation, or other valuable consideration for aiding, promoting, or assisting in the conversion of the mutual insurer to a domestic stock insurer, other than compensation paid to any director, officer, or employee of the insurer in the ordinary course of business; or

(2) Any distribution of the assets, surplus, or capital of the insurer as part of a conversion.

(h) The Commissioner may adopt rules to carry out the provisions of this section. (1999-369, s. 6; 2001-223, s. 9.5.)

§ 58-10-12. Conversion plan requirements.

(a) As used in this section:

(1) "Closed block" means an allocation of assets for a defined group of in-force policies which, together with the premiums of those policies and related investment earnings, are expected to be sufficient to maintain the payments of guaranteed benefits, certain expenses, and continuation of the current dividend scale on the closed block, if experience does not change.

(2) "Converting mutual" means a domestic mutual insurance company that has adopted a plan of conversion and an amendment to its articles of incorporation under this section that will, upon consummation, result in the domestic mutual insurance company converting into a domestic stock insurance company.

(3) "Eligible member" means a person who:

a. Is a member of the converting mutual on the date the converting mutual's board of directors adopts a resolution proposing a plan of conversion and an amendment to the articles of incorporation; and

b. Continues to be a member of the converting mutual on the effective date of the conversion.

(4) "Former mutual" means the domestic stock insurance company resulting from the conversion of a converting mutual to a stock insurance company under a plan of conversion and an amendment to its articles of incorporation under this section.

(5) "Member" means a person that, according to the records, articles of incorporation, and bylaws of a converting mutual, is a member of the converting mutual.

(6) "Membership interests" means:

a. The voting rights of members of a domestic mutual insurance company as provided by law and by the company's articles of incorporation and bylaws; and

b. The rights of members of a domestic mutual insurance company to receive cash, stock, or other consideration in the event of a conversion to a stock insurance company under this section or a dissolution as provided by the company's articles of incorporation and bylaws.

(7) "Parent company" means a corporation that, upon the effective date of a conversion, owns all of the stock of the former mutual.

(8) "Plan of conversion" means the plan of conversion described in subsection (b) of this section.

(b) The plan of conversion under G.S. 58-10-10 shall:

(1) Describe the manner in which the proposed conversion will occur and the insurance and any other companies that will result from or be directly affected by the conversion, including the former mutual and any parent company.

(2) Provide that the membership interests in the converting mutual will be extinguished as of the effective date of the conversion.

(3) Require the distribution to the eligible members, upon the extinguishing of their membership interests, of aggregate consideration equal to the fair value of the converting mutual.

(4) Describe the manner in which the fair value of the converting mutual has been or will be determined.

(5) Describe the form or forms and amount, if known, of consideration to be distributed to the eligible members.

(6) Specify relevant classes, categories, or groups of eligible members and describe and explain any differences in the form or forms and amount of consideration to be distributed to or among the eligible members.

(7) Require and describe the method or formula for the fair and equitable allocation of the consideration among the eligible members.

(8) Provide for the determination and preservation of the reasonable dividend expectations of eligible members and other policyholders with policies that provide for the distribution of policy dividends, through establishment of a closed block or other method acceptable to the Commissioner.

(9) Provide that each member and other policyholder of the converting mutual will receive notification of the address and telephone number of the converting mutual and the former mutual, if different, along with the notice of hearing as approved by the Commissioner.

(10) Include other provisions as the converting mutual determines to be necessary.

(c) After the adoption by the board of directors of the resolution proposing the plan of conversion under G.S. 58-10-10 and the amendment to its articles of incorporation, the converting mutual shall file with the Commissioner an application for approval of the plan and amendment. The application must contain the following information, together with any additional information as the Commissioner may require:

(1) The plan of conversion and a certificate of the secretary of the converting mutual certifying the adoption of the plan by the board of directors.

(2) A statement of the reasons for the proposed conversion and why the conversion is in the best interests of the converting mutual, the eligible members, and the other policyholders. The statement must include an analysis of the risks and benefits to the converting mutual and its members of the proposed conversion and a comparison of the risks and benefits of the conversion with the risks and benefits of reasonable alternatives to a conversion.

(3) A five-year business plan and at least two years of financial forecasts of the former mutual and any parent company.

(4) Any plans that the former mutual or any parent company may have to:

a. Raise additional capital through the issuance of stock or otherwise;

b. Sell or issue stock to any person, including any compensation or benefit plan for directors, officers, or employees under which stock may be issued;

c. Liquidate or dissolve any company or sell any material assets;

d. Merge or consolidate or pursue any other form of reorganization with any person; or

e. Make any other material change in investment policy, business, corporate structure, or management.

(5) Any plans for a delayed distribution of consideration to eligible members or restrictions on sale or transfer of stock or other securities.

(6) A copy of the form of trust agreement, if a distribution of consideration is to be delayed by more than six months after the effective date of the conversion.

(7) A plan of operation for a closed block, if a closed block is used for the preservation of the reasonable dividend expectations of eligible members and other policyholders with policies that provide for the distribution of policy dividends.

(8) Copies of the amendment to the articles of incorporation proposed by the board of directors and proposed bylaws of the former mutual and copies of the existing and any proposed articles of incorporation and bylaws of any parent company.

(9) A list of all individuals who are or have been selected to become directors or officers of the former mutual and any parent company, or the individuals who perform or will perform duties customarily performed by a director or officer, and the following information concerning each individual on the list unless the information is already on file with the Commissioner:

a. The individual's principal occupation.

b. All offices and positions the individual has held in the preceding five years.

c. Any crime of which the individual has been convicted (other than traffic violations) in the preceding 10 years.

d. Information concerning any personal bankruptcy of the individual or the individual's spouse during the previous seven years.

e. Information concerning the bankruptcy of any corporation or other entity of which the individual was an officer or director during the previous seven years.

f. Information concerning allegations of state or federal securities law violations made against the individual that within the previous 10 years resulted in (i) a determination that the individual violated state or federal securities laws; (ii) a plea of nolo contendere; or (iii) a consent decree.

g. Information concerning the suspension, revocation, or other disciplinary action during the previous 10 years of any state or federal license issued to the individual.

h. Information as to whether the individual was refused a bond during the previous 10 years.

(10) A fairness opinion addressed to the board of directors of the converting mutual from a qualified, independent financial adviser asserting:

a. That the provision of stock, cash, policy benefits, or other forms of consideration upon the extinguishing of the converting mutual's membership interests under the plan of conversion and the amendment to the articles of incorporation is fair to the eligible members, as a group, from a financial point of view; and

b. Whether the total consideration under sub-subdivision a. of this subdivision is equal to or greater than the surplus of the converting mutual.

The Commissioner may waive the fairness opinion in situations involving a straightforward issuance of stock to members of the former mutual.

(11) An actuarial opinion as to the following:

a. The reasonableness and appropriateness of the methodology or formulas used to allocate consideration among eligible members, consistent with this Article.

b. The reasonableness of the plan of operation and sufficiency of the assets allocated to the closed block, if a closed block is used for the preservation of the reasonable dividend expectations of eligible members and other policyholders with policies that provide for the distribution of policy dividends.

(12) If any of the consideration to be distributed to eligible members consists of stock or other securities, subject to the limitations of G.S. 58-10-10(b)(6), a description of the plans made by the former mutual or its parent company to assure that an active public trading market for the stock or other securities will develop within a reasonable amount of time after the effective date of the plan of conversion and that eligible members who receive stock or other securities will be able to sell their stock or other securities, subject to any delayed distribution or transfer restrictions, at reasonable cost and effort.

(13) Any additional information, documents, or materials that the converting mutual determines to be necessary.

(d) Distribution of all or part of the consideration to some or all of the eligible members may be delayed, or restrictions on sale or transfer of any stock or other securities to be distributed to eligible members may be required, for a reasonable period of time following the effective date of the conversion. However, the period of time shall not exceed six months unless otherwise approved by the Commissioner.

(e) Except as specifically provided in a plan of conversion, for five years following the effective date of the conversion, no person or persons acting in concert (other than the former mutual, any parent company, or any employee benefit plans or trusts sponsored by the former mutual or a parent company) shall directly or indirectly acquire, or agree or offer to acquire, in any manner the beneficial ownership of five percent (5%) or more of the outstanding shares of any class of a voting security of the former mutual or any parent company without the prior approval of the Commissioner of a statement filed by that person with the Commissioner. The statement shall contain the information required by G.S. 58-19-15(b) and any other information required by the Commissioner. The Commissioner shall not approve an acquisition under this subsection unless the Commissioner finds that:

(1) The requirements of G.S. 58-19-15(e) will be satisfied.

(2) The acquisition will not frustrate the plan of conversion or the amendment to the articles of incorporation as approved by the members and the Commissioner.

(3) The boards of directors of the former mutual and any parent company have approved the acquisition.

(4) The acquisition would be in the best interest of the present and future policyholders of the former mutual without regard to any interest of policyholders as shareholders of the former mutual or any parent company. (2001-223, s. 9.6.)

Part 2. Assumption Reinsurance.

§ 58-10-20. Scope.

(a) This Part applies to any licensed insurer that either assumes or transfers the obligations or risks on policies under an assumption reinsurance agreement that is entered into on or after January 1, 1996.

(b) This Part does not apply to:

(1) Any reinsurance agreement or transaction in which the ceding insurer continues to remain directly liable for its insurance obligations or risks under the policies subject to the reinsurance agreement.

(2) The substitution of one insurer for another upon the expiration of insurance coverage under statutory or contractual requirements and the issuance of a new policy by another insurer.

(3) The transfer of policies under mergers or consolidations of two or more insurers to the extent that those transactions are regulated by statute.

(4) Except as provided in G.S. 58-10-45, any insurer subject to a judicial order of liquidation or rehabilitation.

(5) Any reinsurance agreement or transaction to which a state insurance guaranty association is a party, provided that policyholders do not lose any

rights or claims afforded under their original policies under Articles 48 or 62 of this Chapter.

(6) The transfer of liabilities from one insurer to another under a single group policy upon the request of the group policyholder. (1995, c. 318, s. 1; 2004-199, s. 20(b).)

§ 58-10-25. Definitions.

(a) As used in this Part:

(1) Assuming insurer. - The insurer that acquires an insurance obligation or risk from the transferring insurer under an assumption reinsurance agreement.

(2) Assumption reinsurance agreement. - Any contract, arrangement, or plan that:

a. Transfers insurance obligations or risks of existing or in-force policies from a transferring insurer to an assuming insurer.

b. Is intended to effect a novation of transferred policies with the result that the assuming insurer becomes directly liable to the policyholders of the transferring insurer and the transferring insurer's insurance obligations or risks under the policies are extinguished.

(3) Home service business. - Insurance business on which premiums are collected on a weekly or monthly basis by an agent of the insurer.

(4) Policy. - A contract of insurance as defined in G.S. 58-1-10.

(5) Policyholder. - Any person that has the right to terminate or otherwise alter the terms of a policy. It includes any group policy certificate holder whose certificate is in force on the proposed effective date of the assumption, if the certificate holder has the right to keep the certificate in force without any change in benefits after termination of the group policy. The right to keep the certificate in force referred to in this subdivision does not include the right to elect individual coverage under the Consolidated Omnibus Budget Reconciliation Act ("COBRA"), section 601, et seq., of the Employee Retirement Income Security Act of 1974, as amended, 29 U.S.C. § 1161, et seq.

(6) Transferring insurer. - The insurer that transfers an insurance obligation or risk to an assuming insurer under an assumption reinsurance agreement.

(b) For the purposes of this Part, a "novation" does not require the formation of a new policy or the amendment of an existing policy between the assuming insurer and the policyholder. (1995, c. 318, s. 1; 1995 (Reg. Sess., 1996), c. 752, s. 2.)

Whenever the board of trustees borrow money from the Club as authorized by this subdivision it shall first advise the Commissioner of the nature and purpose of the loan, and shall obtain his prior approval of such loan. (1987, c. 330.)

Vision Books Order Form

Fax Orders:	1-980-299-5965
Phone Orders:	1-704-898-0770
E-mail Orders:	www.visionbooks.org
Mail Orders:	Vision Books, LLC P.O. Box 42406 Charlotte, NC 28215

Shipp To:
Name_____
Address_____
City_____State_____Zip_____
Phone_____Fax_____
Email_____@_____

Bill To: We can bill a third party on your behalf.
Name_____
Address_____
City_____State_____Zip_____
Phone___(_____)_____Fax_____
Email_____@_____

Pamphlet Number ($15.00 Each)	Qty	Total Cost
_____	_____	_____
_____	_____	_____
_____	_____	_____
_____	_____	_____
_____	_____	_____
_____	_____	_____
_____	_____	_____
<u>Full Volume Set 1-92</u>	<u>92 Pamphlets</u>	<u>1,380.00</u>

Free Shipping Shipping & Handling on Full Volume Orders
Add $1.00 Shipping & Handling per pamphlet $_____

Total Cost $_____

Thank you for your support. Management!

DID YOU ENJOY THIS BOOK?

Vision Books, LLC would like to hear from you! If you or someone you know has been fasely imprisoned, we would like to hear your story. If the 'North Carolina Criminal Law and Procedure' has had an effect in your life or if you have suggestions, we would like to hear from you. Send your letters to:

Vision Books, LLC
Attn: Staff Writers
P.O. Box 42406
Charlotte, NC 28215
Email: staff@visionbooks.org

Order Additional Copies:

Fax Orders:	1-980-299-5965
Phone Orders:	1-704-898-0770
E-mail Orders:	www.visionbooks.org
Mail Orders:	Vision Books, LLC P.O. Box 42406 Charlotte, NC 28215

www.ingramcontent.com/pod-product-compliance
Lightning Source LLC
Chambersburg PA
CBHW051628170526
45167CB00001B/103